Study Guide

Abnormal Psychology

Study Guide

Michele T. Martin
Wesleyan College

Abnormal Psychology

Second Edition

Thomas F. Oltmanns

Robert E. Emery

PRENTICE HALL, Upper Saddle River, New Jersey 07458

© 1998 by PRENTICE-HALL, INC.
Simon & Schuster / A Viacom Company
Upper Saddle River, New Jersey 07458

10 9 8 7 6 5 4 3 2 1

ISBN 0-13-750258-3
Printed in the United States of America

TABLE OF CONTENTS

CHAPTER 1 - EXAMPLES AND DEFINITIONS OF ABNORMAL BEHAVIOR

Chapter Outline

I. Abnormal Psychology: An Overview
    A. Clinical Science
    B. The Uses and Limitations of Case Studies

II. What is Abnormal Behavior?
    A. Descriptive Psychopathology
    B. Defining Abnormal Behavior
        1. Harmful Dysfunction
        2. DSM-IV Definition
        3. Social and Political Considerations

III. Boundaries of Abnormal Behavior
    A. Dimensions Versus Categories
    B. Epidemiology
    C. Culture and Psychopathology

IV. Causes of Abnormal Behavior
    A. Nature and Nurture
    B. Systems of Influence

V. Treatment of Abnormal Behavior

VI. Psychopathology in Historical Context
    A. The Greek Tradition in Medicine
    B. The Creation of the Asylum
    C. Worcester Lunatic Hospital: A Model Institution
    D. Lessons from the History of Psychopathology

VII. The Mental Health Professions

VIII. Goals of This Book

Learning Objectives

After reviewing the material presented in this chapter, you should be able to:

1.   Know a basic definition of abnormal psychology.

2.   Understand the scientist-practitioner model.

3.   Consider the three primary criteria of abnormality (personal distress, statistical rarity, and maladaptiveness) in terms of their strengths and weaknesses.

4. Distinguish the dimensional approach to abnormality from the categorical approach.

5. Know the terms epidemiology, incidence, and prevalence.

6. Describe the nature-nurture controversy in abnormal psychology and explain why it should not be a controversy since nature and nurture interact.

7. Compare the individual, social, and biological systems of influence.

8. Define and understand the advantages and disadvantages of biological reductionism.

9. Understand that changes due to a certain form of treatment do not prove causality.

10. Recognize the differences between a demonological and a natural scientific approach to psychopathology.

11. Know the historical development within institutional treatment of mental disorders.

12. Understand the importance of recognizing cultural bias and using scientific research to establish the validity of approaches to psychopathology.

13. Appreciate the "conservative" approach in research, leading to a reluctance to reject the null hypothesis until evidence establishes the validity of a new theory.

Key Terms - Matching #1

The following terms related to abnormal psychology are important to know. To test your knowledge, match the following terms with their definitions. Answers are listed at the end of the chapter.

a.	Psychology		k.	Bulimia nervosa
b.	Psychological science		l.	Categorical approach
c.	Abnormal psychology		m.	Dimensional approach
d.	Scientist-practitioner model		n.	Threshold model
e.	Case study		o.	Dichotomous decision
f.	Hypotheses		p.	Epidemiology
g.	Psychopathology		q.	Incidence
h.	Psychosis		r.	Prevalence
i.	Delusion		s.	Lifetime prevalence
j.	Disorganized speech		t.	Etiology

1. _____ highly specific and testable predictions about cause and effect
2. _____ the scientific study of behavior, cognition, and emotion

3. _____ the scientific study of the frequency and distribution of disorders within a population
4. _____ the body of knowledge generated by psychological researchers, along with their research methods
5. _____ a symptom often found in schizophrenia of speech that is odd and difficult to comprehend; a problem with the form of speech rather than content
6. _____ a view of classification based on the assumption that behavior is distributed on a continuum from normal to abnormal, and that differences between forms of mental disorder are quantitative rather than qualitative
7. _____ the total number of active cases of a disorder present in a population during a specific period of time
8. _____ the total proportion of people in a population who have been affected by the disorder at some point in their lives
9. _____ a descriptive presentation of the psychological problems of one particular person
10. _____ emphasizes the integration of science and clinical practice
11. _____ a state of being profoundly out of touch with reality
12. _____ the causes of a disorder
13. _____ required in making a diagnosis; determining whether a particular person fits a diagnostic category
14. _____ a form of eating disorder characterized by bingeing and purging
15. _____ the manifestations of, and study of the causes of, mental disorders
16. _____ a view of classification based on the assumption that there are qualitative differences between normal and abnormal behavior and between different types of abnormal behavior
17. _____ the application of psychological science to the study of mental disorders
18. _____ a combination of dimensional and categorical approaches to classification stating that people can exhibit characteristics of a disorder without any harm to their adjustment until they pass a critical threshold, where there is a dramatic increase in the number of problems they encounter
19. _____ the number of new cases of a disorder that appear in a population during a specific period of time
20. _____ an idiosyncratic belief, not shared by other members of the society, that is rigidly held despite its preposterous nature

Key Terms - Matching #2

The following terms related to abnormal psychology are important to know. To test your knowledge, match the following terms with their definitions. Answers are listed at the end of the chapter.

1. Formal thought disorder
2. Insanity
3. Not guilty by reason of insanity
4. Nervous breakdown
5. Descriptive psychopathology
6. Syndrome
7. Schizophrenia
8. Insight
11. Nature-nurture controversy
12. Biopsychosocial model
13. Psychopharmacology
14. Psychotherapy
15. Psychoanalytic theory
16. Moral treatment movement
17. Psychiatry
18. Experimental hypothesis

9. Harmful dysfunction
10. Diagnostic and Statistical Manual of Mental Disorders (DSM-IV)
19. Null hypothesis
20. Clinical psychology
21. Social work

a. _____ a mental disorder characterized by psychotic symptoms, disorganized speech, and emotional flatness and withdrawal

b. _____ any new prediction made by a researcher

c. _____ a group of symptoms that appear together and are assumed to represent a specific type of disorder

d. _____ a specialization in medicine concerned with the study and treatment of mental disorders

e. _____ the use of medication to treat mental disorders

f. _____ a person's awareness that he or she has symptoms of a mental disorder

g. _____ a legal term indicating a legal defense or finding that, although a person committed a crime, he or she is not criminally responsible for the behavior because of a mental disorder

h. _____ a movement founded on a basic respect for human dignity and the belief that humanistic care would be effective in the treatment of mental illness, that promoted improved conditions at mental hospitals

i. _____ the use of psychological procedures in the context of a relationship with a therapist to treat mental disorders

j. _____ the alternative to the experimental hypothesis; predicts that the experimental hypothesis is not true

k. _____ currently, this is a legal term referring to a person's culpability for criminal acts if he or she has a mental disorder

l. _____ another term for disorganized speech

m. _____ an approach to defining whether a condition is a mental disorder in terms of its harm to the person and whether the condition results from the inability of some mental mechanism to perform its natural function

n. _____ a specialization in psychology concerned with the application of psychological science to the assessment and treatment of mental disorders

o. _____ a theory of understanding human behavior based on the work of Freud

p. _____ the official listing of mental disorders and their diagnostic criteria published by the American Psychiatric Association and updated regularly

q. _____ a profession concerned with helping people achieve an effective level of psychosocial functioning; focuses less on a body of scientific knowledge than on a commitment to action

r. _____ the debate over whether genetic or biological factors versus environmental factors cause mental disorders or abnormal behavior

s. _____ an old-fashioned term indicating that a person became incapacitated because of an unspecified mental disorder

t. _____ the analytic approach toward etiology combining the influences of biological, psychological, and social systems

u. _____ psychopathology based on the signs and symptoms of a mental disorder rather than on its inferred causes

Names You Should Know - Matching

The following people or legal cases have played an important role in abnormal psychology. To test your knowledge, match the following names with the descriptions of their contributions. Answers are listed at the end of the chapter.

    a. Jerome Wakefield   c. Dorothea Dix   e. Samuel Woodward
    b. Hippocrates   d. Blue Shield v. McCready and Wyatt v. Stickney

    1. _____   an early advocate for the humane treatment of the mentally ill; promoted the creation of mental institutions for treatment
    2. _____   saw mental disorders as diseases having natural causes, like other forms of physical disease
    3. _____   held that licensed clinical psychologists and social workers should be able to treat patients without the supervision of a psychiatrist
    4. _____   proposed the harmful dysfunction approach to defining mental disorder
    5. _____   argued that mental disorders could be traced to immoral behavior, stress, or improper living environments; optimistic about curing mental illnesses

Review of Concepts - Fill in the Blank and True/False

This section will help focus your studying by testing whether you understand the concepts presented in the text. After you have read and reviewed the material, test your comprehension and memory by filling in the following blanks or circling the right answer. Answers are listed at the end of the chapter.

1. Most of the important scientific advances in abnormal psychology have been made by researchers who work directly with clinical problems and patients but also promote the method of scientific inquiry in clinical practice: **true**   **false**
2. Case studies are particularly important in understanding mental disorders that are _____.
3. Case studies can prove that a certain factor is the cause of a disorder:
        true   **false**
4. One limitation of case studies is that one person may not be _____ of the disorder as a whole.
5. There are several laboratory tests available to test for the presence of certain forms of mental disorders: **true**   **false**
6. One symptom is usually enough to establish a diagnosis: **true**   **false**
7. An unusual behavior or symptom that goes away after a few days is not clinically significant; that is, it does not indicate that a person has a disorder:
        true   **false**
8. What is the problem with defining abnormal behavior based on the individual's

experience of personal distress? _____

9. What is the problem with defining abnormal behavior based on statistical norms of rarity? _____

10. The DSM-IV defines mental disorder in terms of personal _____ or impairment of _____ or with significantly increased risk of suffering some form of harm, whether death, injury, or loss of freedom.

11. Why was the behavior of the Yippie Party of the 1960's, whose members threw money off the balcony at a stock exchange, not considered to be a symptom of a mental illness? _____

12. The DSM-IV is not influenced by social or political forces: **true**   **false**

13. Why does the DSM no longer consider homosexuality to be a mental disorder?

_____

14. What type of approach does the DSM take to classifying mental disorders?
dimensional   **categorical**

15. Much of our current estimates of the prevalence of mental disorders is based on the _____ study.

16. Most psychopathologists view mental disorders as being culture-free:
true   **false**

17. Psychotic disorders are less influenced by culture than are nonpsychotic disorders: **true**   **false**

18. Scientists have come to fairly well-agreed-upon conclusions about the etiology of most mental disorders: **true**   **false**

19. A psychopathologist who hypothesizes that schizophrenia is caused by an infectious agent, like a virus, would be arguing for which side of the controversy:
nature   **nurture**

20. Almost all patients who are being treated in psychotherapy are not treated with medication at the same time: **true**   **false**

21. Most people who have a diagnoseable mental disorder receive some form of treatment for it: **true**   **false**

22. Why is it an error to conclude that when a treatment is successful in relieving a mental disorder, that treatment indicates the cause of the disorder?

_____

_____

23. Many ancient theories of abnormal behavior see as its cause the disfavor of the gods or demonic possession: **true**   **false**

24. Cutting patients to make them bleed and reduce the amount of blood in the body was a form of treatment for mental illness in the 19th century: **true**   **false**

25. Urbanization was one of the reasons that _____ were built.

26. What led to the creation of the medical specialty of psychiatry? _____

_____

27. Samuel Woodward saw masturbation, among other "morally objectionable" behaviors, as the cause of _____.

28. Woodward claimed a success rate in treating his institutionalized mental patients of: **about 30%**   **about 50%**   **about 85%**

29. Fever therapy involved infecting mental patients with _____ to cause a fever because symptoms sometimes disappeared in patients with a high fever.

30. What type of mental health professionals can prescribe medication?

_____

31. What type of mental health professionals are trained in the use of scientific research methods? _____

Multiple Choice Questions

The following multiple choice questions will test your comprehension of the material presented in the chapter. Answers are listed at the end of the chapter.

1) A type of formal thought disorder which has the prominent feature of severe disruptions of verbal communication.

   a. depression
   b. schizophrenia

   c. psychosis
   d. disorganized speech

2) This model combines the dimensional and categorical approaches to classification.

   a. threshold model
   b. scientist-practitioner model

   c. diathesis-stress model
   d. biopsychosocial model

3) When literally translated, the term "psychopathology" refers to:

   a. "deterioration of the psyche"
   b. "pathology of the mind"

   c. "pathology of the psyche"
   d. "deterioration of the mind"

4) A mental disorder is typically defined by:

   a. one distinguishing symptom
   b. statistical rarity
   c. a set of characteristic features
   d. the individual being out of contact with reality

5) Beth shows delusional thinking and hallucinations. Bob shows hallucinations and formal thought disorder. According to DSM-IV:

   a. they could both be classified as schizophrenic
   b. they would be given different diagnoses
   c. they probably have different etiologies
   d. they should get different treatments

6) All of the following are hypotheses of the etiology of abnormal behavior EXCEPT:

   a. diathesis-stress model   c. biological reductionism
   b. biopsychosocial model   d. scientist-practitioner model

7) The approach that defines psychopathology in terms of signs and symptoms rather than inferred causes is:

   a. descriptive psychopathology   c. cross-cultural psychopathology
   b. influential psychopathology   d. experiential psychopathology

8) All of the following are ways in which case studies can be useful EXCEPT:

   a. provide important insights about the nature of mental disorders
   b. allow you to draw conclusions about a disorder from a single experience
   c. aid a clinician in making hypotheses about a specific case
   d. provide a rich clinical description which can be helpful in diagnosing an individual

9) These two disorders are much more common in men than they are in women.

   a. alcoholism; antisocial personality disorder
   b. anxiety disorders; depression
   c. alcoholism; depression
   d. anxiety disorders; antisocial personality disorder

10) All of the following could be considered psychotic symptoms EXCEPT:

   a. delusions   c. disorganized speech
   b. hallucinations   d. illusions

11) Eating disorders can be fatal if they are not properly treated because:

    a. there is a high suicide rate among people with eating disorders
    b. they affect so many vital organs of the body
    c. people with eating disorders are often unaware of the disorder and therefore are prone to developing additional disorders
    d. the majority of people with eating disorders do not view their behavior as problematic and therefore do not seek treatment

12) Blue Shield of Virginia v. McCready and Wyatt v. Stickney were two landmark court decisions in the early 1970s that:

    a. allowed licensed clinical psychologists and social workers to treat patients without the supervision of a psychiatrist
    b. allowed licensed clinical psychologists and social workers to prescribe medication to patients with the supervision of psychiatrist
    c. maintained that licensed clinical psychologists and social workers need to be under the supervision of a psychiatrist while treating patients
    d. allowed licensed clinical psychologists and social workers to treat patients without the supervision of a psychiatrist, however they were not allowed to collect payment for their services from insurance companies

13) This is a general term that refers to a type of severe mental disorder in which the individual is considered to be out of contact with reality.

    a. threshold
    b. syndrome
    c. psychosis
    d. schizophrenia

14) _____ is to experience as _____ is to genes.

    a. nature; nurture
    b. nurture; nature
    c. quantitative; qualitative
    d. qualitative; quantitative

15) In order for a behavior to be considered abnormal, it must include all of the following EXCEPT:

    a. present distress or painful symptoms
    b. conflicts between the individual and society that are voluntary in nature
    c. impairment in one or more important areas of functioning
    d. increased risk of suffering death, pain, disability, or an important loss of freedom

16) Which is true about the role of value judgments in the development of diagnostic systems?

    a. values can be avoided with the use of scientific methods
    b. diagnosis is completely determined by values
    c. values have no place in the attempt to define disease
    d. values are inherent in any attempt to define disease

17) The conclusion of Jane Murphy's study of the Inuit of northwest Alaska and the Yoruba of rural, tropical Nigeria was that severe forms of mental illness:

    a. are not limited to Western cultures or developed countries
    b. do appear to be limited to Western cultures or developed countries
    c. are more prevalent in Western cultures and developed countries
    d. are more prevalent in the Inuit and Yoruba populations studied

18) Olivia grew up in a society where mourners pull out their hair, go into an emotional frenzy, and begin speaking in tongues. On a visit to the U.S., she did these things in public when she heard that a relative had died. According to DSM-IV, this would be considered:

    a. not to be psychopathology, because it is part of her culture
    b. not to be psychopathology, because it caused no disruption in her social relationships
    c. to be psychopathology, because of her personal distress
    d. to be psychopathology, because it impaired her functioning

19) Which of the following is NOT considered a criterion for defining a behavior as a form of mental illness?

    a. negative effects on the person's social functioning
    b. recognition by the person that his or her behavior is problematic
    c. personal discomfort
    d. persistent, maladaptive behaviors

Understanding Research - Fill in the Blank

Cross-Cultural Study of Abnormal Behavior: The text presents a detailed description of a study by Murphy in the Research Close-Up on p. 16. Finding the answers to these questions will help you get a good understanding of this study and why it is important. It is not necessary to memorize the answers; the process of finding them in the textbook will help you learn the material you need to know.

1. What did the textbook mean by the term "non-Western?" _____

_____ What were the two

groups of people that Murphy studied? _____ and _____

She lived with each of them for several _____, learned their languages,

and learned how they think about problem _____. One person told her

about the lives of all _____ people in the Inuit village, and three native _____

told her about the Yoruba.

2. Both cultures recognize certain forms of "crazy" behavior, including aberrant beliefs,

feelings, and actions, hearing _____, _____ at strange times, talking in ways that don't make _____: which are like what diagnosis? _____. The specific _____ of hallucinations and delusions varies from one culture to the next, but the underlying _____ appear to be the same. Both groups saw "crazy behavior" as being different from the behaviors of the _____, who also acted strangely at times when doing their job. "When the shaman is healing, he is out of his mind, but he is not _____."

3. Both groups believe that mental illness originates in _____. Their attitudes toward "crazy" people were neither _____ nor _____. The World _____ Organization studied schizophrenia in _____ countries and found about the same _____ of the disorder in all the countries. They concluded that severe forms of mental illness are not limited to _____ or _____ countries.

The Null Hypothesis and the Burden of Proof: The text discusses this research issue in the Research Methods section on p. 24. Finding the answers to these questions will help you get a good understanding of these issues.

4. What is the rule that scientists agree upon for making and testing any new hypothesis? _____

_____

The two hypotheses set up in any research study are the _____ hypothesis and the _____ hypothesis. This rule is similar to the legal saying: _____. These are both _____ principles designed to protect the field from _____ assertions. Scientists feel that _____ "scientific evidence" is more dangerous than _____ knowledge.

5. List three examples of treatments that were used in the past on many thousands of patients without established effectiveness: _____, _____, and _____. What are some of the modern treatments that should be shown effective before their use: _____ _____. Scientists do not prove the null hypothesis; they only fail to _____ it.

Brief Essay

As a final exercise, write out answers to the following brief essay questions. Then compare your answers with the material presented in the text.

After you have answered these questions, review the "critical thinking" questions that are presented at the end of the text chapter. Answering these questions will help you integrate important issues and themes that have been featured throughout the chapter.

1. Briefly describe the criteria that need to be present in order for a behavior to be considered "abnormal." Why is it important to have criteria in order to define a behavior as "abnormal"?

2. Compare and contrast the various approaches presented in this chapter that attempt to explain the etiology of abnormal behavior. What are the strengths and weaknesses of these models?

3. Choose one of the two case studies presented in this chapter and briefly describe the importance of the case in learning about the disorder. In what ways is this case similar to the other three cases? What are some issues that are unique to this case? What can be learned from studying case studies?

ANSWER KEY

Answers to the exercises are listed below; page numbers where the information is referenced in the textbook are given in parentheses.

Key Terms - Matching #1

			Names You Should Know
1. f (3)	8. s (15)	15. g (4)	1. c (21)
2. a (2)	9. e (3)	16. l (14)	2. b (20)
3. p (14)	10. d (2)	17. c (2)	3. d (25)
4. b (2)	11. h (6)	18. n (14)	4. a (8)
5. j (6)	12. t (17)	19. q (14)	5. e (21-22)
6. m (14)	13. o (14)	20. i (6)	
7. r (14)	14. k (11)		

Key Terms - Matching #2

a. 7 (7)	g. 3 (6)	l. 1 (6)	q. 21 (25)
b. 18 (24)	h. 16 (21)	m. 9 (8)	r. 11 (17)
c. 6 (7)	i. 14 (18)	n. 20 (25)	s. 4 (6)
d. 17 (23)	j. 19 (24)	o. 15 (19)	t. 12 (18)
e. 13 (18)	k. 2 (6)	p. 10 (8-9)	u. 5 (6)
f. 8 (7)			

Multiple Choice

1. d	4. c	7. a	10. d	13. c	16. d	19. b
2. a	5. a	8. b	11. b	14. b	17. a	
3. b	6. d	9. a	12. a	15. b	18. a	

Review of Concepts

1. true (3)
2. rare (3)
3. false (3)
4. representative (4)
5. false (6)
6. false (7)
7. true (7)
8. they may not have insight (7)
9. something rare is not necessarily bad (7-8)
10. distress; functioning (9)
11. it was voluntary and had political meaning (9)
12. false (10)
13. political pressure from gay rights activists (10-11)
14. categorical (14)
15. ECA (15)
16. false (15)
17. true (17)
18. false (17)
19. nature (17)
20. false (18)
21. false (19)
22. it's a logical error, like thinking a lack of aspirin causes headaches (19)
23. true (20)
24. true (20)
25. lunatic asylums (20)
26. creation of institutions to treat mental patients (21)
27. mental illness (21)
28. about 85% (22)
29. malaria (23)
30. psychiatrists (25)
31. Ph.D. clinical psychologists (25)

Understanding Research

1. People living in non-industrialized or undeveloped cultures or countries, or other than the U.S., Canada, and Europe; Inuits and the Yoruba; months; behaviors; 500; healers

2. voices; laughing; sense; schizophrenia; content; processes; shamans; crazy

3. magic; positive; negative; Health; 9; frequency; Western cultures; developed

4. The scientist who makes a new prediction must prove it to be true; experimental; null; innocent until proven guilty; conservative; false; undetected

5. lobotomies; fever therapy; coma therapy; institutionalization, medication, and psychotherapy; reject

CHAPTER 2 - CAUSES OF ABNORMAL BEHAVIOR: FROM PARADIGMS TO SYSTEMS

Chapter Outline

I. Overview

II. Brief Historical Perspective on Approaches to Etiology
    A. General Paresis and the Biomedical Approach
    B. Freud and Psychoanalytic Theory
    C. Experimental Psychology and Behaviorism
    D. Free Will and Humanistic Psychology
    E. Paradigms and the Causes of Abnormal Behavior

III. Systems Theory
    A. Holism
        1. Reductionism
    B. Subsystems and Levels of Analysis
    C. Causality: Multiple Factors and Multiple Pathways
        1. The Diathesis-Stress Model
        2. Equifinality or Multiple Pathways
    D. Reciprocal Causality and Control Processes
    E. Development

IV. Biological Factors
    A. The Neuron and Neurotransmitters
        1. Neurotransmitters and the Etiology of Psychopathology
        2. Mind-Body Dualism
    B. Major Brain Structures
        1. Cerebral Hemispheres
        2. Major Brain Structures and the Etiology of Psychopathology
    C. Psychophysiology
        1. Endocrine System
        2. Autonomic Nervous System
        3. Psychophysiology and the Etiology of Psychopathology

V. Behavior Genetics
        1. Some Basic Principles of Genetics
        2. Twin Studies
        3. Adoption Studies
        4. Family Incidence Studies
        5. Misinterpreting Behavior Genetics Findings
        6. Genetics and the Etiology of Psychopathology

VI. Psychological Factors
    A. Motivation, Emotion, and Temperament
        1. Hierarchy of Needs
        2. Attachment Theory
        3. Dominance Relations

          4. Emotions and Emotional Systems
          5. Temperament
          6. Motivation, Emotion, Temperament, and the Etiology of
             Psychopathology
     B. Learning and Cognition
          1. Modeling
          2. Social Cognition
          3. Learning, Distorted Cognition, and the Etiology of Psychopathology
     C. The Sense of Self
          1. Self Systems and the Etiology of Psychopathology
     D. Stages of Development
          1. Development and the Etiology of Psychopathology

VII. Social Factors
     A. Relationships and Psychopathology
          1. Marital Status and Psychopathology
          2. Social Relationships
     B. Gender and Gender Roles
     C. Race and Poverty
     D. Broad Societal Values

Learning Objectives

After reviewing the material presented in this chapter, you should be able to:

1. Define the biopsychosocial approach and explain how it is a systems
    approach.

2. Name some of the major breakthroughs that led to modern scientific
    abnormal psychology: a) discovery of the biological origins of general
    paresis, b) Freud's talking cure with hysterical patients, and c) emergence of
    scientific academic psychology (Wundt, Pavlov, Skinner, Watson, etc.).

3. Contrast holism from reductionism.

4. Understand various aspects about etiology: pathology can be caused by
    multiple factors/pathways; correlation does not mean cause; equifinality
    means that a disorder may have many different causes for different
    incidences of the disease; diathesis-stress models imply both predisposition
    and a stressful event may precipitate a disorder

5. Describe the basic functions of the hindbrain, midbrain, and forebrain.

6. Distinguish structural from psychophysiological problems.

7. Separate central from peripheral nervous systems; voluntary vs. autonomic
    nervous systems; sympathetic vs. parasympathetic nervous system.

8. Know the basic research design used for twin studies, adoption studies, and family incidence studies.

9. Define temperament and explain its significance in the etiology of psychopathology.

10. Describe some ways in which modeling, social cognition, and sense of self may affect abnormal behavior.

11. Understand that the following social factors are generally correlated (not causative) with psychopathology: relationship difficulties, gender, race, and poverty.

Key Terms - Matching #1

The following terms related to abnormal psychology are important to know. To test your knowledge, match the following terms with their definitions. Answers are listed at the end of the chapter.

a.	Paradigm		l.	Ego
b.	Multifactorial causes		m.	Reality principle
c.	Biomedical approach		n.	Superego
d.	General paresis		o.	Neurotic anxiety
e.	Syphilis		p.	Defense mechanisms
f.	Psychoanalytic theory		q.	Projection
g.	Hysteria		r.	Psychosexual development
h.	Conversion disorder		s.	Oedipal conflict
i.	Libido		t.	Electra complex
j.	Pleasure principle		u.	Unconscious
k.	Id		v.	Moral anxiety

1. _____ a paradigm of abnormal behavior based on the concepts of Freud, which focuses on unconscious processes and conflicts as its cause
2. _____ a set of assumptions about the substance of a theory and the scientific method used to test the theory
3. _____ unconscious processes that reduce conscious anxiety by distorting conflictual memories, emotions, and impulses
4. _____ the mode of operation for the ego, where the need to gratify impulses is balanced with demands of reality
5. _____ Freud's concept that a stage boys go through involves having sexual impulses toward their mothers and aggressive impulses toward their fathers, which is resolved by identifying with their fathers
6. _____ a psychoanalytic diagnostic category involving the conversion of psychological conflicts into physical symptoms
7. _____ Freud's theory of development
8. _____ a sexually transmitted disease caused by bacteria, the end stage of which includes psychiatric symptoms; treatable with antiobiotics
9. _____ a Freudian term for the part of personality which serves as the

conscience, containing societal standards of behavior

10. _____ the modern diagnostic category for hysteria
11. _____ a Freudian term for the part of personality which is the source of basic drives and motivations, including sexual and aggressive impulses
12. _____ the etiology of a disorder results from a combination of biological, psychological, and social factors
13. _____ produced by conflict between the id and the ego
14. _____ Freud's concept that a stage girls go through involves yearning for a penis, which they feel they must have lost
15. _____ a paradigm of abnormal behavior that focuses on biological causation and the analogy between physical and psychological illnesses
16. _____ a defense mechanism where the person perceives his or her own forbidden unconscious impulses as a characteristic of another person
17. _____ a Freudian term for sexual or life energy
18. _____ the mode of operation for the id, where impulses seek immediate gratification
19. _____ a disorder including delusions of grandeur, dementia, and progressive paralysis; progressively worsens, ending in death; caused by untreated syphilis
20. _____ a Freudian term for the part of personality which deals with the realities of the world
21. _____ mental processes or contents outside of a person's awareness, largely unavailable to the person
22. _____ produced by conflict between the ego and superego

Key Terms - Matching #2

The following terms related to abnormal psychology are important to know. To test your knowledge, match the following terms with their definitions. Answers are listed at the end of the chapter.

1. Introspection
2. Classical conditioning
3. Unconditioned stimulus
4. Unconditioned response
5. Conditioned stimulus
6. Conditioned response
7. Extinction
8. Operant conditioning
9. Positive reinforcement
10. Negative reinforcement
11. Punishment
12. Response cost
13. Behaviorism
14. Humanistic psychology
15. Determinism
16. Free will
17. Systems theory
18. Holism
19. Reductionism
20. Subsystems
21. Molecular
22. Molar
23. Levels of analysis
24. Correlational study
25. Correlation coefficient

a. _____ a neutral stimulus that, when repeatedly paired with a stimulus that elicits an automatic reaction, comes to produce that reaction itself
b. _____ the idea that human behavior is not determined but a product of a

person's choice

c. _____ the statistic for measuring how strongly two factors are related; it ranges between -1.0 and +1.0
d. _____ when the onset of a stimulus increases the frequency of a behavior
e. _____ the use of different perspectives, subsystems, or "lenses" to conceptualize causal factors
f. _____ when the removal of a stimulus decreases the frequency of behavior
g. _____ a research technique where subjects report systematically and in detail about their inner experiences
h. _____ how smaller units are perceived according to holism
i. _____ a paradigm that emphasizes interdependence, cybernetics, and holism
j. _____ Pavlov's form of learning through association of paired stimuli
k. _____ a research design where the relation between two factors is studied
l. _____ when the cessation of a stimulus increases the frequency of a behavior
m. _____ a stimulus that elicits an automatic reaction
n. _____ the assumption that human behavior is caused by predictable and potentially knowable internal and/or external events
o. _____ an automatic reaction to an event
p. _____ the most general
q. _____ the belief within psychology that observable behaviors are the only appropriate focus of psychological study
r. _____ a learning theory asserting that behavior is a function of its consequences; that behavior increases if it is rewarded and decreases if it is punished
s. _____ the gradual elimination of a response when learning conditions change
t. _____ the idea that the whole is more than the sum of its parts
u. _____ the most reductionistic
v. _____ the perspective that the whole is the sum of its parts, and that the task for science is to divide the world into smaller and smaller components
w. _____ when the introduction of a stimulus decreases the frequency of a behavior
x. _____ a paradigm of abnormal behavior that rejects determinism and argues that human behavior is the product of free will
y. _____ a response that is elicited by a conditioned stimulus

Key Terms - Matching #3

The following terms related to abnormal psychology are important to know. To test your knowledge, match the following terms with their definitions. Answers are listed at the end of the chapter.

a.	Positive correlations	n.	Prognosis
b.	Negative correlations	o.	Anatomy
c.	Third-variable	p.	Physiology
d.	Diathesis-stress model	q.	Neuroanatomy
e.	Equifinality	r.	Neurophysiology
f.	Reciprocal causality	s.	Neurons
g.	Linear causality	t.	Soma
h.	Cybernetics	u.	Dendrites

i.	Homeostasis		v.	Axon	
j.	Developmental psychopathology		w.	Terminal buttons	
k.	Developmental norms		x.	Synapse	
l.	Premorbid history		y.	Neurotransmitters	
m.	Reverse causality				

1. _____ a communication and control process that uses feedback loops in order to adjust progress toward a goal
2. _____ the study of brain structures
3. _____ a pattern of behavior that precedes the onset of the disorder
4. _____ trunk of the neuron that transmits messages toward other cells
5. _____ the idea that causality is bidirectional
6. _____ cell body
7. _____ predictions about the future course of a disorder
8. _____ the same psychological disorder may have different causes
9. _____ the study of biological structures
10. _____ an approach to abnormal psychology that emphasizes the importance of age-graded averages to determining what constitutes abnormal behavior
11. _____ the study of biological functions
12. _____ buds on the end of the axon where messages are sent out to other neurons
13. _____ as one factor goes up, the other factor goes down
14. _____ age-graded averages
15. _____ as one factor goes up, the other factor goes up
16. _____ causation operates in one direction only
17. _____ branching cell structures that receive messages from other cells
18. _____ the possibility that causation could be operating in the opposite direction; Y could be causing X instead of X causing Y
19. _____ the tendency to maintain a steady state
20. _____ the study of brain functions
21. _____ a small gap between neurons filled with fluid
22. _____ a correlation between two variables could be explained by their joint relation with some unmeasured factor
23. _____ nerve cells
24. _____ chemical substances released into the synapse that carry signals from one neuron to another
25. _____ a view of the etiology of a disorder that assumes it is produced by an interaction between a predisposition and a precipitating event

Key Terms - Matching #4

The following terms related to abnormal psychology are important to know. To test your knowledge, match the following terms with their definitions. Answers are listed at the end of the chapter.

1.	Receptors	13.	Limbic system
2.	Reuptake	14.	Thalamus
3.	Neuromodulators	15.	Hypothalamus

4.	Endorphins	16.	Cerebral hemispheres
5.	Dualism	17.	Lateralized
6.	Hindbrain	18.	Corpus callosum
7.	Medulla	19.	Ventricles
8.	Pons	20.	Cerebral cortex
9.	Cerebellum	21.	Frontal lobe
10.	Midbrain	22.	Parietal lobe
11.	Reticular activating system	23.	Temporal lobe
12.	Forebrain	24.	Occipital lobe

a. _____ a brain grouping including the medulla, pons, and cerebellum

b. _____ regulates emotion and basic learning processes

c. _____ sites on the dendrites or soma of a neuron that are sensitive to certain neurotransmitters

d. _____ the uneven surface of the brain just underneath the skull which controls and integrates sophisticated memory, sensory, and motor functions

e. _____ receives and integrates sensory information and plays a role in spatial reasoning

f. _____ controls bodily functions which sustain life, like heart rate and respiration

g. _____ the process of recapturing some neurotransmitters from the synapse before they reach the receptors of another neuron

h. _____ receives and integrates sensory information from the sense organs and from higher brain structures

i. _____ four connected chambers in the brain filled with cerebrospinal fluid

j. _____ each cerebral hemisphere serves a specialized role in brain function; the left hemisphere is involved in language and the right hemisphere in spatial relations

k. _____ regulates stages of sleep

l. _____ connects the two cerebral hemispheres and coordinates their different functions

m. _____ helps coordinate physical movement

n. _____ processes sound and smell, regulates emotions, and is involved in learning, memory, and language

o. _____ controls a number of complex functions like reasoning, planning, emotion, speech, and movement

p. _____ the view that mind and body are separable

q. _____ regulates sleep and waking

r. _____ a brain grouping which evolved last and is the location of most sensory, emotional, and cognitive processes

s. _____ the two major structures of the forebrain and the site of most sensory, emotional, and cognitive processes

t. _____ chemicals that may be released from neurons or endocrine glands which influence communications of many neurons by affecting the functioning of neurotransmitters

u. _____ a brain grouping which controls some motor activities, especially fighting and sex, and includes part of the reticular activating system

v. _____ receives and interprets visual information

w. _____ controls basic biological urges such as eating, drinking, and sex

x. _____ one type of neuromodulator which is chemically similar to the drug opium

Key Terms - Matching #5

The following terms related to abnormal psychology are important to know. To test your knowledge, match the following terms with their definitions. Answers are listed at the end of the chapter.

a. Psychophysiology
b. Endocrine system
c. Hormones
d. Hyperthyroidism/Graves' disease
e. Central nervous system
f. Peripheral nervous system
g. Somatic nervous system
h. Autonomic nervous system
i. Sympathetic nervous system
j. Parasympathetic nervous system
k. Genes
l. Chromosomes
m. Behavior genetics

n. Genotype
o. Phenotype
p. Alleles
q. Locus
r. Polygenic
s. Monozygotic (MZ)
t. Dizygotic (DZ)
u. Concordance
v. Shared environment
w. Nonshared environment
x. Probands
y. Individual differences
z. Species-typical characteristics

1. _____ the study of changes in the functioning of the body that result from psychological experiences
2. _____ an individual's actual genetic structure
3. _____ fraternal twins produced from separate fertilized eggs; the twins are as genetically related as nontwin siblings
4. _____ the voluntary nervous system that governs muscular control
5. _____ chainlike structures in the nucleus of all cells
6. _____ the component of the family environment that offers the same or very similar experiences to all siblings
7. _____ a division of the human nervous system including all connections to the body's muscles, sensory systems, and organs
8. _____ the component of the family and outside of the family environment that is unique to that sibling
9. _____ a specific location on a chromosome
10. _____ a division of the human nervous system including the brain and spinal cord
11. _____ characteristics all people have in common as part of human nature
12. _____ units of DNA, located on the chromosomes, that carry information about heredity
13. _____ caused by more than one gene
14. _____ chemical substances that affect the functioning of distant body systems
15. _____ the study of genetic influences on the evolution and development of normal and abnormal behavior
16. _____ a collection of glands located throughout the body that produce psychophysiological responses by releasing hormones into the blood-stream
17. _____ the involuntary nervous system that regulates body organs
18. _____ identical twins produced from a single fertilized egg; the twins have identical genotypes

19. _____ the expression of a given genotype
20. _____ agreement; when twin pairs either both have a disorder or both are free of the disorder
21. _____ alternate forms of a genetic trait
22. _____ how people are different from one another
23. _____ a disease where the thyroid gland secretes too much of the hormone thyroxin, causing restlessness, agitation, and anxiety
24. _____ a division of the autonomic nervous system that controls the slowing of arousal and energy conservation
25. _____ index cases; people who have a disorder and then their relatives are examined to see if they also have the disorder
26. _____ a division of the autonomic nervous system that is associated with increased arousal and expenditure of energy

Key Terms - Matching #6

The following terms related to abnormal psychology are important to know. To test your knowledge, match the following terms with their definitions. Answers are listed at the end of the chapter.

1.	Hierarchy of needs	11.	Agreeableness
2.	Attachment theory	12.	Conscientiousness
3.	Ethology	13.	Anxious attachments
4.	Imprinting	14.	Goodness of fit
5.	Dominance	15.	Modeling
6.	Emotions	16.	Identification
7.	Temperament	17.	Social cognition
8.	Neuroticism	18.	Attributions
9.	Extraversion	19.	Learned helplessness theory
10.	Openness to experience	20.	Cognitive errors

a. _____ internal feeling states
b. _____ a personality dimension of active and talkative vs. passive and reserved
c. _____ a personality dimension of trusting and kind vs. hostile and selfish
d. _____ learning through imitation of others
e. _____ the study of animal behavior
f. _____ an ordering of human motivations according to priority by Maslow
g. _____ the study of how humans process information about themselves and others
h. _____ the theory that infants form special and selective bonds with their care-givers early in life
i. _____ uncertain or ambivalent parent-child relationships resulting from incon-sistent and unresponsive parenting particularly in the first year of life
j. _____ may be related to depression; wrongly attributing negative events to internal, global, and stable causes
k. _____ a personality dimension of nervous and moody vs. calm and pleasant
l. _____ the match between children's temperaments and their environment
m. _____ automatic and distorted perceptions of reality; negative ones may be

linked to depression

n. _____ a process where children not only imitate a model but want to be like it and adopt its values

o. _____ the hierarchical ordering of a social group into more and less powerful members

p. _____ an inflexible process of forming selective bonds in the first hours of life which occurs in some species

q. _____ a personality dimension of imaginative and curious vs. shallow and imperceptive

r. _____ people's beliefs about cause-effect relationships

s. _____ characteristic styles of relating to the world that are very stable

t. _____ a personality dimension of organized and reliable vs. careless and negligent

Key Terms - Matching #7

The following terms related to abnormal psychology are important to know. To test your knowledge, match the following terms with their definitions. Answers are listed at the end of the chapter.

a.	Identity	k.	Fixation
b.	Role identities	l.	Regression
c.	Self-schema	m.	Social roles
d.	Irrational beliefs	n.	Labeling theory
e.	Self-control	o.	Self-fulfilling prophesy
f.	Socialization	p.	Social support
g.	Self-concept	q.	Gender roles
h.	Self-efficacy	r.	Relational
i.	Developmental stage	s.	Instrumental
j.	Developmental transition	t.	Androgyny

1. _____ the belief that one can achieve desired goals
2. _____ a return to an earlier stage or style of coping or behaving
3. _____ internal rules for guiding appropriate behavior
4. _____ abnormal behavior is created by social expectations or roles
5. _____ oriented toward others
6. _____ styles of behaving according to the expectations of the social situation
7. _____ possessing both female and male gender-role characteristics
8. _____ various senses of self which correspond with life roles
9. _____ the emotional and practical assistance received from others
10. _____ definition of self
11. _____ cognitive conceptualizations about oneself
12. _____ impossible, absolute standards
13. _____ when psychological development is arrested at a particular stage
14. _____ roles associated with social expectations about gendered behavior
15. _____ people's actions conforming to the expectations created by a label given to them
16. _____ the process where parents, teachers, and peers use discipline, praise,

and example to teach children prosocial behavior and set limits on antisocial behavior
17. _____ feelings about one's worthiness and capability
18. _____ the idea that stressful and important changes occur during times of rapid biological, psychological, or social development
19. _____ oriented toward action and achievement
20. _____ a period of continuous and slow change

Names You Should Know - Matching

The following people have played an important role in research and theory of anxiety disorders. To test your knowledge, match the following names with the descriptions of their contributions to the study of abnormal psychology. Answers are listed at the end of the chapter.

a. Sigmund Freud
b. B.F. Skinner
c. Rene Descartes
d. John Bowlby

e. Wilhelm Wundt
f. John B. Watson
g. Gregor Mendel

h. Ivan Pavlov
i. Thomas Kuhn
j. Abraham Maslow

1. _____ attempted to balance religious teachings with emerging scientific reasoning by proposing dualism
2. _____ founded behaviorism and applied learning theory to the study of abnormal behavior
3. _____ developed attachment theory, based in part on ethology
4. _____ developed psychoanalytic theory; focused on the importance of early childhood experiences and unconscious conflicts
5. _____ conducted a series of studies on classical conditioning
6. _____ applied the idea of paradigm to the historical study of science
7. _____ discovered genetic inheritance; made the distinction between genotypes and phenotypes
8. _____ a humanistic psychologist who explored motivation
9. _____ one of the first experimental psychologists; pioneered the scientific study of psychological phenomena
10. _____ conducted a series of studies on operant conditioning

Review of Concepts - Fill in the Blank and True/False

This section will help focus your studying by testing whether you understand the concepts presented in the text. After you have read and reviewed the material, test your comprehension and memory by filling in the following blanks or circling the right answer. Answers are listed at the end of the chapter.

1. It is likely that continuing research will answer the "nature-nurture" debate by

demonstrating on a disorder-by-disorder basis what the cause of each disorder is:

true   false

2. What three major events encouraged advances in the scientific understanding of the etiology of psychopathology in the nineteenth and twentieth centuries?

_____, _____,

and _____

3. The development of a _____ for general paresis inspired a search for its cause, which took 100 years of investigation.

4. General paresis was eliminated with the advent of _____.

5. The elimination of general paresis encouraged researchers to adopt what paradigm in their research on etiology of mental disorders? _____

6. What theorist opposed the biomedical paradigm for mental disorders? _____

7. Freud developed his theories largely on the basis of _____ rather than scientific research.

8. What approach did Wundt use in studying psychological phenomena, which was his greatest contribution to psychology? _____

9. Behaviorists are primarily concerned with the _____ of mental disorders rather than understanding their causes.

10. _____ psychology was a reaction against biomedical, psychoanalytic, and behavioral theories of abnormal behavior.

11. Humanistic psychologists tend to blame dysfunctional, abnormal, or aggressive behavior on: **the individual   society**

12. What are the four paradigms the authors of your text focus on in explaining mental disorders? _____, _____, _____, and _____

13. The textbook example of the Martian scientists trying to figure out what causes automobiles to move points out the importance of the _____ that a research approach uses.

14. A predisposition toward developing a disorder is called a:

stress   diathesis

15. A thermostat is a good example which systems theory concept? _____

16. The density and sensitivity of _____ on neurons has been implicated in some types of abnormal behavior.

17. All psychological experience has a representation in the biochemistry of the

_____.

18. A _____ is caused by blood vessels in the brain rupturing and cutting off the supply of oxygen to parts of the brain, thereby killing surrounding brain tissue.

19. Psychophysiological **overarousal** or **underarousal** has been

hypothesized to be responsible for excessive anxiety; while psychophysiological **overarousal** or **underarousal** has been linked with antisocial behavior.

20. The simple mode of dominant/recessive inheritance has been linked with forms of which of the following kinds of abnormal behavior?

schizophrenia   mental retardation   depression

21. The genetic contributions to most disorders are hypothesized to be caused by:

a single gene   multiple genes

22. If a disorder is purely genetic, the concordance for MZ twins would be _____% and the concordance for DZ twins would be _____%.

23. If the concordance rates for MZ and DZ twins are the same, then what type of factors are responsible for the disorder?   **genetic   environmental**

24. Family incidence studies ask whether diseases _____.

25. If a disorder is shown to be genetic, then nothing can change it: **true   false**

26. According to attachment theorists, displays of distress by human infants serve to keep caregivers in _____, which makes infants more likely to survive.

27. Negative emotions occur together, but negative emotions also occur together with _____ emotions.

28. The most effective parents are those who provide both high levels of _____ and _____.

29. Two prominant stage theories are those proposed by which theorists? _____ and _____

30. There is a correlation between marital status of parents and emotional _____ of children.

31. A close relationship with an adult outside the family can protect children from the effects of troubled family circumstances: **true   false**

32. Some theorists have suggested that _____ are responsible for the much higher rates of depression among women.

33. One study found that 12% of school-aged children had seen a _____ in the streets outside their homes in a Washington, D. C. neighborhood.

Multiple Choice Questions

The following multiple choice questions will test your comprehension of the material presented in the chapter. Answers are listed at the end of the chapter.

1) Which of the following is a model that views psychopathology as resulting from physical factors that form a predisposition combined with a threatening or challenging experience?

   a. medical model
   b. diathesis-stress model
   c. threshold model
   d. biopsychosocial model

2) The assumption that biological explanations are more useful than psychological explanations because they deal with smaller units is called:

   a. biological perspective
   b. genetic predisposition
   c. biological reductionism
   d. medical model

3) Which regulates the functions of various organs such as the heart and stomach?

   a. somatic nervous system
   b. autonomic nervous system
   c. sympathetic nervous system
   d. parasympathetic nervous system

4) According to Freud, this is the part of the personality that attempts to fulfill id impulses while at the same time dealing with the realities of the world.

   a. ego
   b. id
   c. superego
   d. libido

5) All of the following are methods of learning EXCEPT:

   a. classical conditioning
   b. operant conditioning
   c. introjection
   d. modeling

6) Leading developmental theory speculates that children whose parents are _____ and _____ are better adjusted than those whose parents are inadequate on one or both of these dimensions.

   a. loving; firm in their discipline
   b. authoritative; hold high expectations of their child
   c. demanding; promote individuality
   d. congenial; encourage separation and independence

7) Freud was trained by this neurologist who successfully used hypnosis to treat what used to be called hysteria.

   a. Harry Stack Sullivan
   b. Ludwig von Bertalanffy
   c. Fritz Perls
   d. Jean Charcot

8) While watching her daughter play kickball in the street of their neighborhood, Mrs. Jones witnesses her daughter fatally being hit by a car. Shortly following this tragedy, Mrs. Jones loses her vision. After visits to numerous doctors, there is no known organic impairment to cause the blindness. Mrs. Jones' condition could be considered which of the following disorders?

a. depression
b. conversion disorder

c. hysteria
d. hypochondriasis

9) Which of the following could be considered an uncertain or ambivalent parent-child relationship that is a consequence of inconsistent and unresponsive parenting, particularly during the first year of life?

a. anxious attachment
b. neurotic attachment

c. oppositional attachment
d. apathetic attachment

10) All of the following are associated with the humanistic approach EXCEPT:

a. Carl Rogers
b. B.F. Skinner

c. Fritz Perls
d. Abraham Maslow

11) In the famous experiments on which classical conditioning was based, the bell served as the _____ and the meat powder was the _____.

a. conditioned response; unconditioned response
b. unconditioned response; conditioned response
c. conditioned stimulus; unconditioned stimulus
d. unconditioned stimulus; conditioned stimulus

12) The enigma written by Lord Byron and presented in this chapter illustrates that:

a. paradigms are unscientific and should not be used in evaluating situations
b. the hidden meanings in life are sometimes difficult to comprehend, however the use of a paradigm can aid in this process
c. we should use our paradigm to reveal the meaning from certain situations
d. assumptions made by a paradigm can at times act as blinders and lead an investigator to overlook what otherwise might be obvious

13) Mike's mother took away his privilege to use the computer for two days because he hit his sister. This is an example of:

a. punishment
b. response cost

c. extinction
d. negative reinforcement

14) Systems theory has roots in all of the following EXCEPT:

a. biology
b. engineering

c. philosophy
d. all of the above

15) _____ are chainlike structures that are found in the nuclei of cells.

a. alleles
b. genes

c. chromosomes
d. loci

16) Which is a pattern of behavior that precedes the onset of the disorder?

    a. prognosis
    b. premorbid history
    c. determinism
    d. self-fulfilling prophesy

17) Advances in the scientific understanding of the etiology of psychopathology did not appear until the nineteenth and early twentieth centuries when all of the following major events occurred EXCEPT:

    a. the number of people diagnosed with psychopathology rapidly increased
    b. the cause of general paresis was discovered
    c. the emergence of Sigmund Freud
    d. the creation of a new academic discipline called psychology

18) According to Freud's theory of psychosexual development, boys harboring forbidden sexual desires for their mothers is called (a/an):

    a. defense mechanism
    b. neurotic anxiety
    c. Electra complex
    d. Oedipal conflict

19) According to the "Big Five" bipolar dimensions of personality, this domain is characterized by trusting and kind versus hostile and selfish.

    a. conscientiousness
    b. agreeableness
    c. neuroticism
    d. extraversion

20) According to the psychodynamic paradigm, the cause of abnormality is:

    a. early childhood experiences
    b. social learning
    c. frustrations of society
    d. genes, infection, or other physical damage

21) The cornerstone of humanistic psychology, _____ is the assumption that human behavior is not determined but is a product of how people choose to act.

    a. holism
    b. self-fulfilling prophesy
    c. individuation
    d. free will

22) Which of the following is a communication and control process that uses feedback loops to adjust progress toward a goal?

    a. homeostasis
    b. neuromodulators
    c. cybernetics
    d. neurotransmitters

23) This nervous system is responsible for controlling activities associated with increased arousal and energy expenditure.

    a. sympathetic nervous system
    b. parasympathetic nervous system
    c. autonomic nervous system
    d. somatic nervous system

24) Freud can be credited with all of the following EXCEPT:

    a. offering specific, empirically-derived hypotheses about his theory
    b. calling attention to unconscious processes
    c. formulating a stage theory of child development
    d. identifying numerous intrapsychic defenses

25) Which of the following are characteristic ways of behaving according to the expectations of the social situation?

    a. prescribed roles   c. gender roles
    b. social roles   d. transitional roles

26) All of the following are true from a systems perspective regarding the etiology of psychopathology EXCEPT:

    a. there may be biopsychosocial contributions to psychopathology, but clear hypotheses must still be supported by empirical evidence
    b. social domains of behavior are the most significant contribution to the causes of abnormal behavior
    c. different types of abnormal behavior have very different causes
    d. causes of almost all forms of abnormal behavior are unknown at present

27) According to the behavioral paradigm, the inborn human nature is:

    a. aggressive
    b. basically good
    c. basically selfish, but having some altruism
    d. neutral, like a blank slate

28) Which of the following is a defense mechanism that includes the insistence that an experience, memory, or internal need did not occur or does not exist?

    a. sublimation   c. denial
    b. reaction formation   d. repression

29) This occurs when a conditioned stimulus is no longer presented together with an unconditioned stimulus.

    a. extinction   c. negative reinforcement
    b. punishment   d. response cost

30) A _____ is an individual's actual genetic structure.

    a. locus   c. proband
    b. phenotype   d. genotype

31) This theory suggests that depression is caused by wrongly attributing bad events to internal, global, and stable causes.

   a. labeling theory
   b. learned helplessness theory
   c. modeling theory
   d. social cognition theory

Understanding Research - Fill in the Blank

Marriage and Mental Health: The text presents a detailed description of a study by Robins and Regier on the ECA in the Research Close-Up on pp. 64-65. Finding the answers to these questions will help you get a good understanding of this study and why it is important. It is not necessary to memorize the answers; the process of finding them in the textbook will help you learn the material you need to know.

1. A factor commonly found to be correlated with psychological well-being is
_____. This study, the _____ study, involved interviewing
_____ of people. There were consistent correlations between marriage
and _____ health. Of people still in their first marriage, _____% were
diagnosed with depression in the past year; of people who were never married, the
rate was _____%; among those divorced once the rate was _____%; among those
divorced more than once the rate was _____%.

2. What other diagnostic category was found to be correlated with marital status?
_____ What percentage of people in their first marriage had ever
had this diagnosis? _____% What percentage of people never married? _____%
What percentage of people divorced once? _____% What percentage of people
divorced more than once? _____% Another disorder that was correlated was
_____. Marital status was correlated with virtually _____
psychological disorder that was diagnosed in this study.

3. One explanation for these findings is that not being married _____
mental disorders, because having a spouse may provide emotional support, and
divorce and _____ and loss of support may increase susceptibility to
disorders.   However, emotional problems may _____ marital status.
Psychologically disturbed people may have more trouble _____ and forming
relationships, and may have shakier marriages. This explanation is called
_____. Another explanation is the _____
interpretation, which states that another factor may cause a _____
correlation between marital status and abnormal behavior. One possible factor to

consider is _____.

4. These different explanations result in very different implications for _____ of mental disorders and social _____. What should be done if the third variable hypothesis is correct? _____

What do most researchers conclude about the correlation between marriage and mental health? It remains after controlling for _____ variables; for disorders like schizophrenia, marital status is a reaction to, not a cause of, the _____ problem; and marital status does have causal impact on disorders like _____.

The Correlational Study: The text discusses this type of research in the Research Methods section on pp. 43-44. Finding the answers to these questions will help you get a good understanding of these issues.

5. In a correlational study, the relation between two _____ is studied systematically. The statistic that measures how strongly two factors are related is the correlation _____, which ranges between _____.

If the correlation is positive, that means that as one factor goes up, the other factor goes _____. What are two examples of positive correlations given?

_____

If the correlation is negative, that means that as one factor goes up, the other factor goes _____. One note of caution is that correlation does not mean

_____.

6. What are the two alternative explanations besides one factor causing the other?

_____ and _____

What does spurious mean? _____

_____

Brief Essay

As a final exercise, write out answers to the following brief essay questions. Then compare your answers with the material presented in the text.

After you have answered these questions, review the "critical thinking" questions that are presented at the end of the text chapter. Answering these questions will help you integrate important issues and themes that have been featured throughout the chapter.

1. Compare and contrast the following behavior genetics investigations: twin studies, adoption, and family incidence studies. In what ways are these findings helpful? In what ways could these findings possibly be misinterpreted?

2. Discuss Maslow's hierarchy of needs theory. In what ways is this similar to attachment theory as proposed by Bowlby? In what ways is it different? Could these theories complement one another? Why or why not?

3. Compare and contrast Freud and Erikson's theories on development. Which theory makes the most sense to you and your personal experience? Why?

4. Discuss why it is not enough to focus on one subsystem or level of analysis when viewing psychopathology. What do you gain by focusing on multifactorial causes?

ANSWER KEY

Answers to the exercises are listed below; page numbers where the information is referenced in the textbook are given in parentheses.

Key Terms - Matching #1

1. f (36)	9. n (37)	17. i (36)
2. a (32)	10. h (36)	18. j (36)
3. p (37)	11. k (36)	19. d (35)
4. m (36)	12. b (32)	20. l (36)
5. s (37)	13. o (37)	21. u (37)
6. g (36)	14. t (37)	22. v (37)
7. r (37)	15. c (35)	
8. e (35)	16. q (37)	

Names You Should Know

1. c (48)	9. e (38)
2. f (39)	10. b (38)
3. d (57)	
4. a (36-7)	
5. h (38)	
6. i (40)	
7. g (53)	
8. j (56)	

Key Terms - Matching #2

a. 5 (38)
b. 16 (39)
c. 25 (43)
d. 9 (38)
e. 23 (42)
f. 12 (38)
g. 1 (38)
h. 20 (41)
i. 17 (41)
j. 2 (38)
k. 24 (43)
l. 10 (38)
m. 3 (38)

n. 15 (39)
o. 4 (38)
p. 22 (42)
q. 13 (39)
r. 8 (38)
s. 7 (38)
t. 18 (41)
u. 21 (42)
v. 19 (41)
w. 11 (38)
x. 14 (39)
y. 6 (38)

Key Terms - Matching #3

1. h (45)
2. q (46)
3. l (46)
4. v (46)
5. f (45)
6. t (46)
7. n (46)
8. e (44)
9. o (46)
10. j (45)
11. p (46)
12. w (47)
13. b (43)

14. k (45)
15. a (43)
16. g (45)
17. u (46)
18. m (43)
19. i (45)
20. r (46)
21. x (47)
22. c (43)
23. s (46)
24. y (47)
25. d (44)

Key Terms - Matching #4

a. 6 (48)
b. 13 (48)
c. 1 (47)
d. 20 (49)
e. 22 (49)
f. 7 (48)
g. 2 (47)
h. 14 (49)
i. 19 (49)
j. 17 (49)
k. 8 (48)
l. 18 (49)

m. 9 (48)
n. 23 (49)
o. 21 (49)
p. 5 (48)
q. 11 (48)
r. 12 (48)
s. 16 (49)
t. 3 (47)
u. 10 (48)
v. 24 (49)
w. 15 (49)
x. 4 (47)

Key Terms - Matching #5

1. a (49)
2. n (53)
3. t (54)
4. g (52)
5. l (53)
6. v (54)
7. f (52)
8. w (55)
9. q (53)
10. e (52)
11. z (56)
12. k (53)
13. r (54)

14. c (52)
15. m (53)
16. b (52)
17. h (52)
18. s (54)
19. o (53)
20. u (54)
21. p (53)
22. y (56)
23. d (52)
24. j (52)
25. x (55)
26. i (52)

Key Terms - Matching #6

a. 6 (58)
b. 9 (59)
c. 11 (59)
d. 15 (59)
e. 3 (57)
f. 1 (56)
g. 17 (60)
h. 2 (57)
i. 13 (59)
j. 19 (60)

k. 8 (59)
l. 14 (59)
m. 20 (60)
n. 16 (59)
o. 5 (57)
p. 4 (57)
q. 10 (59)
r. 18 (60)
s. 7 (58)
t. 12 (59)

Key Terms - Matching #7

1. h (61)
2. l (62)
3. e (61)
4. n (63)
5. r (66)
6. m (63)
7. t (66)
8. b (61)
9. p (65)
10. a (60)

11. c (61)
12. d (61)
13. k (62)
14. q (66)
15. o (63)
16. f (61)
17. g (61)
18. j (62)
19. s (66)
20. i (61)

Review of Concepts

1. false (32)
2. discovery of the cause of general paresis; Freud; birth of psychology (35)
3. diagnostic category (35)
4. penicillin (36)
5. biomedical (36)
6. Freud (36)
7. introspection (37)
8. the scientific method (38)
9. treatment (39)
10. Humanistic (39)
11. society (39)
12. systems theory; biological factors; psychological factors; social factors (41-67)
13. level of analysis (42)
14. diathesis (44)
15. cybernetics (45)
16. receptors (47)
17. brain (48)
18. stroke (49)
19. overarousal; underarousal (53)
20. mental retardation (53)
21. multiple genes (54)
22. 100%; 50% (54)
23. environmental (54)
24. run in families (55)
25. false (56)
26. proximity (57)
27. positive (58)
28. love; discipline (59)
29. Freud; Erikson (61)
30. problems (63)
31. true (65)
32. gender roles (66)
33. dead body (66)

Multiple Choice

1. b	6. a	11. c	16. b	21. d	26. b	31. d
2. c	7. d	12. d	17. a	22. c	27. d	
3. b	8. b	13. b	18. d	23. a	28. c	
4. a	9. a	14. d	19. b	24. a	29. a	
5. c	10. b	15. c	20. a	25. b	30. d	

Understanding Research

1. marital status; ECA; thousands; mental; 1.5%; 2.4%; 4.1%; 5.8%

2. alcoholism; 8.9%; 15%; 16.2%; 24.2%; schizophrenia; every

3. causes; conflict; cause; dating; reverse causality; third variable; spurious; poverty

4. treatment; policy; intervention should focus on changing the third variable; third; emotional; depression

5. factors; coefficient; -1.00 and +1.00; up; height and weight, years of education and income; down; causation

6. reverse causality, third variable; the correlation is an artifact of the relation of both variables with a third variable

CHAPTER 3 - TREATMENT OF PSYCHOLOGICAL DISORDERS

Chapter Outline

I. Overview

II. Traditional Treatment Paradigms
    A. Brief Historical Perspective
    B. Biological Treatments
        1. Electroconvulsive Therapy
        2. Psychosurgery
        3. Psychopharmacology
    C. Psychodynamic Psychotherapies
        1. Freudian Psychoanalysis
        2. Current Status of Freudian Psychoanalysis
        3. Ego Analysts and Psychodynamic Psychotherapy
        4. Short-Term Psychodynamic Psychotherapy
    D. Behavior Therapy
        1. Classical Conditioning Techniques
            a. Systematic Desensitization
            b. In Vivo Desensitization
            c. Flooding
            d. Aversion Therapy
        2. Operant Conditioning Techniques
            a. Contingency Management
            b. Social Skills Training
    E. Cognitive Behavior Therapy
        1. Attribution Retraining
        2. Self-Instruction Training
        3. Cognitive Therapy
        4. Rational-Emotive Therapy
        5. Integration: The Evolution of Cognitive Behavior Therapy
    F. Humanistic Therapies
        1. Client-Centered Therapy
        2. Gestalt Therapy
        3. Humanistic Psychotherapy: A Means, Not an End?

III. Research on Psychotherapy
    A. Psychotherapy Outcome Research
        1. Meta-Analysis
        2. Improvement Without Treatment
        3. No Treatment Control Groups
        4. Efficacy and Effectiveness: The *Consumer Reports* Study
        5. Two Predictors of Treatment Outcome: Treatment Length and the YAVIS Client
        6. Outcome Research on Different Paradigms for Psychotherapy
    B. Psychotherapy Process Research: Toward the Integration of Psychotherapies
        1. The Placebo Effect

2. Psychotherapy as Social Support
3. Psychotherapy as Social Influence

IV. Changing Social Systems: Couples, Family, and Group Therapy
    A. Couples Therapy
    B. Family Therapy
    C. Group Therapy
    D. Community Psychology and Prevention

V. Specific Treatments for Specific Disorders

Learning Objectives

After reviewing the material presented in this chapter, you should be able to:

1. Understand the systems approach to psychotherapy: using different approaches for different disorders, when appropriate and effective.

2. Make broad comparisons between biological, psychodynamic, behavioral, and humanistic approaches to treatment.

3. Distinguish the two historical trends toward spiritual/religious treatment from the natural/scientific approach to treatment.

4. Describe electroconvulsive therapy and psychosurgery as they are practiced today.

5. Evaluate the overall effectiveness of psychopharmacology in the treatment of mental illness.

6. Describe the basic goals and primary techniques involved in psychoanalysis.

7. Explain the theory behind ego analysis and the differences between psychoanalysis and psychodynamic psychotherapy.

8. Articulate the ways in which classical conditioning principles are utilized in behavior therapy techniques such as systematic desensitization, in vivo desensitization, flooding, and aversion therapy.

9. Describe contingency management and social skills training programs.

10. Understand the basic principles of attribution therapy, self-instruction training, cognitive therapy, and rational emotive therapy.

11. Know how client-centered therapy and Gestalt therapy reflects the underlying principles of humanistic psychology.

12. Describe the basic findings produced from meta-analysis of psychotherapy outcome studies.

13. Compare efficacy research to effectiveness research on psychotherapy: what are the strengths and weaknesses of each?

14. Use Sloane's study to compare behavioral therapy with psychodynamic psychotherapy in terms of outcomes.

15. Define psychotherapy process research and describe some of its basic findings.

16. Compare the goals, techniques, and known outcomes of couples therapy, family therapy, and group therapy; describe the differences between these approaches and individual psychotherapy.

17. List some basic recommendations that the authors suggest will improve the effectiveness of psychotherapy.

Key Terms - Matching #1

The following terms related to the treatment of psychological disorders are important to know. To test your knowledge, match the following terms with their definitions. Answers are listed at the end of the chapter.

a.	Psychotherapy	m.	Trephining
b.	Psychotherapy outcome research	n.	Symptom alleviation
c.	Psychotherapy process research	o.	Electroconvulsive therapy
d.	Eclectic	p.	Bilateral ECT
e.	Biological therapies	q.	Unilateral ECT
f.	Psychodynamic therapies	r.	Psychosurgery
g.	Behavior therapies	s.	Prefrontal lobotomy
h.	Cognitive therapies	t.	Cingulotomy
i.	Humanistic therapies	u.	Human subject committee
j.	Defensive style	v.	Informed consent
k.	Homework	w.	Psychopharmacology
l.	Genuineness	x.	Psychoactive drugs

1. _____ investigates similarities in practice by studying aspects of the therapist-client relationship
2. _____ an ancient form of surgery to treat mental disorders consisting of chipping a hole in the patient's skull
3. _____ treatments based on Freud's writings and later related theorists; focus on exploring the patient's past and unconscious to promote insight
4. _____ electroconvulsive therapy through both brain hemispheres
5. _____ treatments based on the perspective that mental illness is like physical illness
6. _____ a procedure in which the frontal lobes of the brain are surgically destroyed
7. _____ ability to be oneself with other people and to oneself
8. _____ a panel that reviews the ethics of proposed research with human

subjects

9. _____ treatments focusing on present feelings which encourage the client to take responsibility for their actions
10. _____ a type of behavior therapy focused on changing the client's cognitions
11. _____ surgical destruction of specific regions of the brain
12. _____ treatment for mental illness involving the deliberate induction of a seizure by passing electricity through the brain
13. _____ electroconvulsive therapy through one brain hemisphere
14. _____ protecting oneself from being aware of inner feelings
15. _____ compares the effectiveness of alternative forms of treatment
16. _____ obtaining a research participant's consent to participate in research after he or she has been fully briefed about the study's risks and benefits and the voluntary nature of his or her participation
17. _____ a form of limited psychosurgery that may be effective for very severe cases of obsessive-compulsive disorder
18. _____ the study of the use of medications to treat psychological disturbances
19. _____ the use of psychological techniques to try to produce change in the context of a special, helping relationship
20. _____ activities assigned to the client designed to continue treatment outside the therapy session
21. _____ an approach of picking different treatments according to the needs of individual disorders and individual clients
22. _____ chemical substances that affect psychological state
23. _____ reducing the dysfunctional symptoms of a disorder but not eliminating its root cause
24. _____ treatments based on an emphasis on applying findings of basic psychological research; focuses on changing learned patterns; seen as a form of education

Key Terms - Matching #2

The following terms related to the treatment of psychological disorders are important to know. To test your knowledge, match the following terms with their definitions. Answers are listed at the end of the chapter.

1. Catharsis
2. Free association
3. Psychoanalysis
4. Insight
5. Interpretation
6. Therapeutic neutrality
7. Transference
8. Countertransference
9. Psychodynamic
10. Ego analysis
11. Short-term psychodynamic psychotherapy
12. Behaviorism
13. Experiment
14. Hypothesis
15. Independent variable
16. Experimental group
17. Control group
18. Random assignment
19. Dependent variable
20. Statistically significant
21. Confounded
22. Internal validity
23. External validity

a. _____ bringing formerly unconscious material into conscious awareness
b. _____ a form of treatment involving active focus on a particular emotional issue rather than free association, usually completed in about 25 sessions
c. _____ subjects who receive an active treatment
d. _____ an analyst's suggestion to the patient of what is the hidden meaning of his or her symptoms, dreams, or verbalizations
e. _____ the outcome that is hypothesized to vary according to the manipulations of the independent variable
f. _____ the sudden release of pent-up emotions in therapy which reduces psychic strain
g. _____ the belief that observable behaviors rather than cognitive or emotional states are the appropriate focus of psychological study
h. _____ subjects who receive no treatment or a placebo
i. _____ a purposeful stance the therapist takes of being distant and uninvolved to minimize his or her influence on free association
j. _____ changes in the dependent variable can be accurately attributed to changes in the independent variable
k. _____ a therapeutic technique where patients report without censorship whatever thoughts cross their mind, no matter how trivial
l. _____ a type of scientific investigation which can establish cause and effect
m. _____ the factor that is controlled and manipulated by the experimenter
n. _____ revisions of psychoanalysis where the therapist is more engaged and direction and treatment is often briefer
o. _____ where the independent variable is unknowingly related to some other unmeasured factor which is not evenly distributed among the treatment groups, and this factor is causing the observed effect
p. _____ the form of psychological therapy developed by Freud
q. _____ the experimenter's specific prediction about cause and effect
r. _____ the probability that the observed difference between the groups occurred by chance alone rather than the effect of the independent variable is less than 5%
s. _____ the process whereby patients transfer their feelings about key people in their lives onto their therapist
t. _____ ensuring that each subject has a statistically equal chance of receiving different levels of the independent variable
u. _____ the process whereby therapists' feelings and reactions toward their patients affects their responses to them
v. _____ findings of an experiment can be validly generalized to other circum-stances
w. _____ innovations on psychoanalytic theory giving more importance to the ego and the role of society and culture

Key Terms - Matching #3

The following terms related to the treatment of psychological disorders are important to know. To test your knowledge, match the following terms with their definitions. Answers are listed at the end of the chapter.

a.	Counterconditioning	n.	Cognitive behavior therapy
b.	Systematic desensitization	o.	Attribution retraining
c.	Progressive muscle relaxation	p.	Self-instruction training
d.	Hierarchy of fears	q.	Collaborative empiricism
e.	In vivo desensitization	r.	Rational-emotive therapy (RET)
f.	Flooding	s.	Emotional awareness
g.	Aversion therapy	t.	Client-centered therapy
h.	Contingency management	u.	Empathy
i.	Token economy	v.	Self-disclosure
j.	Social skills training	w.	Unconditional positive regard
k.	Assertiveness training	x.	Gestalt therapy
l.	Role playing	y.	Empty chair technique
m.	Social problem solving		

1. _____ the therapist's description of his or her own feelings and reactions
2. _____ a technique for challenging negative distortions in thinking where the therapist gently confronts the client's fallacies and asks the client to evaluate the accuracy of his or her thinking
3. _____ teaching clients new, desirable ways of behaving that are likely to be rewarded in the everyday world
4. _____ ordering fears ranging from very mild to very frightening
5. _____ a treatment for impulsive children where an adult first models an appropriate behavior while saying the self-instruction aloud, then the child does so, and gradually shifts from saying the self-instruction aloud to saying it silently to themselves
6. _____ nonjudgmentally valuing clients for whom they are regardless of their behavior
7. _____ gradually being exposed to the feared stimulus in real life while simultaneously maintaining a state of relaxation
8. _____ the client has a dialogue with another part of himself or herself that is imagined sitting in an empty chair
9. _____ a humanistic therapy that follows the client's lead where the therapist offers warmth, empathy, and genuineness but the client solves his or her own problems
10. _____ an improvisational acting technique that allows clients to rehearse new social skills
11. _____ emotional understanding of others' unique feelings and perspectives
12. _____ exposure at full intensity to the feared stimulus with prevention of avoidance of the stimuli until the fear response is eliminated through extinction
13. _____ a technique of problem solving where the problem is first assessed in detail, alternative solutions are brainstormed, the different options are evaluated, one alternative is implemented, and its success is evaluated objectively
14. _____ a formalized contingency management system adopted in an institutional setting
15. _____ teaching clients to be direct about their feelings and wishes
16. _____ a cognitive behavior therapy technique designed to directly challenge irrational beliefs about oneself and the world

17. _____ a method of inducing a calm state through the contraction and subsequent relaxation of all the major muscle groups
18. _____ trying to change how a person ascribes causes to various events in his or her life by abandoning intuitive strategies for more scientific methods
19. _____ a form of humanistic therapy that underscores affective awareness and expression, genuineness, and experiencing the moment
20. _____ a treatment for overcoming fears involving systematic exposure to imagined, feared events while simultaneously maintaining relaxation
21. _____ altering existing responses by pairing new responses with old stimuli
22. _____ pairing an unpleasant response with the stimuli that was previously sought; used for helping people stop smoking and drinking alcohol
23. _____ recognizing and experiencing true feelings
24. _____ the application of behavior therapy into the cognitive realm
25. _____ focuses on directly changing the rewards and punishments for various behaviors: rewarding the desired behavior and punishing the undesirable behavior

Key Terms - Matching #4

The following terms related to the treatment of psychological disorders are important to know. To test your knowledge, match the following terms with their definitions. Answers are listed at the end of the chapter.

1. Outcome research
2. Process research
3. Meta-analysis
4. Spontaneous remission
5. Efficacy study
6. Effectiveness study
7. Acculturation
8. Ethnic identity
9. Conformity
10. Dissonance
11. Resistance and immersion
12. Introspection
13. Synergetic articulation and awareness
14. Placebo effect
15. Double-blind study
16. Allegiance effect

17. Couples therapy
18. Communication skills
19. Negotiation skills
20. Conflict resolution
21. Family therapy
22. Parent management training
23. Alliances
24. Group therapy
25. Psychoeducational groups
26. Experiential group therapy
27. Encounter group
28. Self-help groups
29. Community psychology
30. Primary prevention
31. Secondary prevention
32. Tertiary prevention
33. Paraprofessional

a. _____ the finding that psychotherapy researchers typically find that their favorite treatment is the most effective one
b. _____ a branch of clinical psychology that attempts to improve individual well-being by promoting social change
c. _____ correlational studies without random assignment
d. _____ teaching members of a couple effective means to resolve conflicts
e. _____ seeing intimate partners together in therapy

f. _____ experiments with randomly assigned patients in either alternative treatments or no treatment at all

g. _____ a form of experiential group therapy where members may question the self-disclosure of others when it is phony but support honesty

h. _____ teaching members of a couple to give and take productively

i. _____ a period of conflict between self-depreciation and appreciation of one's ethnicity

j. _____ a stage of self-appreciation and ethnocentrism, accompanied by depreciation of the majority group

k. _____ designed to teach members specific information or skills relevant to psychological well-being

l. _____ studies qualities of the therapist-client relationship that predict successful outcome irrespective of the theoretical orientation of the therapist

m. _____ therapy in which the relationships among group members form the primary component of treatment

n. _____ helping members of a couple more effectively express and listen to each other's feelings and thoughts

o. _____ improving the environment in order to prevent new cases of a mental disorder from developing

p. _____ a time of self-depreciation and discrimination

q. _____ the process of learning or adopting the cultural patterns of the majority group

r. _____ neither the physician nor the patient knows whether the prescribed pill is the real medication or the placebo

s. _____ treatment of more than one unrelated person at a time

t. _____ a statistical technique that allows results from different studies to be combined in a standardized way

u. _____ a phase of questioning the basis of self-appreciation and depreciation of the majority group

v. _____ early detection of emotional problems in order to prevent them from becoming more serious and difficult to treat

w. _____ examines the result of psychotherapy; how effective it is in relieving symptoms, eliminating disorders, and improving functioning

x. _____ bringing together people who share a common problem to share information and experiences in an attempt to help themselves and one another

y. _____ therapy with two or more family members present in the session

z. _____ a type of treatment that contains no known active ingredients but is effective in some way in treating the condition

aa. _____ improvement without any treatment

bb. _____ providing intervention to an existing disorder as well as addressing some of the adverse, indirect consequences of mental illness

cc. _____ both self-appreciation and appreciation of the basis of majority group values

dd. _____ an ethnic minority member's understanding of self in terms of his or her own culture

ee. _____ strategic loyalties among family members

ff. _____ teaching parents new skills for rearing troubled children

gg. _____ people who have limited professional training but have personal experience with the problem they are treating

Names You Should Know - Matching

The following people have played an important role in the development, research and theory of treatment for psychological disorders. To test your knowledge, match the following names with the descriptions of their contributions to the study of abnormal psychology. Answers are listed at the end of the chapter.

a.	Egas Moniz	h.	John B. Watson
b.	Joseph Breuer	i.	Joseph Wolpe
c.	Sigmund Freud	j.	Aaron Beck
d.	Harry Stack Sullivan	k.	Albert Ellis
e.	Erik Erikson	l.	Carl Rogers
f.	Karen Horney	m.	Frederich (Fritz) Perls
g.	John Bowlby	n.	Jerome Frank

1. _____ proposed a theory that people have conflicting ego needs to move toward, against, and away from others
2. _____ developed attachment theory
3. _____ developed client-centered therapy
4. _____ abandoned the cathartic method for free association
5. _____ an ego analyst who focused on interpersonal relationships rather than intrapsychic dynamics
6. _____ developed rational-emotive therapy
7. _____ pioneered the cathartic method
8. _____ investigated the common factors of different psychotherapies
9. _____ developed behaviorism
10. _____ won a Nobel Prize for discovering prefrontal lobotomy
11. _____ developed a cognitive behavior therapy for depression
12. _____ developed Gestalt therapy
13. _____ developed systematic desensitization
14. _____ developed a psychosocial stage theory of development

Review of Concepts - Fill in the Blank and True/False

This section will help focus your studying by testing whether you understand the concepts presented in the text. After you have read and reviewed the material, test your comprehension and memory by filling in the following blanks or circling the right answer. Answers are listed at the end of the chapter.

1. There are hundreds of different types of psychotherapy: **true**   **false**

2. The surgical removal of sexual organs was one biological treatment used for emotional problems in the past: **true**   **false**

3. The development of ECT originated in attempts to treat schizophrenia that were based on the incorrect conclusion that schizophrenia was rare among people who had _____.

4. Which type of ECT produces less memory loss: **unilateral**   **bilateral**

5. Which type of ECT is more effective: **unilateral**   **bilateral**

6. Research has shown electroconvulsive therapy to be quite effective in treating what type of mental illness?   _____

7. Psychosurgery is a reversible treatment: **true**   **false**

8. What percentage of people treated with prefrontal lobotomy died?
   1-2%   **11%**   **25%**

9. What is the problem with courts referring sexual offenders into psychological treatment?   _____

10. What is the ethical concern with conducting research on prisoners?   _____
    _____

11. What was the number one selling prescription medical for any type of ailment in the 1990's?   _____

12. What was the number one selling prescription medical for any type of ailment in the 1970's?   _____

13. Uncovering unconscious material and sharing the _____ view of their intrapsychic life is necessary for cure according to psychoanalysis.

14. Why is timing so important in interpreting the patient's dynamics to him or her in psychoanalysis?   _____

15. Psychoanalysis is thought to be more effective for what types of disorders?
    _____

16. Sullivan hypothesized that there are two basic dimensions of interpersonal relationships: _____ and _____

17. Horney stressed the need for a person to have _____ among the three styles in which they relate to others.

18. Research shows that systematic desensitization is an effective form of treatment for fears and phobias: **true**   **false**

19. Research shows that aversion therapy is effective in the long-term alleviation of substance use: **true**   **false**

20. What is the shortcoming of the use of token economies?   _____
    _____

21. Attribution retraining is effective for what of mental disorder?   _____

22. One of the main strengths of the behavior therapy approach is its focus on demonstrating its effectiveness through _____.

23. Humanistic psychotherapists are very active in directing therapy: **true false**

24. When a client in Gestalt therapy is phony, the therapist is _____.

25. There is no research evidence that psychotherapy works: **true**   **false**

26. Research has documented that psychotherapy is more effective in treating mental disorders than chemotherapy is in treating breast cancer: **true**   **false**

27. What proportion of people improve without any treatment:

    one quarter   **one third**   **two thirds**

28. Efficacy studies have strong   **internal** or **external**   validity and uncertain   **internal** or **external**   validity.

29. The quickest improvements in therapy occur in the first several months of therapy:

    true   **false**

30. What does YAVIS stand for? _____

_____

31. Behavior therapy may be more effective in the treatment of _____.

32. In the classic study by Sloane and colleagues comparing behavior therapy and psychodynamic psychotherapy, both forms of therapy were more effective than no treatment, but were not significantly different from each other: **true false**

33. In that same study, the single most important aspect of both types of therapy for the client was his or her _____.

34. Potent placebo effects have been demonstrated in cancer treatment and in surgery: **true**   **false**

35. All forms of therapy emphasize the importance of _____ in the therapist-client relationship.

36. According to family systems therapists, a well-functioning family is one where the primary alliance is between _____.

37. One shortcoming of self-help groups is the lack of _____.

Multiple Choice Questions

The following multiple choice questions will test your comprehension of the material presented in the chapter. Answers are listed at the end of the chapter.

1) According to attribution theory, depressed people often attribute _____ to themselves and _____ to others.

    a. success; failure
    b. failure; success

    c. irrational beliefs; rational beliefs
    d. rational beliefs; irrational beliefs

2) Treatment outcome researchers widely accept the finding that approximately _____ of clients improve as a result of psychotherapy.

    a. one-third
    b. two-thirds

    c. one-quarter
    d. one-half

3) Empathy involves:

    a. trying to put yourself in someone else's shoes in order to understand his or her feelings and perspectives
    b. trying to understand the etiology of someone else's behavior
    c. feeling sorry for someone because of his or her life situation
    d. all of the above

4) The "placebo effect" is:

    a. treatment in which the client has a dialogue with an imagined part of himself or herself
    b. treatment in which the client is taught relaxation skills for the condition being evaluated
    c. treatment that contains no "special ingredient" for treating the condition being evaluated
    d. treatment which involves full intensity exposure to feared stimuli

5) Every day that Sally completes all of her chores at home her mother gives her a star. After Sally has accumulated 15 stars, her mother will take her out for ice cream. Sally's mother is most likely using which of the following to get Sally to do her chores?

    a. token economy   c. in vivo desensitization
    b. counterconditioning   d. classical conditioning

6) Which of the following would most likely ask a patient to do homework?

    a. a biological therapist   c. a humanistic therapist
    b. a psychodynamic therapist   d. a behavior therapist

7) The following is a/are possible side effect(s) of electroconvulsive therapy (ECT):

    a. fractures   c. long-term memory loss
    b. death   d. all of the above

8) All of the following are examples of behavior therapy EXCEPT:

    a. flooding   c. aversion therapy
    b. social skills training   d. empty chair technique

9) An experiment has internal validity if:

    a. the findings can be generalized to other circumstances
    b. changes in the dependent variable can be accurately attributed to changes in the independent variable
    c. the researcher can control all aspects of the experimental environment
    d. the researcher is able to control and manipulate the dependent variable

10) This type of therapy is primarily used to treat substance abuse disorders such as alcoholism and cigarette smoking.

a. cognitive therapy
b. psychodynamic therapy
c. aversion therapy
d. contingency therapy

11) Sam is a first-year college student who is extremely afraid of heights. He entered therapy after failing his first semester chemistry course because it was located on the fifth floor of a building, and Sam was too afraid to go the fifth floor to attend class. Sam's therapist gradually exposes Sam to increasing heights while having Sam simultaneously maintain a state of relaxation. Sam's therapist is using which technique to help Sam alleviate his fear of heights?

a. in vivo desensitization
b. systematic desensitization
c. flooding
d. countercondioning

12) Albert Ellis is to _____ as Aaron Beck is to _____.

a. client-centered therapy; ego analysis
b. ego analysis; client-centered therapy
c. rational-emotive therapy; cognitive therapy
d. cognitive therapy; rational-emotive therapy

13) According to Sigmund Freud, all of the following are ways to reveal aspects of the unconscious mind EXCEPT:

a. slips of the tongue
b. countertransference
c. dreams
d. free association

14) One major difference in technique between humanistic and behavior therapists is:

a. humanistic psychotherapists view the nature of the therapist-client relationship differently than behavior therapists
b. humanistic psychotherapists focus on the patients' past and present interpersonal relationships
c. humanistic psychotherapists focus on treatment irrespective of its causes
d. none of the above

15) All have caused a decline in the practice of classical psychoanalysis EXCEPT:

a. the substantial amount of time required
b. the accessibility of treatment only by those who are financially secure
c. research has proven classical Freudian psychoanalysis to be ineffective
d. the limited data available on the outcome of treatment

16) In the 1990's this medication has outsold every prescription medication, including all medications used to treat physical ailments.

a. Valium
b. Prozac
c. Ritalin
d. Lithium

17) All of the following can be viewed as goals of psychoanalysis EXCEPT:

   a. to rid the patient of his or her defenses
   b. to increase self-understanding
   c. to bring unconscious material into conscious awareness
   d. to release pent-up emotions and unexpressed feelings

18) Pavlov is to _____ as Skinner is to _____.

   a. in vivo desensitization; systematic desensitization
   b. systematic desensitization; in vivo desensitization
   c. operant conditioning; classical conditioning
   d. classical conditioning; operant conditioning

19) Psychotherapy outcome research indicates that:

   a. clients who are young, attractive, verbal, intelligent, and successful tend to improve more in psychotherapy
   b. if psychotherapy is going to be effective, it will be effective rather quickly
   c. psychotherapy is effective when compared with no treatment at all
   d. all of the above

20) Aversion therapy is a type of _____ technique.

   a. classical conditioning
   b. operant conditioning
   c. cognitive-behavioral
   d. social skills training

21) Collaborative empiricism involves:

   a. relieving a client's symptoms through the use of medication
   b. revealing aspects of a client's unconscious drives and conflicts
   c. confronting a client's unrealistic views about the world
   d. challenging a client's negative distortions

22) _____ is the earliest example of a spiritual or religious tradition of healing.

   a. witchcraft
   b. exorcism
   c. trephining
   d. stoning

23) Research indicates that _____ is the most effective approach to treating psychological disorders.

   a. humanistic psychotherapy
   b. psychodynamic psychotherapy
   c. behavior therapy
   d. research generally reveals few differences among approaches

24) The term "unconditional positive regard" refers to:

    a. valuing a client for who he or she is and refraining from judging him or her
    b. only making positive comments to a client and never devaluing him or her as a human being
    c. the relationship between the client and therapist
    d. none of the above

25) _____ has been the most promising avenue of biological treatment.

    a. psychosurgery
    b. classical conditioning
    c. operant conditioning
    d. psychopharmacology

26) In order for a finding to be statistically significant, it would need to occur by chance alone in less than:

    a. 1 out of every 5 experiments
    b. 1 out of every 10 experiments
    c. 1 out of every 15 experiments
    d. 1 out of every 20 experiments

27) _____ is used in training clients to use relaxation techniques to cope with thoughts, feelings, or situations that provoke anxiety.

    a. progressive relaxation
    b. specific muscle relaxation
    c. applied relaxation
    d. primary relaxation

28) This method became the cornerstone of Freud's psychoanalysis.

    a. free association
    b. hypnosis
    c. catharsis
    d. interpretation

Understanding Research - Fill in the Blank

Identifying Common Factors and Isolating Specific Treatments: The text presents a detailed description of a study by Borkovec and Costello in the Research Close-Up on p. 107. Finding the answers to these questions will help you get a good understanding of this study and why it is important. It is not necessary to memorize the answers; the process of finding them in the textbook will help you learn the material you need to know.

1. This is an example of psychotherapy _____ research. The researchers were looking at the effectiveness of types of _____ therapy in treating generalized _____ disorder. What were the two types of behavior therapy used? _____ and _____.
What was the third type of therapy used? _____
Why did they include ND? _____
_____. How many sessions were involved? _____

2. How many clients were in the study? _____ How were the clients
assigned to treatment group? _____ Who supervised the ND
cases? _____ How were the sessions
monitored? _____ What were the four times that clients were
measured? _____

_____ When were no differences among the groups
found? _____ What two groups were doing much better
right after treatment? _____
A year after treatment, _____% of the CBT group was functioning in the normal
range of _____, while _____% of the AR and _____% of the
ND clients were.

3. This study showed that both _____ and
_____ were important to treatment outcome. The
best predictor of successful outcome in all three groups was the client's expectation for

_____.

The Experiment: The text discusses this type of research in the Research Methods
section on pp. 86-87. Finding the answers to these questions will help you get a good
understanding of these issues.

4. Why is the experiment the most powerful of all scientific methods? _____
_____ What are the two types of variables?
the _____ variable and the _____ variable
In the example given, what are the three groups of the independent variable?
Patients receiving _____, _____,
or _____. Why is random assignment to these three
groups essential? _____

_____

5. Why is the dependent variable named that? _____
_____. What is one limitation of experiments?
_____

_____
What example of this shortcoming is given? _____
_____ What are two types
of threats to internal validity? _____

51

What does external validity mean? _____

Brief Essay

As a final exercise, write out answers to the following brief essay questions. Then compare your answers with the material presented in the text.

After you have answered these questions, review the "critical thinking" questions that are presented at the end of the text chapter. Answering these questions will help you integrate important issues and themes that have been featured throughout the chapter.

1. Compare and contrast the biological, psychodynamic, behavioral, and humanistic approaches to treating psychological disorders. In what ways might these approaches be similar in working with a patient diagnosed with depression? In what ways might they be different?

2. Discuss how the ideas of ego analysts differ from the original ideas of Freud. In what ways are they still similar?

3. Discuss some of the ethical concerns that psychologists have encountered in the past. What are some ways in which ethical issues are now being handled in the field of psychology?

ANSWER KEY

Answers to the exercises are listed below; page numbers where the information is referenced in the textbook are given in parentheses.

Key Terms - Matching #1

1. c (73)	13. q (78)
2. m (77)	14. j (76)
3. f (74)	15. b (73)
4. p (78)	16. v (80)
5. e (74)	17. t (79)
6. s (79)	18. w (80)
7. l (77)	19. a (73)
8. u (80)	20. k (76)
9. i (74)	21. d (74)
10. h (74)	22. x (80)
11. r (79)	23. n (78)
12. o (78)	24. g (74)

Names You Should Know

1. f (84)	13. i (87-8)
2. g (84-5)	14. e (84)
3. l (91-2)	
4. c (82-3)	
5. d (84)	
6. k (91)	
7. b (82)	
8. n (99-100)	
9. h (85)	
10. a (79)	
11. j (90)	
12. m (93)	

Matching #2

a. 4 (83)   m. 15 (86)
b. 11 (85)   n. 9 (84)
c. 16 (86)   o. 21 (87)
d. 5 (83)   p. 3 (82)
e. 19 (86)   q. 14 (86)
f. 1 (82)   r. 20 (86)
g. 12 (85)   s. 7 (83)
h. 17 (86)   t. 18 (86)
i. 6 (83)   u. 8 (83)
j. 22 (87)   v. 23 (87)
k. 2 (82)   w. 10 (84)
l. 13 (86)

Matching #3

1. v (92)   14. i (89)
2. q (90)   15. k (89)
3. j (89)   16. r (91)
4. d (88)   17. c (87)
5. p (90)   18. o (90)
6. w (93)   19. x (93)
7. e (88)   20. b (87)
8. y (93)   21. a (87)
9. t (91)   22. g (88)
10. l (89)   23. s (91)
11. u (92)   24. n (90)
12. f (88)   25. h (88-9)
13. m (89)

Matching #4

a. 16 (101)   r. 15 (100)
b. 29 (106)   s. 24 (105)
c. 6 (96)   t. 3 (94)
d. 20 (103)   u. 12 (98)
e. 17 (103)   v. 31 (106)
f. 5 (95)   w. 1 (94)
g. 27 (105)   x. 28 (105)
h. 19 (103)   y. 21 (104)
i. 10 (97)   z. 14 (100)
j. 11 (98)   aa. 4 (95)
k. 25 (105)   bb. 32 (106)
l. 2 (99)   cc. 13 (98)
m. 26 (105)   dd. 8 (97)
n. 18 (103)   ee. 23 (104)
o. 30 (106)   ff. 22 (104)
p. 9 (97)   gg. 33 (105)
q. 7 (97)

Multiple Choice

1. b   6. d   11. a   16. b   21. d   26. d
2. b   7. d   12. c   17. a   22. c   27. c
3. a   8. d   13. b   18. d   23. d   28. a
4. c   9. b   14. a   19. d   24. a
5. a   10. c   15. c   20. a   25. d

Review of Concepts

1. true (72)
2. true (78)
3. epilepsy (78)
4. unilateral (78)
5. bilateral (79)
6. severe depression (79)
7. false (79)
8. 25% (79)
9. there is no evidence it is effective (80)
10. it may be coercive (80)
11. Prozac (82)
12. Valium (82)
13. analyst's (83)
14. premature interpretations will be rejected -- too threatening (83)
15. milder forms of depression and anxiety (84)
16. power and closeness (84)
17. balance (84)
18. true (88)
19. false (88)
20. they do not generalize to uncontrolled environments (89)
21. depression (90)
22. research (91)
23. false (92)
24. confrontational (93)
25. false (94)
26. true (95)
27. one third (95)
28. internal; external (95)
29. true (96)
30. young, attractive, verbal, intelligent, and successful (97)
31. anxiety (98)
32. true (99)
33. relationship with the therapist (99)
34. true (100)
35. warmth (101)
36. the parents (104)
37. research on process and outcome (105)

Understanding Research

1. outcome; behavior; anxiety; Applied relaxation and Cognitive behavior therapy; Nondirective therapy; to control for common factors; 12

2. 55; randomly; an expert nondirective therapist; audiotape; immediately before and after therapy, 6 months and 1 year after therapy; before therapy; AR and CBT; 58%; anxiety; 37%; 28%

3. specific treatment factors; common factors; success

4. It can determine cause and effect; independent; dependent; medication; psychotherapy; no treatment; to ensure that differences among groups are caused by the independent variable and not selection bias

5. It is hypothesized to depend on the independent variable; interesting variables cannot always be manipulated practically or ethically; whether abusive parenting causes psychological problems; the independent variable could be manipulated poorly or it could be confounded with other variables; whether the findings can be generalized to the real world

CHAPTER 4 - CLASSIFICATION AND ASSESSMENT

Chapter Outline

I. Overview
    A. Issues and Choices

II. Basic Issues in Classification
    A. Categories versus Dimensions
    B. Monothetic versus Polythetic Classes
    C. From Description to Theory

III. Classification of Abnormal Behavior
    A. Brief Historical Perspective
    B. The DSM-IV System
        1. Diagnostic Axes
        2. Other Domains for Assessment

IV. Evaluation of Classification Systems
    A. Reliability
    B. Validity
    C. Unresolved Questions
    D. Problems and Limitations of the DSM-IV System

V. Basic Issues in Assessment
    A. The Purposes of Clinical Assessment
    B. Assumptions about Behavior
        1. Consistency of Behavior
        2. Levels of Analysis
    C. Evaluating the Utility of Assessment Procedures

VI. Assessment Procedures
    A. Assessment of Psychological Systems
        1. Interviews
            a. Structured Interviews
            b. Advantages
            c. Limitations
        2. Observational Procedures
            a. Rating Scales
            b. Behavioral Coding Systems
            c. Advantages
            d. Limitations
        3. Personality Tests and Self-Report Inventories
            a. Personality Inventories
            b. Advantages
            c. Limitations
            d. Other Self-Report Inventories
        4. Projective Personality Tests
            a. Advantages

b. Limitations
B. Assessment of Social Systems
C. Assessment of Biological Systems
    1. Psychophysiological Assessment
        a. Advantages
        b. Limitations
    2. Brain Imaging Techniques
        a. Static Brain Imaging
        b. Dynamic Brain Imaging
        c. Advantages
        d. Limitations

Learning Objectives

After reviewing the material presented in this chapter, you should be able to:

1. Define classification system, assessment, and diagnosis.

2. Distinguish between a categorical approach to classification and a dimensional approach.

3. Compare monothetic and polythetic classes.

4. Explain why DSM III represented a turning point in the diagnosis of psychiatric disorders.

5. Describe the five axes used in diagnosis in DSM IV.

6. Know the meaning and implications of reliability and validity in diagnosis and classification.

7. Give some of the advantages and also limitations of interview data for purposes of assessment.

8. Compare the three types of observational procedures--informal observations, rating scales, and behavioral coding systems.

9. Describe the strengths and weaknesses of the MMPI-2.

10. List some of the advantages as well as limitations of using projective tests for assessment and diagnosis.

11. Know two methods employed for the assessment of social systems.

12. Describe two uses of psychophysiological assessment procedures and two limitations of this approach.

13. Compare static brain imaging techniques with dynamic brain imaging techniques in terms of the type of data each provides.

Key Terms - Matching #1

The following terms related to classification and assessment are important to know. To test your knowledge, match the following terms with their definitions. Answers are listed at the end of the chapter.

a. Assessment
b. Diagnosis
c. Classification system
d. Categorical approach
e. Dimensional approach
f. Monothetic class
g. Polythetic class
h. Phenylketonuria (PKU)
i. Dementia praecox
j. Manic-depressive psychosis
k. Diagnostic and Statistical Manual of Mental Disorders (DSM)
l. International Classification of Diseases (ICD)

m. Labeling theory
n. Multiaxial classification
o. Inclusion criteria
p. Exclusion criteria
q. Reliability
r. Inter-rater reliability
s. Validity
t. Kappa
u. Etiological validity
v. Concurrent validity
w. Predictive validity
x. Comorbidity
y. Test-retest reliability
z. Split-half reliability

1. _____ an old term for what we now call schizophrenia
2. _____ a system for grouping together objects or organisms that share certain properties
3. _____ a system in which the person is rated with regard to several separate aspects of behavior or adjustment
4. _____ the process of gathering and organizing information about a person's behavior
5. _____ looks at the social context in which abnormal behavior occurs; sees mental disorders as maladaptive social roles
6. _____ assumes that distinctions between members of different categories are qualitative
7. _____ concerned with factors that contribute to the onset of the disorder
8. _____ the diagnostic system for mental disorders published by the World Health Organization
9. _____ describes the objects of classifcation in terms of continuous dimensions
10. _____ concerned with the present time and with correlations between the disorder and other symptoms, circumstances, and test procedures
11. _____ the simultaneous appearance of two or more disorders in the same person
12. _____ an old term for what we now call bipolar mood disorder
13. _____ the diagnostic system for mental disorders published by the American Psychiatric Association
14. _____ symptoms or characteristic features that must be present in order for a person to meet the diagnostic criteria for a particular disorder
15. _____ the identification or recognition of a disorder on the basis of its characteristic symptoms
16. _____ an inherited metabolic disorder that, uncontrolled, produces mental retardation

17. _____ symptoms or conditions that are used to rule out the presence of a particular disorder
18. _____ a statistic of reliability that reflects the proportion of agreement that occurred above and beyond what would have occurred by chance alone
19. _____ the meaning or systematic importance of a construct or measurement
20. _____ the consistency of measurements over time
21. _____ a category that is defined in terms of features that are necessary and sufficient to identify members of the class
22. _____ concerned with the future and with the stability of the problem over time
23. _____ a category that is defined in terms of a set of criteria that are neither necessary nor sufficient--each member has to possess a certain minimal number of the defining features, but none of the features has to be found in each member of the category
24. _____ agreement among clinicians
25. _____ the internal consistency of items within a test
26. _____ the consistency of measurements

Key Terms - Matching #2

The following terms related to classification and assessment are important to know. To test your knowledge, match the following terms with their definitions. Answers are listed at the end of the chapter.

1. Structured interviews
2. Informal observations
3. Rating scale
4. Behavioral coding systems
5. Self-monitoring
6. Reactivity
7. Personality tests
8. Personality inventories
9. Minnesota Multiphasic Personality Inventory
10. Validity scales
11. Actuarial interpretation
12. Beck Depression Inventory
13. Self-report inventories
14. Projective tests

15. Rorschach test
16. Thematic Apperception Test
17. Camberwell Family Interview
18. Family Environment Scale
19. Family Interaction Coding System
20. Penile plethysmograph
21. Vaginal photometer
22. Computerized tomographic scanning
23. Magnetic resonance imaging
24. Positron emission tomography
25. Single photon emission computed tomography
26. Basal ganglia
27. Yale-Brown Obsessive Compulsive Scale

a. _____ a procedure where clients record their own behavior
b. _____ analysis of test results based on an explicit set of rules derived from empirical research
c. _____ an index of male sexual arousal based on changes in the circumference of the penis
d. _____ objective tests consisting of a series of straightforward statements that the person indicates how true or false they are in relation to himself or herself
e. _____ a projective test also known as the inkblot test

f. _____ an index of female sexual arousal based on changes in blood flow in the vagina

g. _____ a static brain imaging technique which passes X-rays through brain tissue to measure the density of the tissue

h. _____ a dynamic brain imaging technique using special radioactive elements to produce relatively detailed images of the brain, which can reflect changes in brain activity as a person performs various tasks

i. _____ personality tests in which the person is asked to interpret a series of ambiguous stimuli

j. _____ focus on the frequency of specific behavioral events, requiring fewer inferences on the part of the observer

k. _____ a self-report inventory designed to measure the social characteristics of families

l. _____ a brain imaging technique which passes electromagnetic phenomena through brain tissue to provide a static image of brain structures

m. _____ an objective personality inventory aimed at a focal topic or at one aspect of a person's adjustment

n. _____ people altering their behavior, either intentionally or unintentionally, when they know they are being observed

o. _____ a self-report inventory used as an index of severity of depression

p. _____ standardized situations where a person's behavior can be sampled, and reflects on underlying abilities or personality traits

q. _____ a coding system for observations of interactions between parents and children in their homes

r. _____ an assessment interview that follows a specific question-and-answer format

s. _____ a projective test consisting of a series of drawings that depict human figures in various ambiguous situations

t. _____ reflect the person's attitude toward the test and the openness and consistency with which the questions were answered

u. _____ an assessment device where the observer makes judgments that place the person along a dimension

v. _____ a dynamic brain imaging technique using single-photon-emitting compounds

w. _____ a structured interview designed to measure expressed emotion in families

x. _____ a part of the thalamus implicated in obsessions and compulsions

y. _____ a very widely used personality inventory with a true-false format that produces scores on ten clinical scales and four validity scales

z. _____ qualitative observations of a person's behavior and/or environment with no attempt to quantify the observed characteristics

aa. _____ an interview-based rating scale used extensively to assess obsessions and compulsions

Names You Should Know - Matching

The following people have played an important role in the classification and assessment of mental disorders. To test your knowledge, match the following names with the descriptions of their contributions to the study of abnormal psychology.

Answers are listed at the end of the chapter.

a. Emil Kraepelin   b. Thomas Scheff   c. Hermann Rorschach

1. _____ a proponent of labeling theory
2. _____ pioneered the type of categorical classification system currently used
3. _____ developed the best-known projective test, the inkblot test

Review of Concepts - Fill in the Blank and True/False

This section will help focus your studying by testing whether you understand the concepts presented in the text. After you have read and reviewed the material, test your comprehension and memory by filling in the following blanks or circling the right answer. Answers are listed at the end of the chapter.

1. In the field of psychopathology, assigning a diagnosis implies the etiology of the person's problem: **true**   **false**

2. Classification systems can be based on descriptive or _____ similarities.

3. In which type of classification system are all members of a particular category not identical, even with regard to the defining features of the category?
   monothetic   **polythetic**

4. Which type of emphasis typically comes first in the development of scientific classification systems?   **etiological factors**   **description**

5. What were three criticisms of psychiatric classification systems during the 1950s and 1960s? _____,

   _____,

   and _____

6. The major change that occurred in the third edition of the DSM was a focus on clinical description rather than on _____.

7. Labeling theory views symptoms of mental disorders as violations of residual

   _____.

8. Labeling theory predicts that people from lower status groups, like the impoverished, are   **more** or **less**   likely to receive a diagnosis.

9. The authors of your text conclude that labeling theory provides a good account for abnormal behavior: **true**   **false**

10. How many diagnostic axes are there in the DSM-IV? _____

11. The presence of general medical conditions are coded on one of the axes of a DSM-IV diagnosis: **true**   **false**

12. Clinicians have been more willing to drop old categories in revisions of the DSM than to include new categories: **true** **false**

13. Comorbidity rates among mental disorders as defined in the DSM system are very low: **true** **false**

14. What are the three primary goals which guide most assessment procedures?

    _____

    _____

    _____

15. The meaning or importance of an assessment procedure is known as its: **reliability** **validity**

16. There are only a few select assessment procedures available to clinicians today: **true** **false**

17. Clinical interviews provide clinicians with the opportunity to assess a person's appearance and nonverbal behavior: **true** **false**

18. Clinical interviews are either structured or _____.

19. One advantage of structured interviews is that anybody can conduct them, saving the expense of a clinician's time: **true** **false**

20. Clinical interviews are of limited use with young children: **true** **false**

21. Observations provide a more realistic view of behavior than do people's recollections of their actions and feelings: **true** **false**

22. One problem with observational procedures is that they can be time-consuming and expensive: **true** **false**

23. Why do some clinicians prefer to use the original version of the MMPI?

    _____

24. One advantage of the MMPI is that it allows the clinician to use his or her intuition in coming up with scores on the clinical scales: **true** **false**

25. One unique feature of the MMPI is the **clinical** or **validity** scales.

26. Which is a more complex assessment tool? **the MMPI** **the BDI**

27. If a person scores as being significantly depressed on the Beck Depression Inventory, he or she definitely will meet diagnostic criteria for depression: **true** **false**

28. The Exner system, a new scoring system for the Rorschach test, is based more on which of the following? **content** **form**

29. One strength of the original Rorschach scoring system was its high reliability: **true** **false**

30. Projective tests are more likely to be used by a therapist with which type of

theoretical orientation? **psychodynamic** **behavioral**

31. List three types of physiological measures that provide information about a person's psychological state: _____

_____

32. Men who exhibit physiological responses that indicate intense arousal during discussions with their wives about marital conflicts but who do not express their arousal _____ are more likely to divorce.

33. Brain imaging techniques are used to rule out _____ as a cause of behavioral or cognitive deficits.

Multiple Choice Questions

The following multiple choice questions will test your comprehension of the material presented in the chapter. Answers are listed at the end of the chapter.

1) A definitive characteristic of ALL projective tests is:

   a. a true-false response format
   b. the use of a list of open-ended sentences that the individual must answer
   c. the use of items describing various thoughts, feelings, and behaviors that the individual must rate
   d. the use of ambiguous stimuli

2) Which approach to classification is based on an ordered sequence or on quantitative measurements rather than qualitative judgments?

   a. dimensional approach   c. diagnostic approach
   b. categorical approach   d. monothetic approach

3) Which of the following is NOT an axis of DSM-IV?

   a. global rating of adaptive functioning
   b. psychosocial and environmental problems
   c. general medical conditions that may be relevant to the patient's current behaviors or that may affect treatment
   d. familial communication style

4) Which would NOT be considered a limitation of a clinical interview?

   a. the information gathered is subjective and may be influenced or distorted by errors in memory or perception
   b. the person may be reluctant to directly share with the interviewer experiences that are embarrassing or socially undesirable
   c. interviews are expensive and time consuming
   d. people may not be able to give a rational account of their problems due to the presence of limited verbal skills, a psychotic process, etc.

5) Analyzing a test on the basis of an explicit set of rules based on empirical research is referred to as what type of procedure?

    a. actuarial   c. monothetic
    b. self report   d. cookbook

6) A criticism of psychiatric diagnosis in the 1950's and 1960's was that:

    a. the system in use was too detailed and included too many categories
    b. the system was too descriptive and did not make assumptions about etiology
    c. once labelled with a diagnosis, people did not receive appropriate treatment
    d. once labelled with a diagnosis, an individual might be motivated to continue to act in a manner expected from someone who is mentally ill

7) Research on physiological manifestations of marital dissatisfaction suggests that:

    a. wives who do not express their negative emotions often display sleep difficulties
    b. husbands who do not express their negative emotions often display changes in heart rate and skin conductance that indicate intense arousal
    c. wives who verbally report negative emotion do not display any physiological changes
    d. husbands who verbally express their negative emotions also show changes in their sleep patterns

8) Which of the following does NOT reflect a rationale for classifying abnormal behavior?

    a. a diagnostic system can be used to help clinicians more effectively communicate with one another
    b. a diagnostic system can be used to organize information that may be helpful for research purposes
    c. a diagnostic system can be used to label people who are socially deviant
    d. a diagnostic system can be used in making management and treatment decisions

9) When an observer is asked to make judgments about some aspect of an individual's behavior along a dimension, the observer would be using a:

    a. projective instrument   c. self-report inventory
    b. rating scale   d. structured interview

10) Interpretation of a person's responses to the MMPI is based upon:

    a. reviewing the clinical scale for which the person received the highest score
    b. reading through all of the inventory items and noting how the person answered each one
    c. reviewing the clinical scale for which the person received the lowest score
    d. examining the pattern of scale scores, paying particular attention to those scales that have elevated scores

11) An example of a type of observational procedure would be:

    a. the Rorschach test   c. a behavioral coding system
    b. the MMPI   d. dynamic brain imaging

12) Which would NOT be considered a primary goal of assessment?

    a. making predictions
    b. reconstructing people's developmental history
    c. planning interventions
    d. evaluating interventions

13) An advantage of the MMPI is that:

    a. it provides information about the individual's test-taking attitude
    b. it assesses a wide range of problem areas that would take a clinician several hours to review in an interview
    c. it is scored objectively and is not influenced by the clinician's personal opinion about the individual taking the test
    d. all of the above

14) How many axes are included in the DSM-IV?

    a. 3   c. 5
    b. 4   d. 6

15) What would be considered an advantage of a structured clinical interview compared to a regular clinical interview?

    a. it provides the interviewer with a series of systematic questions that allow for the collection of important diagnostic information
    b. it allows for the establishement of a better therapeutic rapport with the client
    c. it allows the interviewer flexibility in gathering information
    d. all of the above

16) Projective techniques place considerable emphasis upon which of the following?

    a. the importance of unconscious motivations such as conflicts and impulses
    b. the importance of familial values that may influence the person's behavior
    c. the presence of symptoms, which suggest that the person has lost contact with reality and is presently psychotic
    d. the importance of the person's cultural background in understanding his or her personality

17) An example of a measure that assesses a social system is:

    a. Positron emission tomography
    b. the Family Interaction Coding System
    c. the Beck Depression Inventory
    d. the Yale-Brown Obsessive-Compulsive Scale

18) Which type of study could be used to validate a clinical syndrome?

    a. a follow-up study that demonstrated a distinctive course or outcome
    b. a family study supporting that the syndrome "breeds true"
    c. a study demonstrating an association between the clinical syndrome and an underlying biochemical abnormality
    d. all of the above

19) An advantage of psychophysiological assessment is that:

    a. they do not rely on self-report and are less under the person's control
    b. physiological reactivity and stability is very consistent across people
    c. physiological assessment is less expensive and less time consuming than the use of personality inventories
    d. physiological procedures are frequently used in clinical settings

20) The most commonly used procedure in psychological assessment is:

    a. self-report inventories
    b. projective testing
    c. clinical interview
    d. behavioral observation

21) A limitation of brain-imaging procedures is that:

    a. brain-imaging procedures can only be used with certain populations
    b. although useful for research, brain-imaging procedures cannot be used for diagnostic purposes because norms have not yet been established
    c. brain-imaging procedures tend to give imprecise information
    d. the results of brain-imaging procedures tend to be overly responsive to outside factors such as whether the person is presently medicated

22) Which of the following problems could NOT be assessed through the use of an observational measure?

    a. hand-washing
    b. crying
    c. low self-esteem
    d. hitting or punching at school

23) A limitation of the use of projective tests is:

    a. information obtained from projective tests tends to duplicate what can already be obtained from a clinical interview
    b. projective tests cannot be used with children
    c. projective tests cannot be used with psychotic individuals
    d. the reliability of scoring and interpretation appears to be low

24) Which type of study could be used to demonstrate the reliability of a set of diagnostic criteria?

    a. a study demonstrating that clinicians using the same set of criteria arrived at the same diagnosis for the same set of individuals
    b. a study supporting that individuals with the same diagnosis responded to the same kind of treatment
    c. a study supporting that the set of diagnostic criteria could be meaningful to other cultures when properly translated
    d. all of the above

25) The L (Lie) Scale of the MMPI is an example of which type of scale?

    a. reactivity   c. projective
    b. clinical   d. validity

26) The first two axes of the DSM-IV primarily focus on which of the following?

    a. symptomatic behaviors   c. medical history
    b. familial functioning   d. intrapsychic functioning

27) Which would NOT be considered a drawback of using a physiological assessment measure?

    a. the equipment used may be intimidating to certain people
    b. physiological responses can be influenced by many outside factors such as age and medication
    c. physiological response measures have not demonstrated adequate validity
    d. the stability of physiological response systems vary from person to person

Understanding Research - Fill in the Blank

The DSM-IV Field Trial for Obsessive-Compulsive Disorders: The text presents a detailed description of a study by Foa and Kozak in the Research Close-Up on pp. 126-127. Finding the answers to these questions will help you get a good understanding of this study and why it is important. It is not necessary to memorize the answers; the process of finding them in the textbook will help you learn the material you need to know.

1. Careful clinical studies are needed to identify the _____ of a disorder.

This study was done to be sure that people with OCD really view their symptoms as

_____ or _____, because that was a defining feature

of the diagnosis in the _____ and to find out whether in people with

OCD compulsions can occur as _____ instead of

as only observable behaviors. The researchers _____ more than

450 people who were seeking _____ for OCD. An experienced

clinician conducted a structured _____ interview and which scale? _____ What statistic was used to assess inter-rater reliability? _____ What did it range from? _____

2. To address the first question, they looked at responses from 250 people with obsessions of a fear of a _____ consequence if they failed to engage in a particular _____. What percent of people said they were uncertain that the feared consequence would occur if they did not perform their ritual? _____% What percent of people said they were certain it would NOT occur? _____% What percent said they were certain it would occur? _____% Why is this significant? _____

3. The authors recommended that the DSM-IV should include the possibility that the patient may have poor _____ into their condition.   How does this change protect the OCD patient? _____
_____
Regarding the second issue, how many people had both a mental and behavioral compulsion? _____% How are they similar? _____
_____
What was required by the authors of the DSM-IV before they made changes in criterion sets? _____

Diagnostic Reliability: The text discusses this type of research in the Research Methods section on pp. 124-125. Finding the answers to these questions will help you get a good understanding of these issues.

4.   Kappa is a measure of how well clinicians agree on a diagnosis above and beyond agreement that would be expected by _____. A _____ kappa value indicates agreement is less than what would be expected by chance. What value indicates perfect agreement? _____ What is the convention for the value of kappa that is relatively good? _____ What level suggests poor agreement? _____ What category of disorder needs a lot of work to improve kappa? _____

5. Clinicians agree much better on the major heading of disorder than they do on the specific _____. This is like having disagreement about whether a passing vehicle is a Chrysler, Ford, or Toyota _____. The clinicians

who were diagnosing in this study were _____ mental health professionals in their countries. This means that the kappa values found in this study are _____.

Brief Essay

As a final exercise, write out answers to the following brief essay questions. Then compare your answers with the material presented in the text.

After you have answered these questions, review the "critical thinking" questions that are presented at the end of the text chapter. Answering these questions will help you integrate important issues and themes that have been featured throughout the chapter.

1. Briefly discuss the major assumptions of labeling theory. Then discuss your personal position about the theory; that is, to what extent do you agree with its major points?

2. Review examples of both scientific and nonscientific factors that affect the development of diagnostic systems. When do you see nonscientific factors playing an important role in this process?

3. Describe the major purposes of clinical assessment. What are the major assumptions regarding the nature of human behavior upon which the assessment process is based?

4. Pretend that you are a clinician who has just received a call from a potential client. The problem for which the client is seeking treatment is depression. What assessment procedures reviewed in your chapter could you use to determine whether or not the client is really depressed? What type of information would you expect to obtain from each method?

ANSWER KEY

Answers to the exercises are listed below; page numbers where the information is referenced in the textbook are given in parentheses.

Key Terms - Matching #1

1. i (117)	14. o (120)
2. c (115)	15. b (112)
3. n (120)	16. h (116)
4. a (112)	17. p (121)
5. m (118)	18. t (124)
6. d (115)	19. s (123)
7. u (125)	20. y (130)
8. l (117)	21. f (116)
9. e (115)	22. w (126)
10. v (125)	23. g (116)
11. x (128)	24. r (123)
12. j (117)	25. z (131)
13. k (117)	26. q (123)

Matching #2

a. 5 (136)	o. 12 (140)
b. 11 (138)	p. 7 (137)
c. 20 (145)	q. 19 (143)
d. 8 (137)	r. 1 (132)
e. 15 (140)	s. 16 (142)
f. 21 (145)	t. 10 (138)
g. 22 (146)	u. 3 (135)
h. 24 (147)	v. 25 (147)
i. 14 (140)	w. 17 (143)
j. 4 (136)	x. 26 (147)
k. 18 (143)	y. 9 (137-8)
l. 23 (146-7)	z. 2 (134)
m. 13 (140)	aa. 27 (135)
n. 6 (137)	

Names You Should Know

1. b (118-9)   2. a (117)   3. c (140-1)

Multiple Choice

1. d	6. d	11. c	16. a	21. b	26. a
2. a	7. b	12. b	17. b	22. c	27. c
3. d	8. c	13. d	18. d	23. d	
4. c	9. b	14. c	19. a	24. a	
5. a	10. d	15. a	20. c	25. d	

Review of Concepts

1. false (112)
2. structural (115)
3. polythetic (116)
4. description (116)
5. lack of consistency in diagnoses among clinicians; diagnoses are problems in living, not medical disorders; labels might increase maladaptive behavior (118)
6. theories of psychopathology (118)
7. rules (118)
8. more (119)
9. false (119)
10. 5 (120)
11. true (120)
12. false (126)
13. false (128)
14. making predictions, planning interventions, and evaluating interventions (129)

15. validity (131)
16. false (131)
17. true (132)
18. nondirective (132)
19. false (133)
20. true (134)
21. true (136)
22. true (137)
23. because of all the research done with it (137)
24. false (138)

25. validity (138)
26. MMPI (140)
27. false (140)
28. form (141)
29. false (141)
30. psychodynamic (142)
31. heart rate, respiration rate, and skin conductance (144)
32. verbally (146)
33. brain tumors (147)

Understanding Research

1. symptoms; unreasonable; excessive; DSM-III-R; mental events; interviewed; treatment; clinical; Y-BOCS; kappa; .55 to .88

2. harmful; compulsion; 30%; 40%; 30%; It shows they did not experience their obsessions as being senseless

3. insight; It reduces the change they will be diagnosed as psychotic and treated with harmful medications; 8%; same function, to prevent harm or reduce discomfort; research evidence

4. chance; negative; +1.0; .70 or above; below .40; personality disorders

5. subtype; minivan; leading; probably higher than what occurs in typical practice

CHAPTER 5 - MOOD DISORDERS

Chapter Outline

I. Overview

II. Typical Symptoms and Associated Features
    A. Emotional Symptoms
    B. Cognitive Symptoms
        1. Suicidal Ideas
    C. Somatic Symptoms
    D. Behavioral Symptoms
    E. Other Problems Commonly Associated with Depression

III. Classification
    A. Brief Historical Perspective
    B. Contemporary Diagnostic Systems
        1. Unipolar Disorders
        2. Bipolar Disorders
        3. Further Descriptions and Subtypes
    C. Course and Outcome
        1. Unipolar Disorders
        2. Bipolar Disorders

IV. Epidemiology
    A. Incidence and Prevalence
    B. Gender Differences
    C. Cross-Cultural Differences
    D. Risk for Mood Disorders Across the Life Span
    E. Comparisons Across Generations

V. Etiological Considerations and Research
    A. Social Factors
        1. Freud's Theory of Depression
        2. Stressful Life Events and Unipolar Disorders
        3. Social Factors and Bipolar Disorders
    B. Psychological Factors
        1. Cognitive Responses to Failure and Disappointment
            a. Beck's Cognitive Model
            b. Hopelessness Theory
        2. Interpersonal Factors and Social Skills
            a. Lewinsohn's Behavioral Model
            b. Research on Interpersonal Factors
            c. Response Styles and Gender
        3. Integration of Cognitive and Interpersonal Factors
    C. Biological Factors
        1. Genetics
            a. Family Studies
            b. Twin Studies

Learning Objectives

After reviewing the material presented in this chapter, you should be able to:

1. Distinguish clinical depression from a depressed mood.

2. Define emotion, affect, mood, depression, mania.

3. Identify the major emotional, cognitive, and somatic symptoms involved in depression.

4. Contrast major depressive disorder with dysthymia.

5. Distinguish bipolar I, bipolar II, and cyclothymia.

6.　　Know the average age of onset for depression and bipolar disorder, as well as the typical recovery rates for each disorder.

7.　　Understand how social factors, especially interpersonal loss, can be influential in the development of depression.

8.　　Contrast Beck's cognitive model with the Abramson/Alloy hopelessness model of depression.

9.　　Appreciate the interaction between social, psychological, and biological factors in the development and maintenance of mood disorders.

10.　　Compare interpersonal therapy with cognitive therapy approaches.

11.　　Compare the effectiveness of cognitive therapy, interpersonal therapy, and antidepressant medication with a placebo control group in the treatment of depression.

12.　　Understand the pros and cons of electroconvulsive shock therapy.

13.　　Comprehend Durkheim's basic theory about suicide and identify the four types of suicide he delineated.

14.　　Have a basic understanding of the etiology, epidemiology, and treatment of suicidal ideation and suicidal behavior.

Key Terms - Matching #1

The following terms related to mood disorders are important to know. To test your knowledge, match the following terms with their definitions. Answers are listed at the end of the chapter.

a.	Emotion	l.	Dysphoria
b.	Affect	m.	Euphoria
c.	Mood	n.	Somatic symptoms
d.	Depression	o.	Psychomotor retardation
e.	Depressed mood	p.	Comorbidity
f.	Clinical depression	q.	Dysthymia
g.	Mania	r.	Hypomania
h.	Mood disorders	s.	Cyclothymia
i.	Unipolar mood disorder	t.	Melancholia
j.	Bipolar mood disorder	u.	Seasonal affective disorder
k.	Manic-depressive disorder		

1.　　_____　a mood disorder with onset of episodes associated with changes in the seasons

2.　　_____　a state of incredible well-being and elation

3.　　_____　a term for a mood or a clinical syndrome that involves sadness, despair,

and disappointment
4. _____ significant slowing of movements or speech
5. _____ chronic, mild depression lasting for at least two years
6. _____ observable behaviors associated with a person's feelings
7. _____ having more than one mental disorder at the same time
8. _____ a disturbance in mood which can include elation, decreased need for sleep, pressured speech, inflated self-esteem
9. _____ symptoms related to bodily functions, like sleep and appetite disturbance
10. _____ an especially severe form of depression
11. _____ subjective states of feeling, often accompanied by physiological changes
12. _____ a category of mental disorders involving episodes of disturbance of mood, characterized either by clinical depression or mania
13. _____ chronic, mild form of bipolar disorder with episodes of hypomania and depression lasting at least two years
14. _____ a pervasive, long-standing emotional response that affects a person's perception of his or her world
15. _____ a classification of mood disorder involving periods of depression only
16. _____ a classification of mood disorder involving periods of depression and mania, or sometimes mania alone
17. _____ a mood state involving sadness and despair that is not a psychiatric syndrome
18. _____ the former term for bipolar disorder
19. _____ a psychiatric syndrome involving sadness and despair as well as fatigue, sleep disturbance, loss of energy, or changes in appetite
20. _____ a state of depression, despondency, sadness
21. _____ an episode of increased energy that is not as extreme as mania

Key Terms - Matching #2

The following terms related to mood disorders are important to know. To test your knowledge, match the following terms with their definitions. Answers are listed at the end of the chapter.

1. Remission
2. Relapse
3. Neurasthenia
4. Schema
5. Learned helplessness theory
6. Hopelessness
7. Catecholamine hypothesis
8. Indolamine hypothesis
9. Hypothalamic-pituitary-adrenal axis
10. Dexamethasone suppression test
11. Analogue studies
12. Tricyclics
13. Monoamine oxidase inhibitors
14. Selective serotonin reuptake inhibitors
15. Lithium carbonate
16. Electroconvulsive therapy

a. _____ studies that focus on behaviors that are similar to mental disorders, or features of mental disorders; often animal models of psychopathology
b. _____ a theory that depression is associated with lowered levels and mania with an excess of catecholamines, particularly norepinephrine, in the brain
c. _____ a category of antidepressant medication which must not be taken with

certain foods, especially cheese and chocolate

d. _____ a theory that depression may be related to a person's expectation that good things will not happen and bad things will, regardless of his or her actions

e. _____ a lasting and highly organized cognitive structure that influences how people perceive and interpret events in their environment

f. _____ a period of recovery from a mental disorder

g. _____ a diagnostic term referring to multiple complaints involving physical symptoms, such as headaches and weakness

h. _____ a medication often used to treat bipolar disorder

i. _____ a theory that depression is associated with abnormalities in levels of serotonin in the central nervous system

j. _____ a pathway in the endocrine system that regulates hormone secretions by the adrenal glands; may be involved in the etiology of depression

k. _____ a series of treatments in which electric current is run through the patient's brain; effective in the treatment of severe depression

l. _____ the return of active symptoms in a person who had recovered from a previous episode

m. _____ used to study endocrine dysfunction in people with mood disorders; half of depressed patients show an abnormal response to this test

n. _____ a new class of antidepressants which have fewer side effects than older medications

o. _____ an older class of antidepressants which benefit many depressed people

p. _____ a theory that depression is like the passive behavior of animals exposed to uncontrollable electric shock, that depressed people do not see a relation between their behavior and events that occur in their lives

Names You Should Know - Matching

The following people have played an important role in research and theory of mood disorders. To test your knowledge, match the following names with the descriptions of their contributions to the study of abnormal psychology. Answers are listed at the end of the chapter.

a. Aaron Beck
b. James Coyne
c. Emile Durkheim
d. Sigmund Freud
e. Emil Kraeplin
f. Peter Lewinsohn
g. Adolf Meyer
h. Martin Seligman

1. _____ conceptualized depression as cognitive in origin, arising from distortions, errors, and biases common in the thinking of depressed people

2. _____ identified four types of suicide based on the type of society in which the person lives

3. _____ proposed the first classification system for mental disorders, dividing them into dementia praecox and manic-depressive psychosis

4. _____ proposed the interpersonal perspective of depression, where depressed people's behavior drives away important people in their lives

5. _____ compared clinical depression with the normal process of grieving, but hypothesized that depressed people direct their anger at the lost loved

one toward themselves instead

6. _____ widened the focus of depression to include milder forms, included environmental influences, and preferred the term "depressive reactions"
7. _____ proposed a behavioral model of depression where adaptive behavior is not positively reinforced by the environment and therefore decreases
8. _____ proposed the learned helplessness model of depression

Review of Concepts - Fill in the Blank and True/False

This section will help focus your studying by testing whether you understand the concepts presented in the text. After you have read and reviewed the material, test your comprehension and memory by filling in the following blanks or circling the right answer. Answers are listed at the end of the chapter.

1. Many depressed and manic patients are irritable: **true** **false**

2. People who are depressed often have trouble with their thinking: they have trouble _____, and can't make _____.

3. The depressive triad is typical of depressed patients: they focus on the negative aspects of 1) _____, 2) _____, and 3) _____.

4. People with _____ can be easily distracted, incoherent, and grandiose.

5. People with _____ can be preoccupied with thoughts of suicide and may actually make a suicide attempt that may be successful.

6. Sometimes depressed people have trouble falling asleep and wake up throughout the night or very early in the morning, but it is much more common for a depressed person to sleep much more than usual: **true** **false**

7. Depressed people typically eat more than usual: **true** **false**

8. People with _____ are less likely to initiate sexual activity and people with _____ are more likely to do so.

9. List three types of disorders that have high comorbidity with mood disorders (and are also found in higher rates than expected among relatives of people with mood disorders): _____, _____, and _____.

10. Some people with mood disorders become psychotic (lose touch with reality, experience hallucinations and delusions) during their episodes of depression or mania: **true** **false**

11. Most people with unipolar disorder experience only a single, isolated episode during their lifetimes: **true** **false**

12. People with Bipolar I Disorder have clearcut _____ episodes, while people

with Bipolar II Disorder do not.

13. Rapid cycling bipolar patients typically do not respond as well to treatment as other bipolar patients: **true**   **false**

14. People with seasonal depression are more likely to gain weight and sleep more than people with nonseasonal depression patterns: **true**   **false**

15. The average age of onset of a first episode of unipolar disorder is at which age:
    adolescence (15-25)   **young adulthood** (25-35)   **middle age** (40-50)

16. The average number of lifetime depressive episodes of people with unipolar disorder is _____.

17. A person's risk of _____ of depression goes down the longer they are in remission.

18. The average age of onset of a first episode of bipolar disorder is at which age:
    adolescence (15-25)   **young adulthood** (25-35)   **middle age** (40-50)

19. People with bipolar disorder tend to have more episodes than those with unipolar disorder: **true**   **false**

20. Lifetime risk for major depressive disorder is _____%; for dysthymia is _____%; and for bipolar disorder is _____%.

21. Many, even most, people with mood disorders do not seek treatment: **true**   **false**

22. What sex is more likely to experience major depression and dysthymia? _____

23. There are no significant gender differences in rates of _____.

24. Some studies indicate similar frequencies of mood disorders in different countries and cultures, but differences in specific symptoms. For example, depressed people in Europe and North America are more likely to exhibit _____ while depressed people in non-Western countries, like China, are more likely to exhibit _____.

25. Mood disorders are less common among the elderly than among young and middle-aged adults: **true**   **false**

26. The frequency of depression has decreased in recent years: **true**   **false**

27. Freud hypothesized that people who are prone to depression tend to form narcissistic relationships in which they depend on others to maintain their _____.

28. One complicating factor in interpreting the research linking depression and stressful life events was the direction of the _____.

29. Prospective research design has demonstrated that which one comes first, depression or stressful events? _____

30. Research has shown that the _____ of an important person or role precipitates depression.

31. Once a person is depressed, his or her behavior does lead to an increase in his or her levels of stress: **true**   **false**

32. Bipolar patients who leave the hospital to live with hostile, critical family members are more likely to experience _____.

33. List the four vulnerability factors that identify women who are more likely to become depressed: _____,
_____, _____,
and _____.

34. Beck described several types of cognitive distortions he thought were related to depression. Research has shown that these distortions are present during an episode of depression but not before or after an episode: **true**   **false**

35. A depressogenic attributional style is characterized by a tendency to explain negative events, like failing an exam, in which of the following terms:
external or **internal**; **stable** or **unstable**; **specific** or **global**

36. Lewinsohn hypothesized that some depressed behaviors may initially be reinforced by friends and family and the strength and frequency of these behaviors are: **increased**   **decreased**

37. Coyne hypothesized that depressed people actually do have smaller and less supportive social networks, and that it is not just their perceptions but the actual situation that is negative. Does the research evidence support this? _____

38. People with a ruminative style have   **more** or **less**   depression that people with a distracting style. Men are   **more** or **less**   likely to have a ruminative style than women.

39. Among relatives of people with unipolar disorder, there   **is** or **is not**   an increased risk for unipolar disorder, and there   **is** or **is not**   an increased risk for bipolar disorder.

40. Which disorder, major depressive disorder, bipolar disorder, or dysthymia, shows the highest rate of twin concordance (genetic heritability)? _____
Which shows the lowest? _____

41. Researchers think that the genetic influence on mood disorders is due to:
a single gene   **multiple genes**

42. Current research on the role of neurotransmitters in the etiology of depression suggests that the early theories (the catecholamine hypothesis and the indolamine hypothesis) were too complex: **true**   **false**

43. Rats exposed to stressful events in the laboratory develop symptoms similar to those of depressed people, and antidepressant drugs given to these animals can reverse or prevent these symptoms: **true   false**

44. In treating depressed people, _____ therapy focuses on changing the client's negative schemas and irrational beliefs, and _____ therapy focuses on changing current relationships.

45. Prozac, an antidepressant medication, causes increased violent behavior and suicide: **true   false**

46. Antidepressant medication is far more effective in treating depression than either cognitive or interpersonal therapy: **true   false**

47. Among patients with seasonal affective disorder, exposure to broad-spectrum light is actually <u>not</u> effective in reducing depression: **true   false**

48. What percentage of people with mood disorders will eventually commit suicide?
       1–3%   15–20%   50–55%

49. Suicide is increasing among adolescents in recent decades: **true   false**

50. There are gender differences in rates of suicide: more   **males**   or   **females**   make suicide attempts, and more   **males**   or   **females**   actually complete a suicide.

51. Which group has the highest rate of suicide:
       young black men   middle-aged white women   older white men

52. Does suicide run in families?   _____

53. Media coverage of a suicide increases the rate of suicides committed:
       true   false

54. Suicide hotlines decrease suicide rates: **true   false**

Multiple Choice Questions

The following multiple choice questions will test your comprehension of the material presented in the chapter. Answers are listed at the end of the chapter.

1) Which of the following is NOT a general area describing the signs and symptoms representative of mood disorders?

   a. emotional symptoms   c. somatic symptoms
   b. psychological symptoms   d. cognitive symptoms

2) A promising form of treatment for seasonal affective disorder is:

   a. light therapy   c. nutritional therapy
   b. lithium carbonate   d. meditation

3) What is the percent of completed suicides that occur as a result of a primary mood disorder?

  a. under 15%
  b. under 30%

  c. over 50%
  d. over 78%

4) Which is an example of a somatic symptom?

  a. suicidal ideation
  b. loss of interest

  c. sleep disturbance
  d. low self-esteem

5) An advantage of an analogue study is that:

  a. experimental procedures may be employed
  b. it is easy to generalize the results beyond the laboratory
  c. human subjects are not used
  d. it is easy to reproduce a clinical disorder in the laboratory

6) Which symptom would NOT be considered diagnostic for clinical depression?

  a. racing thoughts
  b. fatigue or loss of energy

  c. feelings of worthlessness
  d. difficulty concentrating

7) Why might it be more difficult to diagnose depression in the elderly?

  a. cognitive impairment or other problems common in the elderly may mask the symptoms of depression
  b. the elderly are more reluctant to seek treatment for depression
  c. the symptoms and features of depression change as age increases
  d. the elderly are less likely to report somatic symptoms associated with depression

8) Results from the Treatment of Depression Collaborative Research Program indicate that:

  a. both types of psychological treatment (interpersonal and cognitive) were as effective as antidepressant medication
  b. patients who received interpersonal therapy did not show gains with cognitive problems
  c. placebo was equally effective to antidepressant medication
  d. cognitive therapy was superior to interpersonal therapy in its effectiveness

9) Which age group has experienced increased rates of suicide since the 1960s?

  a. adolescents
  b. people who are in their 30's
  c. people between the ages of 45 - 55
  d. people over 65

10) When two loci occupy positions close together on the same chromosome they are:

a. polygenic
b. matched

c. homogenous
d. linked

11) Which is a social factor which may contribute to the onset of depression?

a. the belief that one cannot control events in one's life
b. cognitive distortions
c. stressful life events
d. neuroendocrine disturbances

12) Which disorder is often comorbid with a mood disorder?

a. schizophrenia
b. dissociative disorder

c. paranoid personality disorder
d. alcoholism

13) Which is a fundamental assumption about Freud's theory of depression?

a. depressed people are not able to experience guilt
b. depression is an extension of the normal process of grieving
c. depressed people do not depend on others to maintain their self-esteem
d. depressed people are really angry with someone else

14) What age would a person most likely have a first episode of bipolar disorder?

a. 18 - 23 years
b. 28 - 33 years

c. 38 - 43 years
d. 48 - 53 years

15) Which of the following is a common element of suicide?

a. the common goal of suicide is cessation of consciousness
b. the common emotion in suicide is anger
c. the common purpose of suicide is to get revenge
d. the common stressor in suicide is financial difficulties

16) Which of the following is NOT a factor which has been found to increase vulnerability to depression in women?

a. loss of mother at an early age
b. lack of employment away from the home
c. children leaving the home for educational and professional pursuits
d. lack of an intimate, confiding relationship

17) Decreased need for sleep, pressure to keep talking, grandiosity, and distractibility are common symptoms of which disorder?

a. mania
b. dysthymia

c. major depression
d. cyclothymia

18) Advantages of selective serotonin reuptake inhibitors include all EXCEPT:

    a. fewer side effects
    b. less likely to have multiple episodes of depression
    c. less dangerous in the case of an overdose
    d. easier for the patient to take

19) Which is an example of a depressogenic premise?

    a. "I find time in my day to relax"
    b. "I should be at the top of my performance at all times"
    c. "I congratulate myself when I finish a hard day at work"
    d. "I try to forgive myself when I screw things up"

20) Research on electroconvulsive therapy supports that:

    a. memory impairment may be permanent
    b. only bipolar depressed patients respond to ECT
    c. ECT is as effective as placebo
    d. some depressed patients may respond to ECT more than to antidepressants

21) Which statement is NOT true about unipolar depression?

    a. episodes of unipolar depression tend to be longer in duration, compared to episodes of depression in bipolar disorder
    b. at least half of unipolar patients will experience more than one episode
    c. female patients tend to relapse more quickly than male patients
    d. unipolar patients have their first episode at a much younger age than do bipolar patients

22) Some depressed people exhibit a depressogenic attributional style that is characterized by the tendency to explain negative events in terms of:

    a. internal, stable, global factors
    b. internal, unstable, specific factors
    c. external, unstable, specific factors
    d. external, stable, specific factors

23) A standard part of cognitive treatment for depression would be:

    a. gaining insight into suppressed anger in close relationships
    b. developing a better understanding of family relationships
    c. substituting more flexible self-statements for rigid and absolute ones
    d. nondirect discussions of unexpressed emotions

24) An important assumption of the hopelessness theory of depression is:

    a. loss of a parent early in life increases risk for depression
    b. desirable events will not occur regardless of what the person does
    c. depressed people are more likely to feel in control of the events of their lives
    d. depressed people have a positive impact on other people's moods

25) Which type of coping behavior is associated with longer and more severely depressed moods?

    a. processing style   c. intellectual style
    b. ruminative style   d. distracting style

26) Studies investigating genetic transmission of mood disorders indicate that:

    a. the genetic factors are more influential in bipolar disorders than major depressive disorder
    b. the concordance rate for mood disorders is higher for DZ than MZ twins
    c. there is no increased risk of bipolar disorder for relatives of bipolar patients
    d. genetic factors account for about 90% of the variance for dysthymia

27) How do depressed people often respond to a test dose of dexamethasone?

    a. they show a suppression of cortisol secretion
    b. they show a failure of suppression of cortisol secretion
    c. they show a dramatic increase of cortisol secretion
    d. they show an abnormal fluctuation of cortisol secretion

28) An example of a DSM-IV subtype of depression is:

    a. retarded   c. narcissistic
    b. dysphoric   d. melancholic

Understanding Research - Fill in the Blank

Social Origins of Depression in Women: The text presents a detailed description of a study by Brown, Bifulco, and Harris in the Research Close-Up on pp. 170-171. Finding the answers to these questions will help you get a good understanding of this study and why it is important. It is not necessary to memorize the answers; the process of finding them in the textbook will help you learn the material you need to know.

1. Did men or women participate? _____ Ages of subjects were from _____ to _____. Why did all subjects selected have children living at home? _____

_____

2. What information did they gather for each subject?

Psychological adjustment (like symptoms of _____ _____

and self- _____)

Living circumstances (like _____ relationships and social _____)

3. At follow-up one year later, they asked about _____ events and difficulties of the previous year, and they asked again about _____ of mental disorders. Judges rating each description of life events could use all information for making ratings but _____ and

_____.

4. How many women were NOT depressed at Time I? _____ What percent of women who did not experience a severe event during the follow up year became depressed? _____% What percent of women who became depressed had experienced a severe event prior to becoming depressed? _____% What does this show are associated? _____

5. Many women (_____%) who had a severe event in the follow-up year did not become depressed. Those who had an event in an area previously identified as a difficulty were _____ likely to become depressed than if the event did not match a prior difficulty. When the severe event was in an area the woman had shown high commitment to she was _____ likely to become depressed than if it was not.

6. Why is the use of a prospective design important here? _____
_____. What is the direction of effect indicated by these findings?

_____ cause(s) _____

Analogue Studies of Psychopathology: The text discusses this type of research in the Research Methods section on pp. 181-182. Finding the answers to these questions will help you get a good understanding of this research method.

7. What is the key difference between a correlational study and an experiment?

_____

_____

8. Why can't researchers do experiments about the causes of psychopathology with human subjects? _____

_____

9. Harlow's research showed that rhesus monkey infants separated from their mothers showed symptoms similar to symptoms of _____ in people. What can protect these infant monkeys from the detrimental effects of maternal separation?

_____

_____

10. What is one criticism of analogue models of depression? _____

_____

_____

11. Not all analogue studies use animals. The Little Albert study involved a human infant repeatedly exposed to the pairing of a white _____ with a loud, startling noise. The infant's behavior was seen as an analogue of clinical _____. What is a criticism of analogue studies in general? _____

_____

_____

Brief Essay

As a final exercise, write out answers to the following brief essay questions. Then compare your answers with the material presented in the text.

After you have answered these questions, review the "critical thinking" questions that are presented at the end of the text chapter. Answering these questions will help you integrate important issues and themes that have been featured throughout the chapter.

1. What are the primary issues that have been at the center of the controversy about definitions of mood disorders? Would you advocate the use of subtyping in mood disorders? Why?

2. Discuss the methodological problems that one encounters in studying mood disorder across cultures. How have cross-cultural investigations assisted our understanding of mood disorders?

3. Describe the model of depression that emphasizes the interplay between cognitive and interpersonal factors.

ANSWER KEY

Answers to the exercises are listed below; page numbers where the information is referenced in the textbook are given in parentheses.

Key Terms - Matching #1

1. u (163)
2. m (156)
3. d (152)
4. o (158)
5. q (160-1)
6. b (152)
7. p (158)
8. g (152)
9. n (157)
10. t (162-3)
11. a (152)
12. h (152)
13. s (162)
14. c (152)
15. i (153)
16. j (153)
17. e (152)
18. k (153)
19. f (152)
20. l (155)
21. r (162)

Names You Should Know

1. a (172)
2. c (188-9)
3. e (159)
4. b (174)
5. d (168-9)
6. g (159)
7. f (174)
8. h (173)

Key Terms - Matching #2

a. 11 (181)
b. 7 (179)
c. 13 (184)
d. 6 (173)
e. 4 (173)
f. 1 (164)
g. 3 (166)
h. 15 (185)
i. 8 (179)
j. 9 (180)
k. 16 (186)
l. 2 (164)
m. 10 (180)
n. 14 (184)
o. 12 (183)
p. 5 (173)

Review of Concepts

1. true (156)
2. concentrating, decisions (157)
3. themselves, their environment, the future (157)
4. mania (157)
5. depression (157)
6. false (157)
7. false (157)
8. depression; mania (157)
9. alcoholism, eating disorders, anxiety disorders (158)
10. true (159-60)
11. false (160)
12. manic (160-2)
13. true (163)
14. true (163)
15. middle age (164)
16. 5 or 6 (164)
17. relapse (164)
18. young adulthood (164)
19. true (164)
20. 5%; 3%; 1% (165)
21. true (165)
22. females (165)
23. bipolar disorder (165)
24. guilt and suicidal feelings; somatic symptoms (167)
25. true (167-8)
26. false (168)
27. self-esteem (169)
28. effect (169)
29. stressful event (169)
30. loss (169)
31. true (171)
32. relapse (171)
33. absence of intimate relationship, several young children at home, no employment, loss of mother when young (172)
34. true (172)
35. internal, stable, global (173)
36. increased (174)

37. yes (174)
38. more; less (175)
39. is; is not (176)
40. bipolar disorder, dysthymia (177)
41. multiple genes (178)
42. false (179)
43. true (180-1)
44. cognitive, interpersonal (182-3)
45. false (184)

46. false (185)
47. false (187)
48. 15-20% (188)
49. true (189)
50. females, males (189)
51. older white men (189-90)
52. yes (192)
53. true (193)
54. false (193-4)

Multiple Choice

1. b	6. a	11. c	16. c	21. d	26. a
2. a	7. a	12. d	17. a	22. a	27. b
3. c	8. a	13. d	18. b	23. c	28. d
4. c	9. a	14. b	19. b	24. b	
5. a	10. d	15. a	20. d	25. b	

Understanding Research

1. women; 18 to 50; because they found that women with children at home are more likely to become depressed

2. mental; disorders; esteem; personal; support

3. life; symptoms; the woman's mental status; how she responded to the stressful event

4. 303; 2; 90; stressful life events and depression

5. 78; more; more

6. It shows that the depression follows the stressful life event; stressful life events cause depression

7. You can't make a case that one thing causes another in a correlational study but you can in an experiment.

8. It is unethical to attempt to cause psychopathology in people.

9. depression; lots of experience with peers and adult monkeys other than the mother

10. Cognitive symptoms of depression can't be measured in (and may not be experienced by) animals.

11. rat; phobia; Results in an artificial laboratory situation may not be generalizable to the real world.

CHAPTER 6 - ANXIETY DISORDERS

Chapter Outline

I. Overview

II. Typical Symptoms and Associated Features
    A. Anxiety
    B. Excessive Worry
    C. Panic Attacks
    D. Phobias
        1. Agoraphobia
    E. Obsessions and Compulsions

III. Classification
    A. Brief Historical Perspective
        1. Psychoanalytic Theory
        2. From DSM-I to DSM-IV
    B. Subclassification
    C. Contemporary Diagnostic Systems (DSM-IV)

IV. Epidemiology
    A. Prevalence
    B. Comorbidity
    C. Gender Differences
    D. Anxiety Across the Life Span
    E. Cross-Cultural Comparisons

V. Etiological Considerations and Research
    A. Social Factors
        1. Stressful Life Events
        2. Childhood Adversity
        3. Attachment Relationships and Separation Anxiety
    B. Psychological Factors
        1. Learning Processes
            a. Preparedness
            b. Observational Learning
        2. Cognitive Factors
            a. Perception of Control
            b. Catastrophic Misinterpretation
            c. Attention to Threat and Shifts in Attention
            d. Thought Suppression: Obsessive-Compulsive Disorder
    C. Biological Factors
        1. Genetic Factors
            a. Family Studies
            b. Twin Studies
        2. Neurochemistry
        3. False Suffocation Alarms: An Integrated Systems Model

VI. Treatment

A. Psychological Interventions
   1. Exposure: Systematic Desensitization and Flooding
   2. Prolonged Exposure and Response Prevention
   3. Applied Relaxation
   4. Cognitive Therapy
B. Biological Interventions
   1. Antianxiety Medications
   2. Antidepressant Medications

Learning Objectives

After reviewing the material presented in this chapter, you should be able to:

1.   Contrast anxiety with fear and define anxiety and worry.

2.   Name some of the key physical and cognitive symptoms involved in panic attacks.

3.   Compare specific phobias with agoraphobia.

4.   Define obsessions and compulsions.

5.   Understand the Freudian theory of anxiety.

6.   Trace the historical development of the current classification system for anxiety disorders.

7.   Know the basic classification system that DSM-IV uses for panic disorder, specific phobia, social phobia, generalized anxiety disorder, obsessive-compulsive disorder, and agoraphobia.

8.   Rank the prevalence rates of the anxiety disorders in order.

9.   Understand the role of evolution in anxiety and anxiety disorders.

10. Recognize the role of social factors (stressful life events, childhood adversity, and attachment) in the development of anxiety disorders.

11. Understand the way in which Seligman's preparedness model helps to explain why certain phobias are "easier" (fear-relevant) to develop.

12. Name four cognitive factors that are considered influential in the development of anxiety disorders.

13. Describe the results of family studies and twin studies of incidence of anxiety disorders.

14. Recognize the role of neurochemistry in anxiety disorders.

15. Appreciate the differences between systematic desensitization and flooding in treatment of phobias.

16. Describe how cognitive therapy is used in the treatment of anxiety disorders.

17. Know the advantages and disadvantages of using benzodiazepines and tricyclics in the treatment of various anxiety disorders.

Key Terms - Matching #1

The following terms related to anxiety disorders are important to know. To test your knowledge, match the following terms with their definitions. Answers are listed at the end of the chapter.

a.	Fear	g.	Social phobia
b.	Anxiety	h.	Specific phobia
c.	Worry	i.	Preparedness
d.	Panic attack	j.	Observational learning
e.	Phobia	k.	Experimental neurosis
f.	Agoraphobia		

1. _____ induced in laboratory animals under stressful performance requirements, such as making extremely difficult discriminations; characterized by anxiety and agitation, increased startle responses, and disruption of feeding
2. _____ a sudden, overwhelming experience of focused terror
3. _____ an emotion experienced in the face of real, immediate danger
4. _____ phobia of public spaces, or being in situations where escape might be difficult
5. _____ phobia cued by doing something, such as speaking or eating, in front of other people who might scrutinize the performance
6. _____ an emotional reaction out of proportion to threats from the environment
7. _____ a phobia cued by the presence of a specific object or situation
8. _____ persistent, irrational fears associated with a specific object or situation that lead the person to avoid the feared stimulus
9. _____ proposes that organisms are biological predisposed, on the basis of neural pathways, to learn certain types of associations more quickly
10. _____ a more or less uncontrollable sequence of negative, emotional thoughts and images concerned with possible future danger
11. _____ learning behaviors through imitation of a model

Key Terms - Matching #2

The following terms related to anxiety disorders are important to know. To test your knowledge, match the following terms with their definitions. Answers are listed at the end of the chapter.

1. Obsessions
2. Compulsions
3. Neurosis
4. Signal anxiety
5. Generalized anxiety disorder
6. Catastrophic misinterpretation
7. Thought suppression
8. Pharmacological challenge procedures
9. False suffocation alarm
10. Flooding
11. Benzodiazepines

a. _____ indicates that an instinctual impulse previously associated with punishment and disapproval is about to be acted upon
b. _____ exposure beginning with the most frightening stimuli
c. _____ repetitive, unwanted, intrusive thoughts, images, or impulses
d. _____ minor tranquilizers frequently used in the treatment of anxiety disorders
e. _____ an active attempt to stop thinking about something that often leads to the paradoxical effect of an increase in strong emotions associated with unpleasant thoughts
f. _____ repetitive, ritualistic behavior aimed at reducing anxiety; the person perceives it as irrational and tries to resist performing it but cannot
g. _____ a disorder characterized by excessive and uncontrollable worry about a number of events or activities and associated with symptoms of arousal
h. _____ a misfire of the system that detects carbon dioxide, which can also be set off by lactate infusion; may cause panic attacks
i. _____ a psychoanalytic term describing persistent emotional disturbances, such as anxiety or depression, in which anxiety is the key characteristic
j. _____ perceiving bodily sensations as a signal of an impending disastrous event, such as a heart attack
k. _____ a research procedure where a particular brain mechanism is stressed by the artificial administration of chemicals, which if it leads to a panic attack may implicate that brain mechanism in the etiology of panic attack

Names You Should Know - Matching

The following people have played an important role in research and theory of anxiety disorders. To test your knowledge, match the following names with the descriptions of their contributions to the study of abnormal psychology. Answers are listed at the end of the chapter.

a. Donald Klein
b. Susan Mineka
c. David Clark
d. Sigmund Freud
e. Thomas Borkovec
f. John Bowlby
g. Kenneth Kendler
h. Martin Seligman

1. _____ studied the influence of genes and environment on anxiety disorders; found that their influences are fairly disorder-specific
2. _____ conducted a series of studies with rhesus monkeys that combined observational learning with preparedness theory
3. _____ proposed preparedness theory, that people are prepared to develop intense, persistent fears to certain stimuli

4. ____ developed an integrated model of panic attacks and agoraphobia incorporating both psychological and biological factors
5. ____ developed a theory of anxiety based on work with many patients; sees anxiety as serving to warn the person her or she is about to do or think something that is unacceptable and triggering ego defenses to prevent the thought or action
6. ____ saw anxiety as an innate response to separation or threat of separation from caregiver
7. ____ conducted research on catastrophic misinterpretation
8. ____ researched uncontrollable worry; conceptualized it as a verbal rather than visual event which distracts the person from imagery that would trigger unpleasant somatic arousal

Review of Concepts - Fill in the Blank and True/False

This section will help focus your studying by testing whether you understand the concepts presented in the text. After you have read and reviewed the material, test your comprehension and memory by filling in the following blanks or circling the right answer. Answers are listed at the end of the chapter.

1. There is a lot of overlap between anxiety disorders and depression: **true false**

2. Maladaptive anxiety, or anxious apprehension, consists of:

   1) _____,

   2) _____, and

   3) _____.

3. Panic attacks have what type of onset: **gradual   sudden**

4. Panic attacks can happen when the person is in bed: **true   false**

5. Agoraphobia is different from other phobias in that agoraphobics are often afraid they will lose _____ in public.

6. List two ways that obsessions are different from worry; obsessions:

   1) _____, and

   2) _____.

7. Normal people seldom experience obsessions: **true   false**

8. Which is a common compulsion?   **scratching   coughing   cleaning**

9. People with anxiety disorders typically require hospitalization: **true   false**

10. The Freudian explanation of obsessive-compulsive disorder is that the patient has serious difficulties in dealing with what emotion? _____

11. Experts who classify mental disorders can be described as "lumpers" or "splitters;" earlier classification systems used the   **lumping** or **splitting**   approach and contemporary systems use the   **lumping** or **splitting**   approach.

12. Intrusive thoughts about real problems are one form of obsession: **true false**

13. Anxiety disorders are the most common form of mental disorder: **true   false**

14. What percent of people who meet the criteria for one anxiety disorder also meet the criteria for another anxiety disorder?   **5%**   **20%**   **50%**

15. Anxiety and depression are closely related concepts, but Clark and Watson have proposed a model using positive and negative affect to help distinguish between them. Anxiety and depression both share high negative affect, but anxiety alone is characterized by _____ and depression alone is characterized by _____.

16. Depressive disorders and anxiety disorders show high comorbidity; another disorder with high comorbidity with anxiety disorders is _____.

17. Which are more likely to experience specific phobias?   **men   women**

18. Which anxiety disorder occurs equally frequently among men and women?

_____

19. What age group has the lowest prevalence of anxiety disorders? _____

20. Anxiety disorders are almost entirely specific to people in Western societies; very few people in nonindustrialized countries experience them: **true   false**

21. Stressful life events have been linked to both depressive disorders and anxiety disorders. In one study, women who experienced an event involving _____ were more likely to experience depression and those who experienced an event involving _____ were more likely to experience anxiety.

22. Interpersonal conflict such as marital discord often precedes what type of anxiety disorder? _____

23. Two types of childhood adversity were linked to adult anxiety disorders, especially panic disorder; they were _____ and _____; specific phobia was unrelated to childhood adversity.

24. People who have agoraphobia were more likely to have had an _____ attachment to their parents as toddlers.

25. Seligman identified several shortcomings with the classical conditioning model of phobias. They are 1) Conditioned fear responses learned in a laboratory are easy to _____, while phobic responses are extremely persistent; 2) Phobias developed after traumatic experiences, in contrast to those learned in the laboratory, are developed after _____ trial, and 3) The theory states that any stimulus can be conditioned to provoke fear, but phobias of guns, cars, and electrical outlets, potentially dangerous objects, are _____.

26. Rhesus monkeys raised in the wild   **are** or **are not**   afraid of snakes, while those raised in a laboratory   **are or are not**   afraid of snakes.

27. Monkeys can learn to fear snakes by watching videotapes of other monkeys exhibiting fear reactions toward snakes: **true**   **false**

28. People who believe they can control their environment are   **more** or **less** likely to show symptoms of anxiety than people who believe they are helpless.

29. One piece of evidence of the limitations of the catastrophic misinterpretation model of panic attacks is that they can occur while a person is _____.

30. In contrast to a depressed person, who is convinced that failure will occur, an anxious person is _____ that failure will occur.

31. Thought suppression has been found to be quite effective in reducing worrying and intrusive thoughts: **true**   **false**

32. Relatives of people with panic disorder are more likely to have panic disorder but not more likely to have generalized anxiety disorder: **true**   **false**

33. Relatives of people with generalized anxiety disorder are more likely to have GAD but not more likely to have panic disorder: **true**   **false**

34. Relatives of people with obsessive-compulsive disorder are more likely to have OCD but not more likely to have other anxiety disorders: **true**   **false**

35. There is no evidence that the findings that anxiety disorders run in families can be explained in part by genetic influences: **true**   **false**

36. Injecting anxiety disorder patients with lactate almost always triggered a panic attack, while only a few control subjects experienced one: **true**   **false**

37. Which of the following substances can trigger panic attack in anxiety patients?
    alcohol   caffeine   aspirin

38. Exposure to the feared object, situation, or behavior is an effective treatment for anxiety disorders: **true**   **false**

39. The best form of behavior therapy for OCD is _____.

40. Cognitive therapy for anxiety disorders often involves analyzing errors in the patient's _____ as well as the process of _____.

41. Antianxiety medications are particularly effective in reducing a person's worry and rumination: **true**   **false**

42. Benzodiazepines are more effective in the treatment of _____ and _____ and less effective in the treatment of _____ and _____.

43. Benzodiazepines are addictive: **true**   **false**

44. Antidepressants are effective in treating some anxiety disorders: **true**   **false**

Multiple Choice Questions

The following multiple choice questions will test your comprehension of the material presented in the chapter. Answers are listed at the end of the chapter.

1) The most frequently used types of minor tranquilizers for the treatment of anxiety disorders are:

   a. tricyclics
   b. benzodiazapines

   c. serotonin
   d. GABA inhibitors

2) Which of the following is LEAST likely to be present in an anxiety disorder?

   a. lack of insight
   b. social impairment

   c. significant personal distress
   d. negative emotional response

3) Which of the following is an example of a potential unconditioned stimulus (UCS) which could contribute to the development of a phobia?

   a. loss of a relationship
   b. chronic occupational difficulties
   c. a painfully loud and unexpected noise
   d. a sad song

4) _____ is experienced in the face of real, immediate danger, _____ is a diffuse reaction that is out of proportion to threats from the environment.

   a. anxiety, fear
   b. worry, anxiety

   c. fear, anxiety
   d. worry, fear

5) Results of family studies investigating transmission of anxiety disorders suggest:

   a. there appears to be no genetic component to OCD
   b. social phobia is the most inheritable form of anxiety disorder
   c. panic disorder and GAD are etiologically separate disorders
   d. the most inheritable anxiety disorder is specific phobia

6) The two most common types of compulsions are:

   a. counting and repeating
   b. cleaning and checking

   c. sorting and counting
   d. checking and writing

7) A junior in college, Sam is acutely distressed at the thought of having to write in front of other people. He is afraid that he will drop his pen, lose control of his writing, or do something else embarassing while other people are watching him. While he is able to write in the privacy of his room, this fear has impaired his ability to take notes in classes. His most likely diagnosis would be:

   a. specific phobia
   b. agoraphobia

   c. generalized anxiety disorder
   d. social phobia

8) The discovery of laboratory procedures that reliably induce panic attacks is important because:

   a. they offer investigators the opportunity to research the antecedents and consequences of panic attacks
   b. brain activities that occur during a panic attack may be monitored
   c. such procedures may be fruitful in developing a map of the specific areas of the brain that mediate anxiety symptoms
   d. all of the above

9) Which of the following is the most common type of abnormal behavior?

   a. phobias
   b. major depression
   c. generalized anxiety disorder
   d. dysthymia

10) Specific phobias may be best understood in terms of learning experiences. The association between the object and intense fear can develop through all BUT which of the following?

   a. direct experience
   b. observational learning
   c. exposure to fear-irrelevant stimuli
   d. exposure to warnings and instructions about dangerous situations

11) Which is TRUE regarding the relationship between anxiety and other disorders?

   a. substance dependence is rarely associated with anxiety disorders
   b. anxiety disorders overlap considerably with other anxiety disorders
   c. anxiety disorders usually overlap with psychotic disorders
   d. anxiety disorders do not appear to be associated with depressive disorders

12) "Free-floating" anxiety would be most characteristic of which anxiety disorder?

   a. social phobia
   b. panic disorder
   c. obsessive-compulsive disorder
   d. generalized anxiety disorder

13) Which of the following is NOT consistent with Freud's model of anxiety?

   a. repression is the product of anxiety
   b. anxiety is the result of a harsh superego in conflict with the defense mechanisms that are employed by the ego
   c. the specific form of overt symptoms is determined by the defense mechanisms that are employed by the ego
   d. different types of anxiety disorders can be distinguished by many factors within the analytic framework, for example, the developmental stage at which the person experiences problems

14) Anxiety disorder categories did not emerge in psychiatric classifications during the last century primarily because:

    a. the prevalence of anxiety disorders was much lower during the last century
    b. they were considered to be neurological disorders
    c. very few cases of anxiety disorders required institutionalization
    d. physicians were not trained to recognize the symptoms of anxiety disorders

15) Which of the following is NOT a symptom of a panic attack?

    a. feeling of choking   c. nausea
    b. trembling   d. headache

16) Research on the relationship between stressful life events and anxiety disorders suggests that:

    a. the onset of agoraphobia may be associated with interpersonal conflict
    b. marital distress is associated with the onset of simple phobia
    c. the onset of agoraphobia may be associated with the experience of a
        conditioning event, such as a sudden painful injury
    d. severe loss is associated with the onset of an anxiety disorder

17) Which cognitive factor shares an important relationship with panic attacks?

    a. perception of control over events in one's environment
    b. thought suppression
    c. cognitive minimization of traumatic events
    d. all-or-none thinking about future events

18) Which is NOT included in the DSM-IV's classification of anxiety disorders?

    a. panic disorder   c. cyclothymia
    b. agoraphobia   d. obsessive-compulsive disorder

19) If a panic attack only occurs in the presence of a particular stimulus, it is said to be:

    a. a situationally cued attack   c. a "below threshold" attack
    b. an anticipated attack   d. a cognitively processed attack

20) Karen has consistent worries that she is going to lose her job, something is going to happen to her husband and she will be alone, and her health will deteriorate. She knows that her worries cause friction in her marital relationship, but feels she cannot control them, though she repeatedly tries to put them out of her mind. Although she has always been a "worrier", the intensity and frequency of her worries has gotten worse in the past year. Her most likely diagnosis is:

    a. agoraphobia   c. generalized anxiety disorder
    b. panic disorder   d. simple phobia

21) The most serious adverse side effects of benzodiazepines is:

   a. heart palpitations
   b. significant weight gain
   c. the dietary restrictions which patients must observe while using them
   d. their potential for addiction

22) The types of symptoms most characteristic of a panic attack are:

   a. interpersonal difficulties   c. emotional reactions
   b. physical sensations   d. cognitive reactions

23) Cross-cultural research on anxiety disorders suggests that:

   a. anxiety disorders are not experienced in certain cultures
   b. phobic avoidance is the most commonly reported symptom across cultures
   c. the focus of typical anxiety complaints can vary dramatically across cultures
   d. anxiety disorders are more common in preliterate cultures

24) An important consideration in diagnosing panic disorder is that the person must:

   a. experience recurrent, situationally cued panic attacks
   b. experience recurrent panic attacks in anticipation of a feared event
   c. report the experience of feeling out of control
   d. experience recurrent unexpected panic attacks

25) Which of the following is NOT included in the DSM-IV as criteria to establish the boundary between normal behavior and compulsive rituals?

   a. the rituals cause marked distress
   b. the rituals can be observed by other people
   c. the rituals interfere with normal occupational and social functioning
   d. the rituals take more than one hour per day to perform

26) Which of the following would be a typical situation that would cause problems for an agoraphobic?

   a. travelling on the subway   c. cleaning the house
   b. speaking to a friend on the phone d. encountering a snake

27) According to recent research, what percent of the people who qualify for an anxiety disorder diagnosis actually seek treatment for their disorder?

   a. 15%   c. 40%
   b. 25%   d. 50%

28) What is an important difference between compulsions and some addictive behaviors such as gambling?

    a. addictive behaviors reduce anxiety more effectively than compulsions
    b. compulsions are more resistant to treatment
    c. addictive behaviors are not repetitive in nature
    d. compulsions reduce anxiety but they do not produce pleasure

29) Women are about twice as likely as men to experience all BUT which of the following anxiety disorders?

    a. social phobia
    b. agoraphobia
    c. specific phobia
    d. panic disorder

Understanding Research - Fill in the Blank

Panic and Perception of Control: The text presents a detailed description of a study by Sanderson, Rapee, and Barlow in the Research Close-Up on pp. 223-224. Finding the answers to these questions will help you get a good understanding of this study and why it is important. It is not necessary to memorize the answers; the process of finding them in the textbook will help you learn the material you need to know.

1. All of the procedures researchers have used to induce a panic attack in a laboratory situation produce a range of peripheral _____ sensations, such as _____, chest _____, and _____- headedness.

2. In this study they used air enriched with _____ but manipulated the subjects' impressions of whether they were in _____ of the air mixture. All subjects met diagnostic criteria for _____ disorder.

3. Each person sat _____ in a quiet room, breathing through a gas _____, and rated his or her _____ level. They were told when the box was ____ they could adjust the mixture of carbon dioxide by using the dial on their _____. In reality the dial had _____ effect. All patients received _____ minutes of compressed air, then _____ minutes of carbon-dioxide enriched air. For _____ of the _____ patients the light went on, and for the rest it never went on.

4. Following the procedure, subjects were all interviewed to see if they experienced a _____. Eight of the 10 subjects in the _____ group had a panic attack. Two of the 10 subjects in the _____ group had a panic attack. Those in the no illusion group reported more than _____

as many symptoms that those in the illusion of control group. Both groups had symptoms of breathlessness and _____ sensations, dizziness, _____ headedness, and pounding _____.

5. This study is important because it shows how biological and psychological factors _____ to produce the experience of panic. Biological factors were important but alone were not _____ to produce an attack. Feelings of _____ were particularly important.

Statistical Significance and Clinical Importance: The text discusses this type of research in the Research Methods section on pp. 231-232. Finding the answers to these questions will help you get a good understanding of these issues.

6. Does a statistical difference always mean the finding is clinically significant? _____
What disorder is used in the hypothetical example? _____
What is the null hypothesis? _____
What is the other hypothesis? _____
_____

7. Statistically significant tests are ones where the probability of finding the difference that you are observing among the groups by chance alone is less than _____ times out of 100. In the hypothesized study, outcome was rated on a scale of anxiety ranging from _____ to _____. Both groups had a mean rating of _____ prior to treatment, and after treatment the difference between the two treatment groups was _____ points.

8. Why is this difference not clinically important? _____
_____
_____

Brief Essay

As a final exercise, write out answers to the following brief essay questions. Then compare your answers with the material presented in the text.

After you have answered these questions, review the "critical thinking" questions that are presented at the end of the text chapter. Answering these questions will help you integrate important issues and themes that have been featured throughout the chapter.

1. Learning processes have been theoretically associated with the development of phobias, while cognitive factors have been used to explain the development of panic attacks. Review the prominent learning and cognitive theories that account for each type of disorder. Do you think that differences in etiological processes imply that these disorders are really unrelated? Why or why not?

2. Discuss the overlap between anxiety and depression. Do you think that anxiety and depression are separate types of disorders, or do you think that they represent different manifestations of the same problem? What evidence supports your position?

3. Consider the following psychological interventions used for the treatment of anxiety disorders: desensitization, flooding, prolonged exposure and response prevention, and cognitive therapy. Select an anxiety disorder and discuss how you would approach treatment for this disorder. Which intervention techniques(s) would you choose and why?

4. False suffocation alarm theory is a theoretical model of panic attacks and agoraphobia that integrates biological and psychological factors. Discuss this theory, highlighting both the main assumptions of the model and the research findings which support these assumptions.

ANSWER KEY

Answers to the exercises are listed below; page numbers where the information is referenced in the textbook are given in parentheses.

Key Terms - Matching #1

1. k (222)	7. h (211)
2. d (203)	8. e (204)
3. a (202)	9. i (220)
4. f (205)	10. c (203)
5. g (210)	11. j (221)
6. b (202)	

Names You Should Know

1. g (227)
2. b (221)
3. h (220)
4. a (229)
5. d (209)
6. f (219)
7. c (222)
8. e (224-5)

Key Terms - Matching #2

a. 4 (209)	d. 11 (233)	g. 5 (210)	j. 6 (222)
b. 10 (231)	e. 7 (225)	h. 9 (229)	k. 8 (227)
c. 1 (206)	f. 2 (206)	i. 3 (209)	

Multiple Choice

1. b	6. b	11. b	16. a	21. d	26. a
2. a	7. d	12. d	17. a	22. b	27. b
3. c	8. d	13. b	18. c	23. c	28. d
4. c	9. a	14. c	19. a	24. d	29. a
5. c	10. c	15. d	20. c	25. b	

Review of Concepts

1. true (200)
2. high levels of negative emotion, a sense of uncontrollability, and self-preoccupation (203)
3. sudden (203)
4. true (204)
5. control (205)
6. are out of the blue, and involve socially unacceptable and horrific themes (206)
7. false (207)
8. cleaning (208)
9. false (208)
10. anger or aggression (209)
11. lumping; splitting (210)
12. false (213)
13. true (213)
14. 50% (213)
15. physiological hyperarousal; absence of positive affect (214)
16. alcoholism (215)
17. women (215)
18. OCD (215)
19. the elderly (215-6)
20. false (216)
21. loss; danger (218)
22. agoraphobia (218)
23. parental indifference; physical abuse (219)
24. insecure-anxious (219)
25. extinguish; one; rare (220)
26. are; are not (221)
27. true (221)
28. less (222)
29. asleep (224)
30. not sure (224)
31. false (225)
32. true (226)
33. true (226)
34. false (226)
35. false (227)
36. true (228)
37. caffeine (228)
38. true (230-1)
39. prolonged exposure with response prevention (231-2)
40. thinking; decatastrophizing (233)
41. false (233)
42. GAD; social phobia; specific phobia; OCD (233)
43. true (234)
44. true (234)

Understanding Research

1. somatic; palpitations; tightness; light

2. carbon dioxide; control; panic

3. alone; mask; anxiety; lit; lap; no; 5; 15; 10; 20

4. panic attack; no illusion; illusion of control; twice; smothering; light; heart

5. interact; sufficient; control

6. No; social phobia; two treatments are not different; exposure treatment group will show more improvement than placebo or nondirective treatment

7. 5; 0 to 100; 85; 10

8. Because the average patient in the exposure group still has a score above the cutoff for identifying meaningful psychopathology.

CHAPTER 7 - POSTTRAUMATIC STRESS DISORDER DISSOCIATIVE and SOMATOFORM DISORDERS

Chapter Outline

I. Overview

II. Acute and Posttraumatic Stress Disorders
    A. Typical Symptoms and Associated Features of ASD and PTSD
        1. Reexperiencing
        2. Avoidance
        3. Arousal or Anxiety
        4. Dissociative Symptoms
    B. Classification of Acute and Posttraumatic Stress Disorders
        1. Brief Historical Perspective
        2. Contemporary Classification
            a. Acute Stress Disorder
            b. Traumatic Events
            c. Differential Diagnosis, Comorbidity, and the Grouping of PTSD/ASD
    C. Epidemiology of Trauma and Traumatic Stress Disorders
    D. Etiological Considerations and Research on PTSD and ASD
        1. Biological Factors in Traumatic Stress Disorders
            a. Biological Effects of Exposure to Trauma
        2. Psychological Factors in Traumatic Stress Disorders
        3. Social Factors in Traumatic Stress Disorders
        4. Integration and Alternative Pathways
    E. Prevention and Treatment of ASD and PTSD
        1. Emergency Treatment of Trauma Victims
        2. Treatment of PTSD
            a. Therapeutic Reexposure to Trauma
        3. Course and Outcome
            a. Recovered Memories?

III. Dissociative Disorders
    A. Brief Historical Perspective: Hysteria and Unconscious Mental Processes
        1. Unconscious Processes and Contemporary Cognitive Science
    B. Typical Symptoms of Dissociative Disorders
        1. Trauma and the Onset of Dissociative Symptoms
    C. Classification of Dissociative Disorders
        1. Brief Historical Perspective
        2. Contemporary Classification
        3. The Three Faces of Eve: The Case of Chris Sizemore
    D. Epidemiology of Dissociative Disorders
        1. Disorder or Role Enactment?
    E. Etiological Considerations and Research on Dissociative Disorders
        1. Biological Factors
        2. Psychological Factors
        3. Social Factors

F. Treatment of Dissociative Disorders

IV. Somatoform Disorders
    A. Typical Symptoms and Associated Features of Somatoform Disorders
    B. Unnecessary Medical Treatment
    C. Classification of Somatoform Disorders
        1. Conversion Disorder
        2. Somatization Disorder
        3. Hypochondriasis
        4. Pain Disorder
        5. Body Dysmorphic Disorder
    D. Epidemiology of Somatoform Disorders
        1. Comorbidity
    E. Etiological Considerations and Research on Somatoform Disorders
        1. Biological Factors
            a. Diagnosis by Exclusion
        2. Psychological Factors
            a. Primary and Secondary Gain
        3. Social Factors
    F. Treatment of Somatoform Disorders

Learning Objectives

After reviewing the material presented in this chapter, you should be able to:

1. Define and list the DSM IV symptoms of Post Traumatic Stress Disorder.

2. Distinguish PTSD from acute stress disorder and adjustment disorder.

3. Describe some of the treatment approaches utilized with victims of PTSD.

4. Distinguish dissociative and somatoform disorders.

5. Describe the views on hysteria of: early Greeks, Charcot, Janet, and Freud and compare these perspectives with the contemporary perspective.

6. Define dissociation and psychogenic amnesia.

7. Explain the connection between psychological trauma and fugue, amnesia, and multiple personality disorder.

8. Define retrograde, posttraumatic, anterograde, and selective amnesia.

9. Identify the DSM criteria for depersonalization disorder and multiple personality disorder.

10. Define prosopagnosia and explain the significance of this biologically based disorder for the biological approach to dissociation.

11. Understand the psychological view of dissociative disorders, but be aware that little scientific research has been conducted to verify these theories.

12. Describe the ways in which hypnosis and abreaction presumably aid in the integration of dissociated memories.

13. Give the DSM IV criteria for body dysmorphic disorder, hypochondriasis, somatization disorder, pain disorder, and conversion disorder.

14. Understand the way in which misdiagnosis of somatoform disorder can be dangerous.

15. Know Freud's theory of primary and secondary gain used to explain somatoform symptoms.

16. Describe the behavioral therapy approach to treatment of chronic pain.

17. Outline the way physicians should treat the patient who presents "excessive" physical concerns that are not physiologically based.

Key Terms - Matching #1

The following terms are important to know. To test your knowledge, match the following terms with their definitions. Answers are listed at the end of the chapter.

a.	Traumatic stress	k.	Dissociative amnesia
b.	Acute Stress Disorder (ASD)	l.	Selective amnesia
c.	Posttraumatic stress disorder (PTSD)	m.	Depersonalization disorder
d.	Dissociative Disorders	o.	Multiple personality disorder
e.	Somatoform Disorders	p.	Hypnosis
f.	Malingering	q.	Prosopagnosia
g.	Factitious Disorder	r.	Retrospective reports
h.	Flashbacks	s.	State-dependent learning
i.	Depersonalization	t.	Iatrogenesis
j.	Derealization	u.	Abreaction

1. _____ a disorder characterized by the sudden inability to recall extensive and important personal information
2. _____ a sense of feeling cut off from oneself or one's environment
3. _____ impairment of face recognition sometimes resulting from brain damage
4. _____ characterized by persistent, maladaptive disruptions in the integration of memory, consciousness, or identity
5. _____ a marked sense of unreality about oneself or one's environment
6. _____ recollections about the past that have questionable reliability and validity
7. _____ an altered state of consciousness during which people are especially susceptible to suggestion
8. _____ occurs within 4 weeks of exposure to a trauma; characterized by dissociative symtoms, reexperiencing of the event, avoidance of

reminders of the event, and anxiety or arousal

9. _____ lasts over a month after exposure to a trauma, or has a delayed onset (6 or more months after trauma); characterized by dissociative symptoms, reexperiencing of the event, avoidance of reminders of the event, and anxiety or arousal

10. _____ creation of a disorder by attempts at treatment

11. _____ exposure to some event that involves actual or threatened death or serious injury to self or others

12. _____ the emotional reliving of a past traumatic experience

13. _____ a dissociative disorder characterized by the existence of two or more distinct personalities in a single individual, which repeatedly take over the person's behavior outside of his or her awareness

14. _____ the previous term for dissociative identity disorder

15. _____ sudden, intrusive, vivid memories during which a trauma is replayed in images or thoughts

16. _____ pretending to have a psychological disorder in order to achieve some external gain

17. _____ pretending to have a psychological disorder in order to assume the sick role

18. _____ a dissociative disorder characterized by severe and persistent feelings of being detached from oneself

19. _____ learning that occurs in one state of affect or consciousness is recalled most accurately while in that same state

20. _____ a form of amnesia in which people do not lose their memory completely but are unable to remember only certain personal events and information

21. _____ characterized by unusual physical symptoms that occur in the absence of a known physical illness

Key Terms - Matching #2

The following terms are important to know. To test your knowledge, match the following terms with their definitions. Answers are listed at the end of the chapter.

1. Victimization
2. Two-factor theory
3. Trauma desensitization
4. Eye Movement Desensitization and Reprocessing (EMDR)
5. Recovered memories
6. False memories
7. Dissociative fugue
8. Hysteria
9. Amnesia
10. Psychogenic amnesia

11. Conversion disorder
12. Somatization disorder
13. La belle indifference
14. Briquet's syndrome
15. Hypochondriasis
16. Pain disorder
17. Body dysmorphic disorder
18. Diagnosis by exclusion
19. Primary gain
20. Secondary gain
21. Alexithymia

a. _____ a pattern of response among victims of violent crime that includes fear, guilt, self-blame, powerlessness, and lowered self-esteem

b. _____ a somatoform disorder characterized by preoccupying fear or belief that one is suffering from a physical illness, even in the face of a clean bill of health by a physician

c. _____ a somatoform disorder characterized by physical symptoms that mimic those found in neurological diseases, but which often do not make sense anatomically

d. _____ amnesia that is psychologically caused, resulting from trauma or emotional distress

e. _____ a process of identifying somatoform disorders by ruling out physical causes that could account for the symptoms

f. _____ a name sometimes used to refer to somatization disorder

g. _____ a controversial treatment using rapid back-and-forth eye movements to induce relaxation while reliving a traumatic event

h. _____ a somatoform disorder characterized by constant preoccupation with some imagined or grossly exaggerated defect in physical appearance

i. _____ dramatic recollections of a long-forgotten traumatic experience

j. _____ partial or complete loss of recall for particular events or for a particular time period

k. _____ an unintentionally invented memory of an event that did not actually occur

l. _____ a psychoanalytic term that a symptom protects the ego from an unacceptable thought or impulse by serving as a symbolic, disguised expression of that thought

m. _____ a somatoform disorder characterized by multiple, somatic complaints in the absence of organic impairment

n. _____ a rare disorder characterized by sudden, unplanned travel, the inability to remember details about the past, and identity confusion or assumption of a new identity

o. _____ a psychoanalytic term that a symptom is rewarding because it allows a patient to avoid responsibility or elicit sypathy or attention from others

p. _____ a flippant lack of concern about the physical symptoms of a somatoform disorder

q. _____ an historic diagnostic category that included both dissociative and somatoform disorders; based on the ancient Greek idea that these symptoms were caused by a "dislodged, wandering uterus"

r. _____ a somatoform disorder characterized by preoccupation with pain in which psychological factors are involved

s. _____ explains the development of symptoms following trauma using a combination of classical and operant conditioning, whereby classical conditioning creates fears and operant conditioning maintains them

t. _____ treatment method where the client is first taught to relax, and while relaxed, gradually relives the traumatic event through discussion or fantasy

u. _____ a deficit in the capacity to recognize and express the emotions signaled by physiological arousal

Names You Should Know - Matching

The following people have played an important role in research and theory of PTSD, dissociative, and somatoform disorders. To test your knowledge, match the following names with the descriptions of their contributions to the study of abnormal psychology. Answers are listed at the end of the chapter.

- a. Pierre Janet
- b. Edna Foa
- c. Nicholas Spanos
- d. Jean Charcot
- e. Sigmund Freud

1. _____ argued that multiple personalities are caused by role playing
2. _____ viewed dissociation as a normal process, similar to repression, whereby the ego defends itself against unacceptable thoughts
3. _____ used hypnosis to treat hysteria
4. _____ viewed dissociation as an abnormal process, and indicative of psycho-pathology
5. _____ explains PTSD symptoms using the two-factor theory

Review of Concepts - Fill in the Blank and True/False

This section will help focus your studying by testing whether you understand the concepts presented in the text. After you have read and reviewed the material, test your comprehension and memory by filling in the following blanks or circling the right answer. Answers are listed at the end of the chapter.

1. PTSD is characterized by these three symptoms: _____, _____, and _____.

2. ASD is characterized by the above three symptoms and _____.

3. Sometimes the reexperiencing of PTSD and ASD occurs as a _____ state, which is usually brief.

4. In PTSD, avoidance may manifest as _____, where feelings seem dampened or nonexistent, and they withdraw from others.

5. Many people with PTSD and ASD are jumpy and nervous, showing an "exaggerated _____ response."

6. The development of ASD as a diagnostic category was in part an attempt to _____ the development of PTSD by providing early treatment.

7. What was wrong with earlier definitions of trauma? _____ _____

8. What are five types of experience that often lead to the development of PTSD? _____, _____ _____, _____ and _____

9. Some of the consequences of rape are: 39% of victims sustain injuries on parts of their body other than their genitals; many contract a sexually transmitted

disease; 5% are impregnated; and most develop _____.

10. What three disorders commonly co-occur with PTSD? _____,
_____, and _____.

11. It is thought that about _____% of women and _____% of men will develop
PTSD at some point in their lives.

12. People who experience what type of trauma develop PTSD in the highest
proportions? _____

13. People with a history of emotional problems are   **more** or **less**   likely
to experience trauma and are   **more** or **less**   likely to develop PTSD.

14. Childhood _____ problems increase the risk of experiencing
a traumatic stressor and make it more likely that PTSD will develop in response
to the stressor.

15. What are the three models that attempt to explain why not everybody that
experiences a traumatic event develops PTSD? _____,
_____, and _____.

16. Monozygotic (MZ) twins had a   **higher** or **lower**   concordance rate
than dizygotic (DZ) twins for experiencing trauma in the form of exposure to
combat, and for developing PTSD symptoms in a study of Vietnam veterans.

17. Which of the following is NOT one of the psychological risk factors that may
account for increased risk of trauma exposure and PTSD:
antisocial behavior   depression   intelligence   neuroticism

18. Research has suggested that an increase in the production of the neurotransmitter
_____ in response to trauma causes the increased
arousal and anxiety seen in PTSD, and that the increase in production of
endogenous _____ in response to trauma causes the numbing.

19. One study showed that Vietnam veterans with PTSD showed   **more** or **less**
pain sensitivity following exposure to a film of combat.

20. People cope   **better** or **worse**   with trauma when they anticipate its onset.

21. What three characteristics of an attack increase the chance that victims of sexual
assault will develop PTSD? _____,
_____, _____

22. What three types of experiences among Vietnam veterans increase the risk of
PTSD? _____, _____,
and _____

23. Social support   **increases** or **decreases**   the risk for PTSD.

24. Research   **supports** or **does not support**   the idea that immediate,

emergency psychological treatment is effective in preventing PTSD.

25. What was the conclusion of the study in the Netherlands comparing the effectiveness of trauma desensitization, hypnotherapy, and psychodynamic therapy in improving PTSD? _____

26. Although painful and difficult, _____ is the essential component of effective treatment for PTSD.

27. There is no evidence that repression of memories of traumatic events occurs:
       true   false

28. It is very difficult to establish whether a recovered memory is accurate: **true   false**

29. Freud viewed the unconscious mind as being   **dumb** or **smart**   while contemporary scientists view it as   **dumb** or **smart**.

30. One study found that 80% of patients with dissociative identity disorder also met criteria for what disorder?   _____

31. What traumatic experience is hypothesized to play a role in the etiology of many dissociative disorders?   _____

32. Only 200 case histories of _____ disorder appeared in the entire world literature before 1980; a 1986 report suggested that about 6,000 cases of it had been diagnosed in North America alone, yet the diagnosis remains extremely rare in Europe and Japan.

33. Some professionals question the existence of dissociative identity disorder, arguing that it is created by the power of _____.

34. What is one important way that the multiple identity enactment created in laboratory studies differs from the multiple identities found in dissociative identity disorder?   _____

35. Patients with prosopagnosia demonstrate the normal preference for viewing faces that are familiar. This finding implies a dissociation between _____ and _____ cognitive processes.

36. An adequate test of the hypothesized relation between child abuse and dissociative disorders requires _____ research following trauma victims from childhood into adult life with assessments of dissociation at different times.

37. Some psychologists argue that dissociative identity disorder is produced by iatrogenesis; in other words, who causes the disorder?   _____

38. The goal of treatment for dissociative identity disorder is _____

_____.

39. What kind of professional do people with somatoform disorders typically see?

_____

40. In one study, 27% of women undergoing what type of surgery actually suffered from somatization disorder? _____

41. Somatization disorder must have its onset in:

young adulthood   **middle age**

42. Conversion disorders are   **more** or **less**   common now than in the past.

43. Somatization disorder is more common in which of the following:

women or **men**   **blacks** or **whites**   **less educated** or **more educated**

44. Somatoform disorders show high comorbidity with _____.

45. People with somatization disorder are more likely to have male relatives with

_____ disorder.

46. In one study, what percentage of patients diagnosed with conversion disorders were eventually found to have a neurological disease?   **5%   25% 45%**

47. Patients with somatization disorder are best treated by a physician who expresses

_____ for their problems.

Multiple Choice Questions

The following multiple choice questions will test your comprehension of the material presented in the chapter. Answers are listed at the end of the chapter.

1) Many people who suffer from PTSD also meet the diagnostic criteria for another mental disorder, particularly _____ and _____.

   a. depression; substance abuse
   b. hypomania; antisocial personality disorder
   c. depression; adjustment disorder
   d. hypomania; paranoid personality disorder

2) All of the following are cultural myths of sexual assault EXCEPT:

   a. women who are raped provoke it
   b. women who are raped are "damaged goods"
   c. women who are raped often enjoy it
   d. most women who are raped are raped by an acquaintance

3) Jack, a Vietnam veteran, runs for cover every time he hears an airplane pass by overhead. Jack's reaction can best be described as a:

   a. flashback   c. brief psychotic reaction
   b. dissociative state   d. hallucination

4) According to one study conducted in the St. Louis area, the most common cause of PTSD among men was:

    a. observing domestic violence in the home as a child
    b. being a victim of physical abuse as a child
    c. participation in the Vietnam War
    d. witnessing a friend or relative die from a traumatic event

5) Several surveys have found that approximately _____ of U.S. women have been victims of rape.

    a. 10%   c. 30%
    b. 20%   d. 40%

6) All of the following are factors that increase the risk for experiencing trauma and therefore make PTSD more likely EXCEPT:

    a. having a history of conduct problems during childhood
    b. being male
    c. being less educated
    d. having an introverted personality

7) As many as _____ of all stranger rapes are not reported to authorities.

    a. one-third   c. one-quarter
    b. two-thirds   d. one-half

8) Some research indicates that it is helpful to recount stressful experiences because:

    a. it can reduce the various psychophysiological indicators of the stress response
    b. it helps dissipate negative feelings associated with the stressful experiences
    c. it helps the person "let go" of the experience and continue with his or her life
    d. there is no research that supports the effectiveness of recounting stressful experiences

9) Studies show that _____ is the most effective treatment for PTSD.

    a. hypnotherapy
    b. psychodynamic therapy
    c. trauma desensitization
    d. there were no significant differences detected among any of the above therapies

10) _____ is the help and understanding received from friends and family as well as from professionals.

    a. A personal network   c. Psychotherapy
    b. Social support   d. None of the above

11) Which of the following is NOT typically a symptom of PTSD?

    a. difficulty falling or staying asleep   c. paranoid thoughts or ideas
    b. irritability or outbursts of anger   d. difficulty concentrating

12) A horrifying experience that leads to increases in anxiety and arousal, avoidance of emotionally charged situations, and frequent reliving of the traumatic event is:

    a. posttraumatic stress disorder   c. acute stress disorder
    b. victimization   d. generalized anxiety disorder

13) Sudden, unplanned travel, the inability to remember certain past details, and confusion about one's identity are primary features of:

    a. general amnesia   c. body dysmorphic disorder
    b. Briquet's syndrome   d. dissociative fugue

14) Abnormal fears of having a serious medical disorder, even after a thorough medical evaluation reveals nothing wrong, is characteristic of:

    a. hypochondriasis   c. somatization disorder
    b. depersonalization disorder   d. conversion disorder

15) This term describes people who habitually and deliberately pretend to have a physical illness.

    a. hypochondriasis   c. factitious disorder
    b. psychosis   d. adjustment disorder

16) An unfortunate consequence of having a somatoform disorder is:

    a. the patient does not attend to the medical aspects of the disorder, resulting in underutilization of health care
    b. the psychological nature of the patient's problems go unnoticed, and unnecessary medical procedures are performed
    c. the seriousness of the physical complaints are overlooked, and necessary medical treatments are refused
    d. psychologists, not physicians, are consulted, resulting in poor health care

17) Which disorder does NOT appear to overlap with somatoform disorders?

    a. anxiety disorders   c. antisocial personality disorder
    b. depression   d. multiple personality disorder

18) Freud believed that both dissociative and somatoform disorders were:

    a. expressions of unresolved anger
    b. reactions of the superego toward repressed impulses
    c. expressions of unconscious conflict
    d. conscious reactions to traumatic situations

19) "La belle indifference" is occasionally exhibited by patients with:

    a. multiple personality disorder
    b. pain disorder
    c. psychogenic amnesia
    d. somatization disorder

20) Whenever Tom looks into the mirror, the first thing he notices is his large and somewhat pointed ears. Although friends have reassured him otherwise, he is convinced that his ears are the first thing others notice about him, too. He thinks people may call him Mr. Spock behind his back. He has consulted with several plastic surgeons and his first surgery has scheduled. He displays symptoms of:

    a. somatization disorder
    b. Briquet's syndrome
    c. conversion disorder
    d. body dysmorphic disorder

21) Sally is depressed about her relationship with her boyfriend as she studies for her spring chemistry final. The next fall, she takes another chemistry course and easily remembers the material from her spring course while studying for her first quiz. She is also depressed now due to a fight with her girlfriend. This is:

    a. state-dependent learning
    b. abreaction
    c. hypnotic recall
    d. recovered memory

22) How might antianxiety, antipsychotic, or antidepressant medications be helpful in the treatment of dissociative disorders?

    a. they facilitate reintegration of the dissociated states
    b. they reduce the level of the patient's emotional distress
    c. they increase the likelihood of having one personality become dominant over other personalities
    d. they are not recommended treatment for dissociative disorders

23) A critical consideration in diagnosis of a somatoform disorder is the person may:

    a. be aware of the psychological factors producing the disorder
    b. minimize physical complaints, resulting in not detecting the disorder
    c. also have coexisting multiple personalities
    d. actually have a real but as yet undetected physical illness

24) Which disorder is NOT a type of somatoform disorder?

    a. depersonalization disorder
    b. body dysmorphic disorder
    c. conversion disorder
    d. pain disorder

25) A distinguishing feature of somatization disorder is:

    a. the physical complaints involve multiple systems (gastrointestinal, cardiovascular, reproductive)
    b. the physical complaints are limited to only one somatic system
    c. the patient appears very serious, obsessive, and emotionally withdrawn
    d. the onset of the disorder rarely occurs before age 30

26) The separation of mental processes such as memory or consciousness that are usually integrated is referred to as:

a. abreaction
b. dissocation
c. repression
d. deja vu

27) Which of the following is the best definition of a conversion symptom?

a. a physical symptom in one part of the body that is actually referred pain or trauma from another part of the body
b. a symptom produced by psychological conflict that mimics a symptom found in a neurological disease
c. a symptom produced by injury which is exacerbated by psychological conflict
d. an emotional symptom such as depressed mood produced by physical trauma

28) When is the diagnosis of a dissociative disorder NOT appropriate?

a. when the patient has a history of child sexual abuse
b. when the dissociative process is abrupt in onset
c. when the patient additionally reports feeling depressed
d. when the dissociation occurs in the presence of substance abuse or organic pathology

29) Joe, a housepainter, reports to his family doctor that he has not been able to work for six months because of pain in his legs. In fact, lately he can barely walk to the kitchen from his bedroom because of the pain. No injury occurred that would explain the situation. His wife has been taking care of him but is very concerned about the financial strain this is causing. His doctor orders a thorough examination. If nothing is found, what diagnosis is appropriate?

a. conversion disorder
b. hypochondriasis
c. pain disorder
d. somatoform disorder

30) The onset of a dissociative episode:

a. is typically abrupt and precipitated by a traumatic event
b. is slow and insidious in nature
c. can be traced to certain metabolic deficiencies
d. typically happens following a severe head injury

31) A conversion symptom that serves the function of protecting the conscious mind by expressing the conflict unconsciously is referred to as:

a. la belle indifference
b. primary gain
c. diagnosis by exclusion
d. abreaction

32) While both disorders involve memory loss, a major difference between dissociative amnesia and dissociative fugue is that:

   a. dissociative fugue is characterized by sudden and unexpected travel away from home
   b. the memory loss in dissociative amnesia has a physical basis
   c. dissociative amnesia is characterized by the emergence of at least one additional personality
   d. dissociative fugue additionally includes persistent feelings of being detached from oneself

33) Research on the prevalence of somatoform disorders suggests:

   a. they appear to be more common than depression in the general population
   b. they appear to be less common during war time
   c. they appear to be rare in the general population
   d. their prevalence has increased since Freud's time

34) The sociocultural view of the etiology of somatoform disorders suggests that:

   a. people with education and financial security have greater access to physicians who will listen to their somatic complaints
   b. people in nonindustrialized societies have a greater sense of community and describe their inner distress to others in their social network more
   c. people in industrialized societies have more opportunity to develop a more sophisticated vocabulary for their physical symptoms
   d. people with less education or financial security have less opportunity to learn how to describe their inner turmoil in psychological terms

35) A person with which of the following would be at risk for developing a dissociative disorder?

   a. a family history of depression
   b. a history of child sexual abuse
   c. a history of violent behavior
   d. all of the above

36) Why are people with somatoform disorders likely to reject a referral to a mental health professional from their physicians?

   a. people may have difficulty accepting the possibility of the psychological basis to their physical symptoms
   b. people may feel that their physician is belittling their problems
   c. people may feel that their physician is not being empathic
   d. all of the above

37) Which statement is NOT correct about somatization disorder?

   a. it is more common among higher socioeconomic groups
   b. it is more common among women
   c. it is more common among African Americans than whites
   d. somatic symptoms are more frequent among people who have lost a spouse

38) Every Friday, Sarah's fifth grade class has a spelling test. Every Friday morning, she complains of a stomachache to her mother. This may be an example of:

    a. expressing an emotional concern that has a genuine emotional basis
    b. expressing an emotional concern in terms of a physical complaint
    c. expressing a physical complaint that has been reinforced by the environment
    d. expressing a psychological symptom that has an organic basis

39) Somatoform disorders are characterized by:

    a. physical complaints that can be traced to organic impairment
    b. patients who deliberately lie about the presence of physical symptoms
    c. physical symptoms that cannot be explained on the basis of underlying physical illness
    d. physical symptoms which are consciously linked to psychological difficulties

40) Although their presenting symptoms differ greatly in appearance, a common link between dissociative and somatoform disorders is:

    a. both involve memory loss
    b. both require extensive medical treatment
    c. both apparently involve unconscious processes
    d. all of the above

41) In contrast to Freud, contemporary cognitive scientists:

    a. do not recognize the existence of unconscious processes
    b. believe that unconscious processes are much less influential in shaping both normal and abnormal behavior
    c. believe that unconscious processes are more influential than conscious processes in shaping both normal and abnormal behavior
    d. have a much less restricted view of unconscious processes and their role in shaping behavior

42) The analogue experiments conducted by Spanos and his colleagues on the symptoms of dissociative identity disorder suggest that:

    a. hypnosis had no relationship to the presence of symptoms of this disorder
    b. they disappeared under hypnosis
    c. they can be induced through role-playing and hypnosis
    d. experimental hypnosis increases risk for dissociative identity disorder

43) An example of a sociological theory of the cause of dissociative identity disorder is

    a. it is caused by disturbances in the temporal lobe of the brain
    b. it is caused by a perceptual disturbance that impairs the ability to recognize faces
    c. it is produced by iatrogenesis, specifically, through the leading questions of therapists
    d. it is produced by recovered memories of the loss of a parent

Understanding Research - Fill in the Blank

Hypnosis: Altered State or the Power of Suggestion?: The text presents a detailed description of a study by Miller and Bowers in the Research Close-Up on p. 265. Finding the answers to these questions will help you get a good understanding of this study and why it is important. It is not necessary to memorize the answers; the process of finding them in the textbook will help you learn the material you need to know.

1. In laboratory studies, hypnotized subjects have an increased threshold for _____ when given suggestions that a body part is numb. Some research has identified a hidden _____: even when consciously denying they feel pain, at another level of _____ many people can recognize the denied pain.

2. One indicator of hypnotizability is a person's response to the suggestion to close their eyes and imagine a _____ tied to their wrist. If their arm _____ they are more likely to be hypnotized.

3. There is a debate about whether hypnosis is an _____ _____ of consciousness or a response to suggestion and _____.

4. First Miller and Bowers identified people who were low or high in terms of _____. Then they put them through one of three manipulations to increase _____ tolerance. The first condition was hypnosis, the second was a cognitive _____ procedure to train them with strategies to cope with pain, and the third was the same as the _____ but they were told that the cognitive coping would involve hypnotic _____ of pain.

5. The cold _____ test evaluated subjects' pain tolerance by having them put their hands in ice water. The test was given before and after the subjects were taught one of the coping strategies. All three strategies _____ pain tolerance. Hypnotizability was correlated with increased pain tolerance among ONLY the subjects who were _____. What does this mean? _____ _____

Retrospective Reports: The text discusses this type of research method in the Research Methods section on pp. 276-277. Finding the answers to these questions will help you get a good understanding of these issues.

6. Scientists are skeptical about the accuracy of people's memories of the past, even when people report them _____ and _____. Research

designs using _____ reports are preferred over those using _____ reports.

7. One problem is normal limitations of _____. The second is that memories of people with _____ problems are particularly unreliable. The third is that psychopathology systematically _____ people's memories. Memory processes are said to be "mood- _____." This could lead researchers to speculate that depressed people who remember more _____ experiences are depressed because they had more sad experiences, when really they may have had the same number of sad experiences but just _____ more when asked to report on them.

8. One study suggests that memory for _____ events is fairly reliable, but that people _____ their history with regard to more global experiences. _____ report more negative memories of the past than do _____. Research evidence does not support the hypothesis that memories are _____- congruent, specifically among depressed people.

9. Freud was uncertain whether to believe his patients' memories of _____ _____. In the end he decided they were _____. Current research indicates that Freud was probably _____. The conclusion of the section is that: _____

_____.

Brief Essay

As a final exercise, write out answers to the following brief essay questions. Then compare your answers with the material presented in the text.

After you have answered these questions, review the "critical thinking" questions that are presented at the end of the text chapter. Answering these questions will help you integrate important issues and themes that have been featured throughout the chapter.

1. Briefly describe Posttraumatic Stress Disorder (PTSD). Give an example of an experience that may result in PTSD and identify the various symptoms that might accompany this disorder.

2. While some professionals believe that multiple personalities are real and more common than previously thought, others believe that the condition is role-playing.

Discuss the controversy, citing research and clinical evidence supporting both views.

3. Are recovered memories examples of dissociation or are they produced through the power of suggestion? Defend your own position on this controversial topic.

4. Review the methodological concerns surrounding the use of retrospective reports. What are the important questions that have been raised regarding their reliability and validity? What are the implications of these concerns regarding the use of retrospective reports in research?

5. Pretend you are a primary care physician with a patient who has a number of vague and inconsistent physical complaints. An extensive medical evaluation reveals no organic pathology. Discuss the types of questions you would consider in trying to determine whether the patient has a somatoform disorder. How would you approach the treatment of this patient if a diagnosis of somatization disorder was given?

ANSWER KEY

Answers to the exercises are listed below; page numbers where the information is referenced in the textbook are given in parentheses.

Key Terms - Matching #1

1. k (262)	8. b (240)	15. h (244)	
2. i (244)	9. c (240)	16. f (241)	
3. q (267)	10. t (268)	17. g (241)	
4. d (241)	11. a (240)	18. m (263)	
5. j (244)	12. u (269)	19. s (268)	
6. r (267)	13. n (263)	20. l (262)	
7. p (265)	14. o (263)	21. e (241)	

Names You Should Know

1. c (264, 266)
2. e (260-1)
3. d (260)
4. a (260)
5. b (251)

Key Terms - Matching #2

a. 1 (248)	g. 4 (255)	l. 19 (277)	q. 8 (260)
b. 15 (272)	h. 17 (273)	m. 12 (271)	r. 16 (273)
c. 11 (270)	i. 5 (255)	n. 7 (259)	s. 2 (251)
d. 10 (262)	j. 9 (262)	o. 20 (277)	t. 3 (254)
e. 18 (275)	k. 6 (257)	p. 13 (271)	u. 21 (277)
f. 14 (272)			

Multiple Choice

1. a	8. a	14. a	20. d	26. b	32. a	38. b
2. d	9. d	15. c	21. a	27. b	33. c	39. c
3. b	10. b	16. b	22. b	28. d	34. d	40. c
4. c	11. c	17. d	23. d	29. c	35. b	41. b
5. b	12. a	18. c	24. a	30. a	36. d	42. c
6. d	13. d	19. d	25. a	31. b	37. a	43. c
7. b						

Review of Concepts

1. reexperiencing, avoidance, and arousal or anxiety (243)
2. dissociative symptoms (243)
3. dissociative (204)
4. numbing of responsiveness (244)
5. startle (244)
6. prevent (246)
7. they defined trauma as outside usual experience but trauma is not that rare (246)
8. war, rape, child sexual abuse, spousal abuse, witnessing disasters (247)
9. PTSD (247)
10. depression, anxiety disorders, substance abuse (248)
11. 10%; 5% (248)
12. rape (248-9)
13. more; more (249)
14. behavior (249)
15. threshold; diathesis-stress; illness (249-50)
16. higher (250)
17. intelligence (250)
18. norepinephrine; opioids (250-1)
19. less (251)
20. better (251)
21. rape is completed; if they were physically injured; if their life was threatened (252)
22. being wounded; being involved in death of civilians; witnessing atrocities (252)
23. decreases (252)
24. supports (253)
25. all were equally effective (254)
26. reexposure (255)
27. false (257)
28. true (256)
29. smart; dumb (261)
30. PTSD (262)
31. child sexual abuse (264)
32. dissociative identity (264)
33. suggestion (264)
34. amnesia is absent in the enactment but typical in the disorder (266)
35. conscious and unconscious (267)
36. prospective (268)
37. a therapist (268)
38. to reintegrate the personalities into one (269)
39. physician (270)
40. a hysterectomy (270)
41. young adulthood (272)
42. less (273)
43. women; blacks; less educated (274)
44. depression (274)
45. antisocial personality (274)
46. 25% (275)
47. concern (278)

Understanding Research

1. pain; observer; consciousness
2. balloon; rises
3. altered; state; expectation
4. hypnotizability; pain; behavioral; second; reduction
5. pressor; increased; hypnotized; Hypnosis, not susceptibility to suggestion, can lead to increased pain tolerance
6. readily; confidently; prospective; retrospective
7. memory; emotional; biases; congruent; sad; remember
8. specific; rewrite; children; parents; mood
9. sexual abuse; fantasies; wrong; Retrospective reports of specific past events are reliable and valid enough to use as a first, less expensive research method.

CHAPTER 8 - STRESS AND PHYSICAL HEALTH

Chapter Outline

I. Overview
    A. Defining Stress
        1. Stress as a Stimulus
        2. Stress as a Response
        3. Stress as a Stimulus-Response Combination

II. Typical Symptoms and Associated Features
    A. Physiological Responses to Stress
        1. Immune Function
        2. Adrenal Hormones and Physiological Toughness
        3. Different Physiological Responses to Different Stressors?
        4. Emotional Responses to Stress
    B. Cognitive Responses to Stress
    C. Behavioral Responses to Stress
        1. Health Behavior
    D. Illness as a Cause of Stress

III. Classification of Stress and Physical Illness
    A. Brief Historical Perspective
    B. Contemporary Approaches

IV. The Role of Psychological Factors in Some Familiar Illnesses
    A. Cancer
    B. Acquired Immune Deficiency Syndrome (AIDS)
    C. Pain Management

V. Cardiovascular Disease
    A. Typical Symptoms and Associated Features of Hypertension and CHD
        1. Classification of CVD
    B. Epidemiology of CVD
        1. Risk Factors for CHD
        2. Risk Factors for Hypertension
    C. Etiological Considerations and Research on CVD
        1. Biological Factors in CVD
        2. Psychological Factors in CVD
            a. Cardiovascular Reactivity to Stress
            b. Life Stressors and CVD: Job Strain as an Example
            c. Type A Behavior and Hostility
        3. Social Factors in CVD
        4. Integration and Alternative Pathways
    D. Prevention and Treatment of Cardiovascular Disease
        1. Primary Prevention
        2. Secondary Prevention
        3. Tertiary Prevention

Learning Objectives

After reviewing the material presented in this chapter, you should be able to:

1. Define stress, stress as a stimulus, stress as a response, and stress as a stimulus-response combination.

2. Know what is meant by the emergency reaction and the general adaptation syndrome.

3. Distinguish between Cannon's and Selye's theories regarding the way in which stress causes illness.

4. Define physiological toughness and understand Dienstbier's theory of resilience.

5. Compare problem-focused and emotion-focused coping with stress.

6. Describe the emotional, cognitive, and behavioral responses to stress.

7. Understand how stress is used in classification in DSM-IV.

8. Understand the role of psychological factors in cancer, aids, and in problems with pain.

9. Distinguish primary and secondary hypertension.

10. Describe the major causes of primary hypertension.

11. Understand the impact of low control, high demand job strain on hypertension.

12. Describe the major characteristics of the Type A personality and the current thinking about its role in coronary heart disease.

13. Understand the primary preventive, secondary preventive, and tertiary preventive treatment approaches which are successful in treatment and prevention of cardiovascular disease.

Key Terms - Matching #1

The following terms related to stress and physical health are important to know. To test your knowledge, match the following terms with their definitions. Answers are listed at the end of the chapter.

a.	Stress	k.	Sleep terror disorder
b.	Traumatic stress	l.	Sleepwalking disorder
c.	Psychosomatic disorders	m.	Specificity hypothesis
d.	Behavioral medicine	n.	Carcinogens

e.   Health psychologists
f.   General adaptation syndrome
g.   Primary appraisal
h.   Secondary appraisal
i.   Emergency response
j.   Fight or flight response

o.   Cardiovascular disease (CVD)
p.   Hypertension
q.   Coronary heart disease (CHD)
r.   Myocardial infarction (MI)
s.   Systolic blood pressure

1. _____ an individual's cognitive evaluation of the challenge, threat, or harm posed by a particular event
2. _____ a challenging event that requires physiological, cognitive, or behavioral adaptation
3. _____ a disorder involving abrupt awakening and intense autonomic arousal but little memory of a dream and a quick return to sleep
4. _____ a group of diseases of the heart
5. _____ an individual's assessment of his or her abilities and resources for coping with a difficult event
6. _____ the body's mobilization in reaction to a perceived threat
7. _____ a three-stage model of reaction to stress involving alarm, resistance, and exhaustion
8. _____ a heart attack, the most deadly form of CHD, caused by oxygen deprivation and death of heart muscle tissue
9. _____ stress caused by exposure to a catastrophic event involving actual or threatened death to oneself or others
10. _____ high blood pressure
11. _____ a multidisciplinary field including medical and mental health professionals who investigate psychological factors in the symptoms, etiology, and treatment of physical illness
12. _____ the idea that specific personality types cause specific psychosomatic diseases
13. _____ the highest blood pressure reading, it is the pressure that the blood exerts against the arteries when the heart is beating
14. _____ a response to threat in which psychophysiological reactions prepare the body to take action against danger
15. _____ a disorder involving rising during sleep and walking about in an unresponsive state with no later memory of the episode
16. _____ a term indicating that physical disease is a product of both the mind and the body
17. _____ a group of disorders affecting the heart and circulatory system
18. _____ cancer-causing agents
19. _____ psychologists who specialize in behavioral medicine

Key Terms - Matching #2

The following terms related to stress and physical health are important to know. To test your knowledge, match the following terms with their definitions. Answers are listed at the end of the chapter.

1. Psychoneuroimmunology
2. Glucocorticoids
3. T cells
4. Lymphocytes
5. Antigens
6. Immunosuppression
7. Physiological toughness
8. Problem-focused coping
9. Emotion-focused coping
10. Diastolic blood pressure

11. Angina pectoris
12. Sudden cardiac death (SCD)
13. Secondary hypertension
14. Essential hypertension
15. Myocardial ischemia
16. Atherosclerosis
17. Coronary occlusion
18. Cardiovascular reactivity
19. Type A behavior pattern

a. _____ hypertension resulting from a known problem such as a diagnosed kidney or endocrine disorder
b. _____ the decreased production of immune agents, often a result of stress
c. _____ a competitive, hostile, urgent, impatient, achievement-striving style of responding to challenge
d. _____ sudden oxygen deprivation when arteries are completely blocked by fatty deposits or when blood clots make their way to the heart muscle
e. _____ coping that is internally oriented and involves attempts to alter subjective distress
f. _____ a category of white blood cells that fight off antigens
g. _____ a form of high blood pressure where the hypertension is the principal disorder
h. _____ externally oriented coping that involves attempts to change a stressor
i. _____ temporary oxygen deprivation that accompanies intermittent chest pains which causes no permanent damage
j. _____ a beneficial effect of stress under certain circumstances
k. _____ death within 24 hours of a coronary episode
l. _____ a measure of the intensity of an individual's cardiovascular reactions to stress in the laboratory which predicts future cardiovascular disease
m. _____ a major form of coronary heart disease involving intermittent chest pains brought on by some form of exertion
n. _____ adrenal hormones secreted in response to stress
o. _____ foreign substances like bacteria that invade the body
p. _____ the lowest blood pressure reading, it is the pressure that the blood exerts against the arteries between heartbeats
q. _____ the field of research on the effects of stress on the functioning of the immune system
r. _____ one of the major types of white blood cells of the immune system
s. _____ the thickening of the coronary artery wall as a result of the accumulation of blood lipids with age

Key Terms - Matching #3

The following terms related to stress and physical health are important to know. To test your knowledge, match the following terms with their definitions. Answers are listed at the end of the chapter.

a.	Health behavior	j.	Longitudinal study
b.	Primary sleep disorder	k.	Cross-sectional approach
c.	Dyssomnias	l.	Social ecology
d.	Parasomnias	m.	Antihypertensives
e.	Primary insomnia	n.	Beta blockers
f.	Narcolepsy	o.	Stress management
g.	Breathing-related sleep disorder	p.	Biofeedback
h.	Circadian rhythm sleep disorder	q.	Role playing
i.	Nightmare disorder	r.	Primary hypersomnia

1. _____ activities essential to promoting good health, such as healthy eating, exercise, and avoidance of unhealthy activities like drug use
2. _____ a disorder involving frequent awakening to alertness by terrifying dreams
3. _____ disorders characterized by abnormal events that occur during sleep, like nightmares
4. _____ the interrelations between the individual and the social world
5. _____ the disruption of sleep due to breathing problems such as sleep apnea, the temporary obstruction of the respiratory airway
6. _____ a treatment to teach more effective coping skills, reduce adverse reactions to stress and improve health behavior
7. _____ medications effective in reducing high blood pressure
8. _____ a type of research design in which subjects are studied over time, allowing researchers to make inferences about causation
9. _____ drugs that reduce the risk of myocardial infarction or sudden coronary death
10. _____ irresistible attacks of refreshing sleep
11. _____ a mismatch between the patient's 24-hour sleeping patterns and their 24-hour life demands
12. _____ a condition where sleeping disturbance is the primary complaint
13. _____ a technique used in therapy of improvisational play acting to teach patients how to respond to stressful interactions with less hostility
14. _____ problems in the amount, quality, or timing of sleep
15. _____ a treatment using equipment to monitor physiological processes and provide the patient with feedback about them to help patients gain conscious control over them
16. _____ a type of research design in which subjects are studied at one point in time
17. _____ excessive sleepiness characterized by prolonged or daytime sleep which interferes with functioning
18. _____ difficulties initiating or maintaining sleep, or poor quality of sleeping

Names You Should Know - Matching

The following people have played an important role in research and theory on stress and health. To test your knowledge, match the following names with the descriptions of their contributions to the study of abnormal psychology. Answers are listed at the end of the chapter.

a. Richard Lazarus   b. Hans Selye   c. Walter Cannon

1. ____   defined stress in terms of the general adaptation syndrome; did much research on animal analogue studies of the GAS
2. ____   argued that stress is not just a stimulus but also the individual's response to the stimulus, specifically his or her cognitive appraisal of the event as being potentially harmful and exceeding his or her coping resources
3. ____   one of the first researchers to conduct systematic studies of stress; interested in the emergency response, which prepares the body for fight or flight

Review of Concepts - Fill in the Blank and True/False

This section will help focus your studying by testing whether you understand the concepts presented in the text. After you have read and reviewed the material, test your comprehension and memory by filling in the following blanks or circling the right answer. Answers are listed at the end of the chapter.

1. Stress can be produced by daily _____ as well as by traumatic events.

2. Scientists used to think that psychological factors were

   important or **irrrelevant**   in most physical illnesses; today they think

   they are   **important** or **irrelevant**.

3. The Diagnostic and Statistical Manual no longer contains a list of psychosomatic

   disorders because _____.

4. Holmes and Rahe developed the Social Readjustment Rating Scale, an attempt to

   measure the amount of _____ caused by various life events.

5. List three criticisms of the Social Readjustment Rating Scale:

   _____

   _____

   _____

6. What are the three stages of the GAS?   _____,

   _____, and _____

7. One problem with Lazarus' approach to defining stress is that it runs the risk of

   being tautological, or _____.

8. The fight or flight response is _____ in the modern world.

9. It is   **harder** or **easier**   on the heart when a person responds to stress with

   physical activity.

10. An analogy for   **Cannon's** or **Selye's**   theory is a car in which the engine

    continues to race instead of idling down after running fast, and an analogy for

    Cannon's or **Selye's**   theory is a car that has run out of gas and is damaged because stress keeps turning the key, trying to restart the engine.

11. Another mechanism whereby stress may cause physical illness is the stress response sapping _____ away from routine bodily functions.

12. Stress weakens immune functioning: **true**   **false**

13. Medical students during exam periods and depressed people have both been demonstrated to show _____.

14. In one study with newly married couples, partners who were more _____ during discussions of marital problems showed greater immunosuppression during the next 24 hours.

15. In the same study,   **men** or **women**   showed more immunosuppression.

16. Heightened immune functioning is   **adaptive** or **maladaptive**   in response to immediate threat from an evolutionary perspective.

17. One theory indicates that the moderate release of **glucocorticoids** or **epinephrine and norepinephrine**   serves to protect the body from depletion under future, more intense stress, a process called physiological toughness.

18. Current research has indicated that different categories of stressors do not cause different physiological responses: **true**   **false**

19. People who repress their anxiety show fewer psychophysiological reactions to stress: **true**   **false**

20. Predictability of a stressor   **improves** or **impairs**   our ability to cope with it.

21. Rats who can stop a shock by pressing a bar experience a bigger stress response than rats who receive an identical shock but don't have to worry about stopping it: **true**   **false**

22. One pathway that may explain how stress and illness are linked is that stress can reduce people's _____.

23. The more a stressed monkey can interact with other monkeys, the less immunosuppression it demonstrates: **true**   **false**

24. Stress can cause illness, but illness can also cause _____.

25. Modern research supports the specificity hypothesis, that certain personality types are more prone to certain psychosomatic illnesses: **true**   **false**

26. Why does the DSM-IV not include the rating system for severity of stressors that was included in DSM-III and DSM-III-R? _____

27. Cancer deaths have risen substantially over the past 30 years: **true**   **false**

28. Cancer is the leading cause of death today: **true**   **false**

29. Stress can directly affect the body's ability to fight cancer cells: **true**   **false**

30. Psychological treatments, such as structured self-help groups, have unfortunately not been shown to be effective in reducing the death rate among cancer patients: **true**   **false**

31. Programs to educate the public about how HIV is transmitted are quite effective in changing risky behaviors related to transmission: **true**   **false**

32. A wide range of treatments, such as biofeedback, hypnosis, relaxation training, and cognitive therapy are quite useful in eliminating a person's chronic pain:
     true   **false**

33. Cardiovascular disease is the second leading cause of death in the United States: **true**   **false**

34. Why is hypertension called the "silent killer?" _____

35. The rate of death due to CVD has decreased in the United States in recent years: **true**   **false**

36. Where has the rate of death due to CVD increased? _____

37. Who are more likely to suffer from CHD?   **men**   **women**

38. Who are more likely to suffer from CHD?   **whites**   **blacks**

39. Which of the following are not among the risk factors for CHD?
     drinking   **smoking**   **obesity**   **a fatty diet**

40. Hypertension is twice as common among blacks, but black men living in high-stress neighborhoods had 4 times the risk for hypertension: **true**   **false**

41. Rats with a genetic predisposition to develop hypertension do so only when exposed to salty diets or environmental stress: **true**   **false**

42. Job strain involves a situation with   **high** or **low**   psychological demand with   **high** or **low**   decisional control.

43. The number of _____ a woman has increases her risk for heart disease if she works but not if she is a homemaker.

44. The key feature of the Type A behavior pattern in predicting CHD is _____.

45. People exposed to an experimental media campaign to improve knowledge and change behavior related to CHD risk factors changed their behaviors relating to _____ but not _____.

46. The only two treatment conditions that lowered blood pressure in a study comparing 1) weight reduction, 2) salt reduction, 3) stress management, 4) calcium supplement, 5) magnesium supplement, 6) potassium supplement, and 7) fish oil supplement, were: _____.

Multiple Choice Questions

The following multiple choice questions will test your comprehension of the material presented in the chapter. Answers are listed at the end of the chapter.

1) All of the following are criticisms of the Holmes and Rahe Social Re-Adjustment Rating Scale EXCEPT:

   a. the inclusion of both positive and negative events as stressors
   b. failure to distinguish between transient and chronic life events
   c. a given stressor does not always produce the same number of life change units for all individuals in all situations
   d. all of the above are criticisms of this scale

2) Generally, hypertension is defined by a systolic blood pressure of above _____ and a diastolic blood pressure of above _____.

   a. 110; 60
   b. 120; 70
   c. 130; 80
   d. 140; 90

3) According to Walter Cannon, _____ is the mobilization of the body in reaction to a perceived threat.

   a. stage of alarm
   b. generalized arousal
   c. emergency response
   d. physiological toughness

4) Which of the following is NOT a reaction of the body to sympathetic nervous system arousal?

   a. heart rate increases
   b. blood pressure rises
   c. blood sugar lowers
   d. respiration rate increases

5) Although somewhat stressful, _____ decreases negative responding to an actual stressor.

   a. predictability
   b. anticipation
   c. control
   d. appraisal

6) Anxiety, depression, and _____ are considered to be the primary affective responses to stressors.

   a. anger
   b. tension
   c. an upset stomach
   d. aggression

7) Stress plays a role in:

   a. all physical disorders
   b. some physical disorders
   c. only heart disease
   d. no physical disorders

8) _____ of all deaths from CHD occur within 24 hours of a coronary event.

    a. One-quarter
    b. One-half
    c. One-third
    d. Two-thirds

9) Which would have the greatest risk for suffering from high blood pressure?

    a. African-American male who is homeless
    b. White male who is a stock broker
    c. African-American female who is an attorney
    d. White female who is a homemaker

10) This uses laboratory equipment to monitor physiological processes that occur outside conscious awareness to help people learn to control them voluntarily:

    a. biofeedback
    b. stress management
    c. systematic desensitization
    d. flooding

11) _____ is the most important goal of intervention with cardiovascular disease.

    a. Medication
    b. Prevention
    c. Psychotherapy
    d. Education

12) According to the Social Re-Adjustment Rating Scale, _____ is the most significant life event that constitutes the greatest number of life change units.

    a. pregnancy
    b. divorce
    c. foreclosure of a mortgage or loan
    d. death of one's spouse

13) Psychoneuroimmunology refers to the study of:

    a. decreased production of T cells and other immune agents
    b. inhibition and destruction of various immune agents
    c. the effects of stress on the functioning of the immune system
    d. white blood cells that fight off foreign substances that invade the body

14) (A) _____ amount of stress is healthy for the heart.

    a. small
    b. moderate
    c. large
    d. No

15) Psychologists in this field define disease as "dis-ease", indicating that illness is a departure not only from adaptive biological functioning but also from adaptive social and psychological functioning.

    a. biopsychosocial psychology
    b. behavioral psychology
    c. health psychology
    d. dynamic psychology

16) According to the Framingham Study which was reviewed in your textbook, which of the following is most likely to suffer from heart disease?

    a. a woman who is a homemaker and has two children
    b. a woman who is a homemaker and has four children
    c. a woman who is a sales manager and has two children
    d. a woman who is a waitress and has four children

17) This term indicates that physical disease is a product of both the mind and body.

    a. somatoform   c. dissociative
    b. cognitive error   d. psychosomatic

18) All of the following are examples of cognitive responses to stress EXCEPT:

    a. control   c. appraisal
    b. repression   d. predictability

Understanding Research - Fill in the Blank

Disclosure of Trauma and Immunity: The text presents a detailed description of a study by Pennebaker, Kiecolt-Glaser, and Glaser in the Research Close-Up on pp. 293-294. Finding the answers to these questions will help you get a good understanding of this study and why it is important. It is not necessary to memorize the answers; the process of finding them in the textbook will help you learn the material you need to know.

1. Subjects were asked to write about _____ events in their lives for _____ consecutive days, especially things they _____. A control group wrote about _____topics for 4 days. All writing took place in the _____. There was a total of _____ subjects.

2. Dependent variables included self-reported mood _____ and _____ writing, measures of _____ arousal, like blood pressure and heart rate, and _____ assays of blood before the study, _____ afterwards, and _____ weeks later.

3. Evaluations by researchers of what the students wrote about confirmed that they had written about _____ experiences, like serious _____ conflict. Immediately after writing, subjects in the experimental group were more _____ than those in the control group. However, they had significantly fewer visits to the _____ and better _____ responses over the next 6 weeks. No differences were found on the measures of

_____. If they wrote about previously _____ events they showed better _____ pressure and immunological functioning.

4. This study is important because it suggests that _____
_____.

Longitudinal Research Designs: The text discusses this type of research design in the Research Methods section on p. 307. Finding the answers to these questions will help you get a good understanding of these issues.

5. The basic goal of a longitudinal study is to determine whether:
_____.
This helps rule out the possibility that the effect actually caused the cause, like
_____. But what is a main problem with longitudinal research?   _____

6. Which type of research design is more expensive: retrospective   prospective
Which type is used in this study: a research project measuring Type A behavior and then recontacting subjects in 5 years to see if those with Type A styles had more heart attacks?   _____

7. Why does a longitudinal design not conclusively prove causality?
_____

Brief Essay

As a final exercise, write out answers to the following brief essay questions. Then compare your answers with the material presented in the text.

After you have answered these questions, review the "critical thinking" questions that are presented at the end of the text chapter. Answering these questions will help you integrate important issues and themes that have been featured throughout the chapter.

1. Discuss Holmes and Rahe's Social Re-Adjustment Rating Scale. How do they define a _life change unit_? What could be considered some of the strengths of this scale? What are some of the criticisms of this scale? How would you change this scale to address some of these criticisms?

2. Briefly discuss Hans Selye's and Walter Cannon's approaches to studying stress. In what ways are they similar? In what ways do they differ?

3. What does the chapter mean when it states that cardiovascular disease (CVD) is a *lifestyle disease*? What are the implications of this? How has health psychology attempted to address this?

ANSWER KEY

Answers to the exercises are listed below; page numbers where the information is referenced in the textbook are given in parentheses.

Key Terms - Matching #1

1. g (289)	8. r (302)	14. j (290)	
2. a (284)	9. b (284)	15. l (296)	
3. k (296)	10. p (302)	16. c (284)	
4. q (302)	11. d (285)	17. o (302)	
5. h (289)	12. m (297)	18. n (300)	
6. i (290)	13. s (302)	19. e (285)	
7. f (288)			

Names You Should Know

1. b (288-9)
2. a (289)
3. c (290)

Key Terms - Matching #2

a. 13 (303)	f. 4 (291)	k. 12 (303)	p. 10 (302)
b. 6 (291)	g. 14 (303)	l. 18 (305)	q. 1 (291)
c. 19 (306)	h. 8 (292)	m. 11 (303)	r. 3 (291)
d. 17 (304)	i. 15 (304)	n. 2 (291)	s. 16 (304)
e. 9 (292)	j. 7 (292)	o. 5 (291)	

Key Terms - Matching #3

1. a (295)	6. o (309)	11. h (296)	15. p (309)
2. i (296)	7. m (308)	12. b (295)	16. k (307)
3. d (295)	8. j (307)	13. q (310)	17. r (295)
4. l (307)	9. n (308)	14. c (295)	18. e (295)
5. g (296)	10. f (295)		

Multiple Choice

1. d	4. c	7. a	10. a	13. c	16. d
2. d	5. a	8. d	11. b	14. b	17. d
3. c	6. a	9. a	12. d	15. c	18. b

Review of Concepts

1. hassles (284)
2. irrelevant; important (284)
3. all illnesses are now seen as psychosomatic (284)
4. stress (287)
5. doesn't account for different ages and backgrounds; includes positive life changes; doesn't consider different meanings for different people (287-8)
6. alarm, resistance, exhaustion (288-9)
7. circular (289)
8. maladaptive (290)
9. easier (290)
10. Cannon; Selye (290)
11. energy (290)
12. true (291)
13. immunosuppression (291)
14. hostile or negative (291)
15. women (291)
16. maladaptive (291)
17. epinephrine and norepinephrine (292)
18. false (292)
19. false (293)
20. improves (294)
21. false (294)
22. health behaviors (295)
23. true (296)
24. stress (297)
25. false (297)
26. the ratings were unreliable (299)
27. true (299)
28. false (299)
29. true (300)
30. false (300)
31. false (301)
32. false (301)
33. false (302)
34. it has no symptoms (302)
35. true (303)
36. Eastern Europe (303)
37. men (303)
38. blacks (303)
39. drinking (303)
40. true (304)
41. true (304)
42. high; low (305)
43. children (305)
44. hostility (306)
45. diet; smoking (308)
46. weight and salt reduction (309)

Understanding Research

1. traumatic; 4; had never told anyone about; trivial; laboratory; 50

2. before; after; autonomic; immunological; immediately; 6

3. upsetting; family; upset; student health center; immune; autonomic arousal; undisclosed; blood

4. immune system functioning may be one mechanism linking stress with illness

5. hypothesized causes come before their assumed effects; illness causing stress; it is expensive

6. prospective; prospective

7. A third variable could cause both.

CHAPTER 9 - PERSONALITY DISORDERS

Chapter Outline

I. Overview

II. Typical Symptoms and Associated Features
   A. Temperament
   B. Dimensions of Personality
   C. Culture and Personality

III. Classification
   A. Cluster A: Paranoid, Schizoid, and Schizotypal Personality Disorders
   B. Cluster B: Antisocial, Borderline, Histrionic, and Narcissistic Personality Disorders
   C. Cluster C: Avoidant, Dependent, and Obsessive-Compulsive Personality Disorders
   D. A Dimensional Perspective on Classification

IV. Epidemiology
   A. Prevalence in Community and Clinical Samples
   B. Gender Differences
      1. Gender Bias and Diagnosis
   C. Stability Over Time

V. Schizotypal Personality Disorder (SPD)
   A. Brief Historical Perspective
   B. Clinical Features and Comorbidity
   C. Etiological Considerations
   D. Treatment

VI. Borderline Personality Disorder (BPD)
   A. Brief Historical Perspective
   B. Clinical Features and Comorbidity
   C. Etiological Considerations
   D. Treatment

VII. Antisocial Personality Disorder (ASPD)
   A. Brief Historical Perspective
   B. Clinical Features and Comorbidity
      1. Antisocial Behavior Over the Lifespan
   C. Etiological Considerations
      1. Biological Factors
      2. Social Factors
      3. Psychological Factors
   D. Treatment

VIII. Dependent Personality Disorder (DPD)
   A. Brief Historical Perspective

B. Clinical Features and Comorbidity
C. Etiological Considerations
D. Treatment

Learning Objectives

After reviewing the material presented in this chapter, you should be able to:

1. Appreciate the fact that the person with a personality disorder experiences his or her behavior as ego-syntonic.

2. Define temperament and the broader term, personality, and explain the relevance of these concepts to the study of personality disorders.

3. Classify the personality disorders into the three clusters according to the categories: eccentric, dramatic, and anxious.

4. Provide a basic description of each of the ten DSM IV personality disorders.

5. Compare and contrast the avoidant personality disorder and the dependent personality disorder.

6. Know the basic prevalence rates for personality disorders in general and which are the most and least common specific personality disorders.

7. Describe the key clinical features of schizotypal personality disorder, borderline personality disorder, and antisocial personality disorder.

8. Compare the treatments of schizotypal, borderline, and antisocial personality disorder patients.

Key Terms - Matching #1

The following terms related to personality disorders are important to know. To test your knowledge, match the following terms with their definitions. Answers are listed at the end of the chapter.

a. Personality
b. Personality disorder
c. Antisocial personality disorder
d. Ego-dystonic
e. Ego-syntonic
f. Narcissistic personality disorder
g. Temperament
h. Neuroticism
i. Extraversion
j. Openness to experience
k. Dependent personality disorder
l. Obsessive-compulsive personality disorder
m. Schizophrenia
n. Schizophrenic phenotype
o. Primary process thinking
p. Splitting
q. Impulse control disorders
r. Intermittent explosive disorder
s. Kleptomania
t. Pyromania

1. _____ characteristic styles of relating to the world; evident in first years of life
2. _____ enduring patterns of perceiving, relating to, and thinking about the environment and oneself, displayed in a wide range of important social and personal contexts
3. _____ the idea that the symptoms of schizotypal personality disorder is seen among people who possess the genotype that makes them vulnerable to schizophrenia
4. _____ out of proportion aggressive behaviors resulting in serious assault or destruction of property
5. _____ stealing objects even though they are not needed or beneficial
6. _____ a dimension of personality describing a person's willingness to consider and explore new ideas, feelings, and activities
7. _____ symptoms that the person is distressed by and uncomfortable with
8. _____ the tendency to see people and events alternatively as all good or all bad
9. _____ disorders characterized by failure to resist a temptation to perform some pleasurable or tension-relieving act that is harmful to self or others
10. _____ where the id relieves tensions by imagining the things it desires
11. _____ a dimension of personality describing a person's activity level, especially interest in interacting with others, and the ease of expressing positive emotions
12. _____ deliberate and purposive fire setting accompanied by fascination with fire and not for personal gain
13. _____ symptoms that are comfortable and acceptable to the person
14. _____ an enduring pattern of dependent and submissive behavior
15. _____ an enduring pattern of thinking and behavior characterized by pervasive grandiosity and preoccupation with one's achievements
16. _____ a psychotic disorder characterized by hallucinations and delusions as well as by negative symptoms like flat affect and poverty of speech
17. _____ an enduring pattern of thinking and behavior characterized by perfectionism and inflexibility
18. _____ a pervasive and persistent disregard for, and frequent violation of, the rights of other people, beginning in childhood or adolescence
19. _____ an enduring pattern of inner experience and behavior that deviates markedly from the expectations of the person's culture
20. _____ a dimension of personality describing emotional stability, particularly in the expression of anxiety, depression, and anger

Key Terms - Matching #2

The following terms related to personality disorders are important to know. To test your knowledge, match the following terms with their definitions. Answers are listed at the end of the chapter.

1. Agreeableness
2. Conscientiousness
3. Culture
4. Cross-cultural psychology
5. Paranoid personality disorder
6. Schizoid personality disorder

11. Trichotillomania
12. Pathological gambling
13. Primate separation model
14. Dialectical behavior therapy (DBT)
15. Psychopathy
16. Adolescence-limited antisocial behavior

7. Schizotypal personality disorder
8. Borderline personality disorder
9. Histrionic personality disorder
10. Avoidant personality disorder

17. Life-course-persistent antisocial behavior
18. Adoptees
19. Sociotropy

a. _____ an enduring pattern of thinking and behavior characterized by excessive emotionality and attention seeking

b. _____ the scientific study of ways that human behavior and mental processes are influenced by social and cultural factors

c. _____ an enduring pattern of thinking and behavior whose primary feature is a pervasive instability of mood, self-image, and interpersonal relationships

d. _____ another term for antisocial personality disorder

e. _____ the shared way of life of a group of people

f. _____ a common form of social behavior that is often adaptive and disappears by adulthood

g. _____ people separated from their biological parents at an early age and raised by adoptive parents

h. _____ an enduring pattern of thinking and behavior characterized by a pervasive tendency to be inappropriately suspicious of the motives and behaviors of others

i. _____ an enduring pattern of thinking and behavior characterized by pervasive social discomfort, fear of negative evaluation, and timidity

j. _____ pulling out one's hair, resulting in noticeable hair loss

k. _____ an approach to psychotherapy with borderline patients

l. _____ an enduring pattern of thinking and behavior characterized by pervasive indifference to interacting with others and a diminished range of emotional experience and expression

m. _____ a dimension of personality describing willingness to cooperate and empathize with others

n. _____ proposed as an analogue for human mood disorders; after young monkeys are separated from their mothers their relationships are disrupted and they may exhibit self-destructive behaviors

o. _____ antisocial behavior that spans a person's life

p. _____ dependent interpersonal relationships that set the stage for later depression

q. _____ a dimension of personality describing the person's persistence in the pursuit of goals, ability to organize activities, and dependability

r. _____ repeated maladaptive gambling despite repeated efforts to stop

s. _____ an enduring pattern of discomfort with other people coupled with peculiar thinking and behavior, which takes the form of perceptual and cognitive disturbances

Names You Should Know - Matching

The following people have played an important role in research and theory of personality disorders. To test your knowledge, match the following names with the descriptions of their contributions to the study of abnormal psychology. Answers are listed at the end of the chapter.

1. _____ furthered the psychodynamic view of borderline personality disorder by developing reliable, descriptive terms to allow reliable diagnosis
2. _____ advocates a psychodynamic theory of borderline personality disorder focusing on the faulty development of ego structure
3. _____ proposed that there are two forms of antisocial behavior, transient and nontransient
4. _____ wrote early descriptions of psychopathy
5. _____ argued that borderline personality disorder is not a meaningful diagnostic category but a heterogeneous collection of symptoms that are associated with mild forms of brain dysfunction
6. _____ conducted a longitudinal study showing the stability of antisocial behavior of boys into adulthood

Review of Concepts - Fill in the Blank and True/False

This section will help focus your studying by testing whether you understand the concepts presented in the text. After you have read and reviewed the material, test your comprehension and memory by filling in the following blanks or circling the right answer. Answers are listed at the end of the chapter.

1. People with personality disorders are especially likely to seek psychological treatment: **true** **false**
2. What are some reasons why personality disorders are controversial among professionals? _____

   _____

3. The personality disorders are listed on Axis _____ of a diagnosis.
4. Personality disorders are usually ego - **syntonic** or **dystonic**
5. Which of the following is not a dimension of temperament?

   irritability **wealth** **activity level** **fearfulness**
6. Under what circumstances could a difficult temperament be adaptive for an infant?

   _____

7. Cultures differ in displays of _____ and in how much they value individualism versus _____.
8. Typologies of personality are likely to be:

   limited to the culture in which they are developed or

   applicable across many different cultures.
9. The behavior of people who fit Cluster _____ is typically anxious and fearful.
10. The behavior of people who fit Cluster _____ is typically odd, eccentric, or asocial.

11. The behavior of people who fit Cluster _____ is typically dramatic, emotional, or erratic.

12. Only criminals meet the diagnostic requirements for antisocial personality disorder: **true   false**

13. There may be an etiological link between histrionic and _____ personality disorders; both reflect a common, underlying tendency toward lack of inhibition and both form shallow, intense relationships with others.

14. One of the advantages of a categorical system over a dimensional system of personality diagnosis is that it provides a more complete description of each person: **true   false**

15. The DSM-IV uses a **categorical** or **dimensional** system with personality disorders.

16. The overall lifetime prevalence for having any type of personality disorder is:
    1–2%   10–14%   25–30%   46–50%

17. Which personality disorder appears to be the least common? _____

18. Very few people who meet the criteria for one personality disorder also meet the criteria for another personality disorder: **true   false**

19. Which personality disorder is most likely to be represented in inpatient and outpatient treatment settings?   _____

20. Borderline personality disorder is more common among   **men** or **women**; antisocial personality disorder is more common among   **men** or **women**; and dependent personality disorder is more common among
    men or **women**.

21. Some critics argue that criteria for personality disorders are unfairly biased against traditionally   **masculine** or **feminine**   traits.

22. People diagnosed with borderline personality disorder as a young adult are **more** or **less**   likely to still qualify for the diagnosis in their fifties than people diagnosed with schizotypal or schizoid personality disorders.

23. Research indicates that schizotypal personality disorder is genetically related to schizophrenia: **true   false**

24. When people with personality disorders appear for psychological treatment, it is usually because _____.

25. Research has shown that low doses of antipsychotic medications are effective in alleviating symptoms of schizotypal personality disorder: **true   false**

26. The difference between impulsive and compulsive behavior is that the original goal for impulsive behavior is to experience _____ while for

compulsive behavior it is to avoid _____.

27. Borderline personality disorder is often comorbid with what Axis I disorder?

_____

28. Borderline personality disorder patients have often had problematic relationships with their _____.

29. Patients in dialectical behavior therapy for borderline personality disorder are less likely to _____.

30. There is no evidence that psychotropic medication is effective for borderline personality disorder: **true**   **false**

31. Which personality disorder has been studied the most? _____

32. The DSM-IV category of antisocial personality disorder does not include traits relating to _____ that the Cleckley description included.

33. The expression of antisocial personality is likely to _____ as the person ages.

34. Research indicates that antisocial behavior is caused by both _____ and

_____.

35. In one study of adoptees, being raised in an adverse home environment **did** or **did not**   increase the likelihood of antisocial behavior among children with antisocial biological parents; being raised in an adverse home environment   **did** or **did not**   increase the likelihood of antisocial behavior among children with nonantisocial biological parents.

36. Children raised in families with inconsistent or absent _____ were more likely to be antisocial as adults.

37. Children with difficult temperaments due to genetic predisposition to antisocial behavior may induce their parents to _____.

38. There is research evidence that antisocial people lack _____, an emotion that normal people have.

39. Some researchers argue that lack of _____ and pathological egocentricity are more important than low anxiety in understanding antisocial personality disorder.

40. Several forms of treatment have been shown to be effective with antisocial personality disorder: **true**   **false**

41. People with borderline personality disorder become enraged and manipulative and people with dependent personality disorder become clingy and submissive when threatened with _____.

42. What type of parents are likely to foster dependency in their children?

_____

Multiple Choice Questions

The following multiple choice questions will test your comprehension of the material presented in the chapter. Answers are listed at the end of the chapter.

1) John is always on the lookout for potential harm, has difficulty trusting even family members, and is suspicious of their motives. He is oversensitive to minor events, reading into them ulterior meanings. This has caused him problems at work and home. What type of personality disorder does he likely have?

   a. schizoid
   b. obsessive-compulsive

   c. antisocial
   d. paranoid

2) The overall lifetime prevalence of personality disorders is approximately:

   a. 5 - 9%
   b. 10 - 14%

   c. 15 - 19%
   d. 20 - 24%

3) Which is a criterion which is used in DSM-IV to define personality disorders?

   a. the person must be aware of how his or her behavior is maladaptive
   b. the person's behavior must be rigid and inflexible
   c. the person's behavior must cause legal problems
   d. the person's behavioral difficulties must have started in childhood

4) Which of the following statements represents an approach that has been used to conceptualize personality disorders?

   a. they are types of personality styles that are closely associated with specific forms of adult psychopathology
   b. they result from problems in childhood development as conceptualized by psychodynamic theories
   c. they are manifestations of the presence of specific psychological deficits
   d. all of the above

5) The Axis I disorder most often diagnosed with borderline personality disorder is:

   a. depression
   b. substance abuse

   c. anxiety
   d. sexual dysfunction

6) In her longitudinal research on antisocial behavior, Robins found that which was associated with an increased probability of antisocial personality in adulthood?

   a. a sibling with a diagnosis of antisocial personality
   b. a history of substance abuse in the child's mother
   c. inconsistent discipline or absence of discipline in the family
   d. neurological abnormalities in childhood

7) According to the DSM-IV, an important characteristic of personality disorders is:

   a. they are typically experienced as ego-syntonic
   b. the impairment associated with these disorders is more severe than is found in other forms of mental disorder
   c. they are episodic and time limited in nature
   d. they are consistently reliably diagnosed

8) Research focusing on relationships among personality disorders suggests that:

   a. there is little diagnostic overlap across all personality disorder categories
   b. histrionic personality disorder demonstrates the least amount of diagnostic overlap with other personality disorder categories
   c. there is considerable overlap across diagnostic categories
   d. obsessive-compulsive personality disorder demonstrates the greatest amount of overlap with other personality disorders

9) The most common personality disorder in both inpatient and outpatient settings is:

   a. dependent   c. borderline
   b. antisocial   d. paranoid

10) Which statement is correct regarding treatment of personality disorders?

   a. people with personality disorders benefit most from insight-oriented therapy
   b. people with personality disorders who present for treatment often do so because they have another type of mental disorder such as depression
   c. people with personality disorders benefit most from antipsychotic drugs
   d. people with personality disorders who present for treatment usually remain in treatment until it is completed

11) The Axis I disorder most often diagnosed with antisocial personality disorder is:

   a. dissociative fugue   c. schizophrenia
   b. depression   d. substance abuse

12) Which is considered the primary feature of borderline personality disorder?

   a. consistent instability in self-image, mood, and interpersonal relationships
   b. extreme social anxiety
   c. consistent disregard for authority figures
   d. extreme fear of rejection from others

13) About _____ of people with personality disorders do NOT seek treatment.

    a. 40%   c. 80%
    b. 60%   d. 95%

14) Tom is definitely a loner. He has no close friends and appears to be indifferent to relationships. Other people would describe Tom as distant and aloof. In addition, Tom reports that he does not feel strongly about anything. He can't think of anything that really makes him excited; then again, he doesn't get upset or distressed about anything either. Tom might qualify for which of the following personality disorders?

    a. borderline   c. paranoid
    b. schizoid   d. narcissistic

15) Which of the following has NOT been a proposed explanation for the etiology of borderline personality disorder?

    a. early substance abuse
    b. negative consequences resulting from parental loss during childhood
    c. a history of physical and sexual abuse
    d. problematic relationships with parents

16) Personality disorders are listed on which axis of DSM-IV?

    a. I   c. III
    b. II   d. IV

17) Which statement regarding gender differences in personality disorders is correct?

    a. antisocial personality disorder is more frequently diagnosed in women
    b. men seek treatment for their personality disorders more often than women
    c. the overall prevalence of personality disorders is about equal in men and women
    d. histrionic personality disorder is more likely to be diagnosed in men

18) Which of the following would NOT be considered a characteristic feature of antisocial personality disorder?

    a. emotional instability   c. deceitfulness
    b. failure to conform to social norms   d. irritability and aggressiveness

19) Mary feels lonely and isolated. Although she has good relationships with family members, she is so afraid of negative criticism from others that she tends to distance herself from others. She desperately wants to make friends, but is afraid of being rejected. She constantly watches for any sign of disapproval. Which personality disorder diagnosis is most appropriate for Mary?

    a. schizoid   c. narcissistic
    b. histrionic   d. avoidant

20) An advantage of a dimensional system of classifying personality disorders is:

   a. it eliminates the need for diagnosis
   b. personality disorders are more reliably assessed
   c. it is more useful for those individuals whose symptoms and behaviors fall on the boundaries between different personality disorder diagnoses
   d. it requires less time to arrive at a diagnosis

21) Studies investigating the long-term course of antisocial personality disorder indicate that:

   a. antisocial individuals tend to become more careless as they grow older, resulting in increasing numbers of arrests
   b. antisocial individuals continue their criminal activity well into middle age
   c. antisocial individuals reform their behavior after several incarcerations
   d. people exhibiting antisocial behavior tend to 'burn out' when they reach middle age

22) According to the five-factor model of personality, the willingness to cooperate and empathize with other people is the trait referred to as:

   a. conscientiousness   c. agreeableness
   b. affiliation   d. cooperativeness

23) Larry has extreme difficulty making decisions on his own. He tends to cling to other people and continually asks them for assistance in making even minor decisions. In addition, he constantly asks for his friends' advice and wants to be reassured about everything, even his ability to be a friend. A possible diagnosis for Larry is:

   a. dependent personality disorder
   b. avoidant personality disorder
   c. narcissistic personality disorder
   d. borderline personality disorder

24) Individual psychotherapy with borderline patients can be difficult because:

   a. borderline patients frequently cannot afford the cost of such treatment
   b. borderline patients are often so transient that it is difficult for them to remain in treatment for more than a brief period of time
   c. maintaining the type of concentration necessary for individual therapy is particularly difficult for such patients
   d. establishing and maintaining the type of close relationship necessary between therapist and patient is particularly difficult for borderlines

25) The personality disorders listed in DSM-IV are divided into how many clusters?

   a. 2   c. 4
   b. 3   d. 5

26) Research on the genetics of antisocial personality disorder suggests which of the following statements?

    a. genetic and environmental factors combine to produce criminal behavior
    b. the presence of any type of genetic factor in the production of antisocial behavior is dubious
    c. without the presence of genetic factors, environmental factors alone can never predict the development of criminal behavior
    d. environmental factors are much more important than genetic factors in the production of criminal behavior

27) Sally takes pride in efficient performance and rational behavior. While others see her as rigid, perfectionistic, inflexible, and judgmental, Sally believes that others simply do not share the same standards and are not worthy of her high opinion. She does not show affection and finds 'mushy' feelings in others distasteful. Which personality disorder might Sally have?

    a. schizotypal   c. obsessive-compulsive
    b. antisocial   d. schizoid

28) Which statement regarding treatment of antisocial personalities is correct?

    a. treatment is usually successful if the individual does not have a history of legal difficulties
    b. currently the best treatment available for this disorder is family therapy
    c. approximately two-thirds of individuals with this disorder show clinical improvement if treated with psychodynamic therapy
    d. the presence of depression in people with this disorder may be associated with a better prognosis for treatment for this disorder

Understanding Research - Fill in the Blank

Stability of Personality Disorders in Adolescents: The text presents a detailed description of a study by Bernstein, Cohen, et al., in the Research Close-Up on pp. 331-332. Finding the answers to these questions will help you get a good understanding of this study and why it is important. It is not necessary to memorize the answers; the process of finding them in the textbook will help you learn the material you need to know.

1. The researchers wanted to know how _____ adolescents had personality disorders and whether they kept them over time. The subjects were selected from a

_____ sample of more than _____ families with one or more children

between the ages of _____ and 21. _____ child from each family could participate.

The families were representative of the general population in terms of

_____. Half the subjects were _____ and the average

age was _____. How many families were not intact? _____

2. Was the study cross-sectional or longitudinal? _____
Information was collected by asking _____ and _____ about
the adolescent's behavior in interviews and _____. Based on this
data, adolescents were diagnosed as having a moderate or severe form of
_____. What percent had at least one personality
disorder? _____ What percent had a severe one? _____ What was
the most common moderate personality disorder? _____
What was the most common severe one? _____

3. What was the one significant sex difference? _____
_____. Was this expected or
unexpected? _____ What was the age that most adolescents
had a personality disorder? _____ How many teens who had a diagnosis at
Time I had one at Time II? _____ The most persistent types
were paranoid, obsessive-compulsive, borderline, and _____.

4. What are the implications of this study? _____
_____

Making Cross-Cultural Comparisons: The text discusses this issue in research in the
Research Methods section on pp. 323-324. Finding the answers to these questions
will help you get a good understanding of these issues.

5. What type of subject is the most commonly studied? _____
Who in the United States has been neglected in terms of research? _____
_____ How are a culture's expectations for behavior passed down?
_____ Culture shapes people's most basic view of
_____. Among Native Americans, hearing _____ is a
common, normal response.

6. Researchers interested in cross-cultural comparisons look at differences in the
_____ of a disorder in different cultures. They examine how causal
_____ may be different. One difficulty in this type of research is how
to determine who shares a _____ culture. Another difficulty is being sure to
use comparable _____ in the different cultures. _____
the differences that are found is another challenge. Researchers must also be careful
to avoid _____ bias in their interpretations.

Brief Essay

As a final exercise, write out answers to the following brief essay questions. Then compare your answers with the material presented in the text.

After you have answered these questions, review the "critical thinking" questions that are presented at the end of the text chapter. Answering these questions will help you integrate important issues and themes that have been featured throughout the chapter.

1. Describe the five-factor model of personality. What are the five factors and their definitions? What would be characteristics of low and high scorers on these traits?

2. Discuss the problems associated with the treatment of individuals with personality disorders. Why is a poor prognosis for treatment associated with most of these disorders? What treatment approaches seem most promising to you?

3. Review the controversies that surround the issue of stability of personality. What methods have been used in the attempt to demonstrate stable traits? What do you think are methodological limitations of these approaches?

4. Pretend that you are on the committee to develop DSM-V. Would you recommend classifying personality disorders using a dimensional or categorical approach? Why?

ANSWER KEY

Answers to the exercises are listed below; page numbers where the information is referenced in the textbook are given in parentheses.

Key Terms - Matching #1

1. g (320)	8. p (337)	15. f (319-20)	
2. a (316)	9. q (337)	16. m (333)	
3. n (333)	10. o (337)	17. l (327)	
4. r (338)	11. i (321)	18. c (317-9)	
5. s (338)	12. t (338)	19. b (316)	
6. j (321-2)	13. e (319)	20. h (321)	
7. d (319)	14. k (327)		

Names You Should Know

1. c (339)
2. b (337)
3. f (344)
4. a (342)
5. d (339)
6. e (331)

Key Terms - Matching #2

a. 9 (326)	f. 16 (344)	k. 14 (341)	p. 19 (348)
b. 4 (323)	g. 18 (345)	l. 6 (325)	q. 2 (322)
c. 8 (326)	h. 5 (324)	m. 1 (322)	r. 12 (338)
d. 15 (342)	i. 10 (327)	n. 13 (340)	s. 7 (325)
e. 3 (323)	j. 11 (338)	o. 17 (344)	

Review of Concepts

1. false (316)
2. difficult to diagnose reliably; etiology is poorly understood; little evidence they are treatable (316)
3. II (316)
4. syntonic (319)
5. wealth (320)
6. during a famine, while being raised in an institution, in a busy daycare center (321)
7. emotion; collectivism (322)
8. limited to the culture where it was developed (322)
9. C (327)
10. A (324)
11. B (325)
12. false (326)
13. antisocial (326)
14. false (328)
15. categorical (328)
16. 10-14% (329)
17. narcissistic (329)
18. false (330)
19. borderline (330)
20. women; men; women (330)
21. feminine (330)
22. less (332)
23. true (334)
24. have another mental disorder (335)
25. true (336)
26. pleasure; anxiety (338)
27. depression (340)
28. parents (340)
29. leave treatment (341)
30. true (341)
31. antisocial (342)
32. emotions and interpersonal behavior (344)
33. change forms (344)
34. genes; environment (345)
35. did; did not (345)
36. discipline (345-6)
37. be inconsistent or give up in discipline (346)
38. fear or anxiety (346)
39. shame (347)
40. false (347)
41. abandonment (349
42. overprotective, authoritarian (349)

Multiple Choice

1. d	6. c	11. d	16. b	21. d	26. a
2. b	7. a	12. a	17. c	22. c	27. c
3. b	8. c	13. c	18. a	23. a	28. d
4. d	9. c	14. b	19. d	24. d	
5. a	10. b	15. a	20. c	25. b	

Understanding Research

1. many; random; 700; 11; One; socioeconomic status; boys; 16; 39%
2. longitudinal; adolescents; mothers; questionnaires; personality disorder; 31%; 17%; obsessive-compulsive; narcissistic
3. boys more likely to have a dependent personality disorder; unexpected; 12-13 years old; less than half; narcissistic
4. Personality disorders are relatively common among teens and are fairly, although not overwhelmingly, stable over time.
5. college students in the United States; ethnic minorities; social learning; reality; voices of the dead
6. rates; mechanisms; common; measures; Interpreting; cultural

CHAPTER 10 - EATING DISORDERS

Chapter Outline

I. Overview

II. Typical Symptoms and Associated Features of Anorexia Nervosa
- A. Refusal to Maintain a Normal Weight
- B. Disturbance in Perceiving or Evaluating Weight or Shape
- C. Fear of Gaining Weight
- D. Cessation of Menstruation
- E. Medical Complications
- F. Struggle for Control
- G. Comorbid Psychological Disorders

III. Typical Symptoms and Associated Features of Bulimia Nervosa
- A. Binge Eating
- B. Inappropriate Compensatory Behavior
- C. Excessive Emphasis on Weight and Shape
- D. Comorbid Psychological Disorders
- E. Medical Complications

IV. Classification of Eating Disorders
- A. Brief Historical Perspective
- B. Contemporary Classification
  1. Anorexia Nervosa
  2. Bulimia Nervosa
  3. Binge Eating Disorder and Obesity

V. Epidemiology of Eating Disorders
- A. Gender Differences and Standards of Beauty
- B. Age of Onset

VI. Etiologic Considerations and Research
- A. Social Factors
  1. Troubled Family Relationships
- B. Psychological Factors
  1. A Struggle for Control
  2. Depression, Low Self-Esteem, and Dysphoria
  3. Negative Body Image
  4. Dietary Restraint
- C. Biological Factors
- D. Integration and Alternative Pathways

VII. Treatment of Eating Disorders
- A. Treatment of Anorexia Nervosa
- B. Course and Outcome of Anorexia Nervosa
- C. Treatment of Bulimia Nervosa
  1. Antidepressant Medications

2. Cognitive Behavior Therapy
3. Interpersonal Psychotherapy
D. Course and Outcome of Bulimia Nervosa

Learning Objectives

After reviewing the material presented in this chapter, you should be able to:

1. Know a basic definition of eating disorders, anorexia nervosa, and bulimia nervosa.

2. Describe the ways in which those with anorexia have distorted perceptions of their weight and shape.

3. Identify the common medical complications associated with anorexia nervosa and bulimia nervosa.

4. Describe some of the typical symptoms of bulimia nervosa, and the inappropriate compensatory behavior that typifies the disorder.

5. Identify the two subtypes of anorexia nervosa and bulimia nervosa.

6. Know the gender differences involved in eating disorders.

7. Define interoceptive awareness and distorted body image, and understand how they play a role in eating disorders.

8. Identify some of the chief social, psychological, and biological factors responsible for the development of eating disorders.

9. Understand the concept of weight set point.

10. Know the basic goals and techniques utilized in the treatment of anorexia nervosa and bulimia nervosa.

11. Understand the common course and outcome associated with each of these disorders.

Key Terms - Matching

The following terms related to eating disorders are important to know. To test your knowledge, match the following terms with their definitions. Answers are listed at the end of the chapter.

a.	Eating disorders	l.	Binge eating disorder
b.	Anorexia nervosa	m.	Obesity
c.	Bulimia nervosa	n.	Incidence
d.	Body mass index	o.	Cohort effects

e.	Distorted body image	p.	Enmeshed families
f.	Amenorrhea	q.	Perfectionism
g.	Lanugo	r.	Introceptive awareness
h.	Electrolyte imbalance	s.	Effects of dietary restraint
i.	Binge eating	t.	Weight set points
j.	Purging	u.	Hypothalamus
k.	Rumination		

1. _____ a fine, downy hair on the face or trunk of the body
2. _____ number of new cases
3. _____ eating an amount of food in a fixed period of time that is clearly larger than most people would eat under similar circumstances
4. _____ the area of the brain that regulates routine biological functions like appetite
5. _____ absence of al least three consecutive menstrual cycles
6. _____ differences that distinguish one group, born during a particular time period, from another group born at a different time period
7. _____ a disturbance in the levels of potassium, sodium, calcium, and other vital elements found in bodily fluids that can lead to cardiac arrest or kidney failure
8. _____ families whose members are overly involved in one another's lives
9. _____ the endless pursuit of unrealistically high standards
10. _____ repeated episodes of binge eating followed by inappropriate compensatory behaviors with other symptoms related to eating and body image
11. _____ excess body fat; body weight over 20 percent above the expected weight
12. _____ an inaccuracy in how one perceives their body size and shape
13. _____ an intentional act designed to eliminate consumed food from the body
14. _____ severe disturbances in eating behavior that result from obsessive fear of gaining weight
15. _____ direct consequences of restricted eating
16. _____ a controversial diagnosis defined by repeated episodes of binge eating in the absence of compensatory behavior
17. _____ the body's preference for a fixed weight that may have biologically controlled homeostatic mechanisms
18. _____ refusal to maintain a minimally normal body weight along with other symptoms related to eating and body image
19. _____ the regurgitation and rechewing of food
20. _____ recognition of internal cues including various emotional states as well as hunger
21. _____ a calculation derived from weight and height used to determine whether someone is significantly underweight

Names You Should Know - Matching

The following people have played an important role in research and theory of eating disorders. To test your knowledge, match the following names with the descriptions of their contributions to the study of abnormal psychology. Answers are listed at the end of the chapter.

a. Hilde Bruch   b. Christopher Fairburn

1. _____   asserted that a struggle for control and perfectionism is the central psychological issue in the development of eating disorders
2. _____   developed a cognitive behavioral treatment for bulimia nervosa

Review of Concepts - Fill in the Blank and True/False

This section will help focus your studying by testing whether you understand the concepts presented in the text. After you have read and reviewed the material, test your comprehension and memory by filling in the following blanks or circling the right answer. Answers are listed at the end of the chapter.

1. People with anorexia nervosa suffer from a loss of appetite: **true**   **false**

2. Anorexia and bulimia are how much more common in women than in men:

   twice as common   four times as common   ten times as common

3. Males in our society see themselves as thin when they weigh 105 percent of their expected weight, while females see themselves as thin when they weigh 90 percent of their expected weight: **true**   **false**

4. Female anorexics are likely to be proud of their emaciation, while male anorexics are likely to be stigmatized for it: **true**   **false**

5. Eating disorders are more common among men who are wrestlers and men who are gay: **true**   **false**

6. Often eating disorders begin with a _____.

7. What percent of people admitted to hospitals with anorexia nervosa die of starvation, suicide, or medical complications?   _____

8. A person with anorexia often becomes more and more afraid of fat the thinner they become: **true**   **false**

9. It is likely that amenorrhea and lack of interest in sex common among anorexics are a result rather than a predisposition of the weight loss: **true**   **false**

10. Although anorexia is a serious mental disorder, it seldom involves medical complications: **true**   **false**

11. A person with anorexia can be seen as exceptionally successful in what area?

    _____

12. The study with World War II conscientious objectors found that obsessive-compulsive behaviors probably   **precede** or **follow** the change in eating patterns.

13. Anorexia seldom co-occurs with symptoms of bulimia: **true**   **false**

14. Binge eating is often triggered by _____.

15. Lack of control is characteristic of _____ while excessive control is characteristic of _____.

16. Vomiting prevents the absorption of how many of the calories consumed during a binge?   **almost none**   **about half**   **almost all**

17. The two subtypes of anorexia are the _____ type and the _____ type.

18. The two subtypes of bulimia are the _____ type and the _____ type.

19. Research indicates that obesity is primarily caused by lack of willpower in eating habits: **true**   **false**

20. Eating disorders have become somewhat less common since the 1960s and 1970s: **true**   **false**

21. Which type of eating disorder is more common? _____

22. In Third World countries, weighing more is a status symbol: **true false**

23. Studies have shown that physical _____ predicts self-esteem among girls and physical _____ predicts self-esteem among boys.

24. People with which type of eating disorder are more likely to report that their families have high levels of conflict? _____

25. Clinicians note that enmeshed families are more characteristic of people with which type of eating disorder? _____

26. Perfectionism is characteristic of people with which type of eating disorder?

_____

27. Negative evaluations of one's weight, shape, and appearance predict the subsequent development of eating disorders: **true**   **false**

28. There is evidence that diets can be the trigger for the development of an eating disorder: **true**   **false**

29. When food intake is reduced, there is an increase in the metabolic rate: **true**   **false**

30. There is strong evidence that eating disorders are genetic: **true   false**

31. There is evidence that family therapy is more effective that individual therapy in treating adolescents with anorexia: **true**   **false**

32. Current forms of treatment for anorexia are quite effective: **true**   **false**

33. Psychotherapy is more effective than antidepressant medication in the treatment of bulimia: **true**   **false**

34. Interpersonal therapy was found to be as effective as cognitive behavior therapy

in the treatment of bulimia: **true** **false**

35. Bulimia is more likely to lead to death than anorexia: **true** **false**

Multiple Choice Questions

The following multiple choice questions will test your comprehension of the material presented in the chapter. Answers are listed at the end of the chapter.

1) Both bulimia and anorexia nervosa are characterized by which of the following?

   a. struggle for control
   b. considerable shame
   c. obsessive-compulsive disorder
   d. the absence of menstruation

2) All of the following are compensatory behaviors of bulimia nervosa EXCEPT:

   a. misuse of laxatives
   b. complete avoidance of food
   c. intense exercise
   d. misuse of enemas

3) All of the following are symptoms of anorexia nervosa EXCEPT:

   a. an intense fear of gaining weight
   b. refusal to maintain weight at or above minimally normal weight for age and height
   c. acknowledgement of the seriousness of low body weight, but refusal to change eating behavior
   d. amenorrhea, or the absence of menstruation

4) Which of the following theories offers the most promising explanations for eating disorders?

   a. biological
   b. social
   c. psychological
   d. all of the above equally offer promising explanations of eating disorders

5) All of the following are symptoms of bulimia nervosa EXCEPT:

   a. recurrent episodes of binge eating that involve large amounts of food
   b. occurs solely during episodes of anorexia nervosa
   c. recurrent inappropriate compensatory behavior, especially purging
   d. undue influence of weight and body shape on self-evaluation

6) Both bulimia and anorexia nervosa are approximately _____ times more common among women than among men.

   a. 10
   b. 15
   c. 20
   d. 25

7) Many professionals agree that anorexia is a source of which of the following?

    a. shame
    b. pride

    c. gratification
    d. resentment

8) Bulimia nervosa is most prevalent among which of the following groups?

    a. women born after 1960
    b. women born before 1950

    c. girls ages 10-15
    d. women born in the 1950s

9) Which of the following is NOT a finding that provides evidence that social factors are very important in eating disorders?

    a. eating disorders have recently become much more common
    b. eating disorders are much more common among women working in fields that emphasize weight and appearance, such as modeling and ballet
    c. eating disorders are more common among middle- and upper-class whites
    d. eating disorders have a higher concordance rate in MZ rather than DZ twins

Understanding Research - Fill in the Blank

Risk Factors in the Development of Disordered Eating: The text presents a detailed description of a study by Leon in the Research Close-Up on pp. 373-374. Finding the answers to these questions will help you get a good understanding of this study and why it is important. It is not necessary to memorize the answers; the process of finding them in the textbook will help you learn the material you need to know.

1. How many subjects from the original sample were not followed up over the period of three years? _____ What grades were the subjects in? _____ The risk factors studied included: physical _____, _____ status, _____ patterns, attitudes about eating and _____, substance _____, _____ characteristics, multiple self-concept scales, perceived _____, and attitudes about _____. Did the study assess boys? _____

2. What were the variables that were statistically significant risk factors for current eating problems? _____ dissatisfaction, negative _____, low _____ awareness, hypo _____, and low perceived _____ competence   What were the only significant predictors of eating difficulties three years later?   earlier _____ difficulties, low introceptive _____, and _____ race

157

3. What is one possible reason that body image dissatisfaction may not have predicted eating difficulties? _____
_____.

Designing Credible Placebo Control Groups: The text discusses this research issue in the Research Methods section on pp. 380-381. Finding the answers to these questions will help you get a good understanding of these issues.

4.   Which is more difficult, creating a placebo control group for testing a new medication or for testing a new psychological treatment? _____
_____   Why is this hard? _____
_____
_____

5. Psychotherapy outcome researchers typically find a treatment that they ally with to be more effective; what is this called? _____ This effect is usually countered with the _____ approach in medication trials, which is impossible to recreate in psychotherapy studies.   What is one way to overcome the allegiance effect? _____

_____
_____
What are two problems created by this approach? _____,
and _____.

Brief Essay

As a final exercise, write out answers to the following brief essay questions. Then compare your answers with the material presented in the text.

After you have answered these questions, review the "critical thinking" questions that are presented at the end of the text chapter. Answering these questions will help you integrate important issues and themes that have been featured throughout the chapter.

1. Discuss the differences between anorexia nervosa and bulimia nervosa in terms of their symptoms, prevalence, etiology, and treatment.

2. Discuss the evidence that social factors play a role in the etiology of eating disorders.

3. If you were a therapist and a young woman entered therapy for an eating disorder, what would your treatment plan entail? Would your treatment for a male patient differ from treatment for a female patient? Explain why or why not.

ANSWER KEY

Answers to the exercises are listed below; page numbers where the information is referenced in the textbook are given in parentheses.

Key Terms - Matching

1. g (361)	8. p (372)	15. s (375)
2. n (368)	9. q (373)	16. l (367)
3. i (364)	10. c (356)	17. t (376)
4. u (377)	11. m (368)	18. b (356)
5. f (361)	12. e (360)	19. k (366)
6. o (369)	13. j (364)	20. r (373)
7. h (361)	14. a (356)	21. d (360)

Names You Should Know

1. a (372-3)
2. b (379)

Review of Concepts

1. false (356)	19. false (368)
2. ten times as common (356)	20. false (368)
3. true (359)	21. bulimia (369)
4. true (359)	22. true (370)
5. true (359)	23. attractiveness; competence (371)
6. diet (359)	24. bulimia (372)
7. 10 percent (360)	25. anorexia (372)
8. true (361)	26. anorexia (373)
9. true (361)	27. true (375)
10. false (361)	28. true (376)
11. self-control (361)	29. false (376)
12. follow (362)	30. false (376)
13. false (362)	31. true (378)
14. an unhappy mood (364)	32. false (378)
15. bulimia; anorexia (364)	33. true (379)
16. about half (365)	34. true (380)
17. restricting; binge-eating/purging (366)	35. false (381)
18. purging; nonpurging (367)	

Multiple Choice

1. a	4. b	7. b
2. b	5. b	8. a
3. c	6. a	9. d

Understanding Research

1. 360; 7-10; size; pubertal; eating; self; use; personality; autonomy; sexuality; yes

2. body; emotionality; introceptive; mania; scholastic; eating; awareness; white

3. so many of the girls reported it

4. psychological treatment;   It is difficult to design a treatment that contains no active ingredients but that increases the expectation for change.

5. allegiance effect;   double-blind;   having investigators with opposing allegiances participate in the same study;   no placebo control;   can't control for differences among therapists

CHAPTER 11 - SUBSTANCE USE DISORDERS

Chapter Outline

I. Overview

II. Typical Symptoms and Associated Features
    A. The Concept of Substance Dependence
        1. Tolerance and Withdrawal
    B. Alcohol
        1. Short-Term Effects
        2. Consequences of Prolonged Use and Abuse
    C. Barbiturates and Benzodiazepines
        1. Short-Term Effects
        2. Consequences of Prolonged Use and Abuse
    D. Opiates
        1. Short-Term Effects
        2. Consequences of Prolonged Use and Abuse
    E. Nicotine
        1. Short-Term Effects
        2. Consequences of Prolonged Use and Abuse
    F. Amphetamines and Cocaine
        1. Short-Term Effects
        2. Consequences of Prolonged Use and Abuse
    G. Cannabis
        1. Short-Term Effects
        2. Consequences of Prolonged Use and Abuse
    H. Hallucinogens
        1. Short-Term Effects
        2. Consequences of Prolonged Use and Abuse

III. Classification
    A. Brief History of Legal and Illegal Substances
    B. DSM-IV
    C. Proposed Subtypes
    D. Course and Outcome
    E. Other Disorders Commonly Associated With Addictions

IV. Epidemiology
    A. Prevalence of Alcohol Abuse and Dependence
        1. Gender Differences
    B. Prevalence of Drug and Nicotine Dependence
    C. Risk for Addiction Across the Life Span

V. Etiological Considerations and Research
    A. Social Factors
    B. Biological Factors
        1. Genetics of Alcoholism
            a. Twin Studies

                    b. Adoption Studies
            2. Neurochemical Modes of Action
                    a. Endogenous Opioid Receptors
                    b. The Serotonin Hypothesis
        C. Psychological Factors
            1. Expectations About Drug Effects
            2. Attention Allocation
        D. Integrated Systems

VI. Treatment
        A. Detoxification and Pharmacotherapy
            1. Disulfiram (Antabuse)
        B. Self-Help Groups: Alcoholics Anonymous
        C. Controlled Drinking
        D. Relapse Prevention
        E. General Conclusions

Learning Objectives

After reviewing the material presented in this chapter, you should be able to:

1. Distinguish substance abuse, substance dependence, and polysubstance abuse.

2. Define tolerance and withdrawal.

3. Name some of the main short-term effects and consequences of prolonged abuse of alcohol.

4. Describe some of the properties, short-term effects, and consequences of prolonged use and abuse of the following drugs: barbiturates and benzodiazepines, opiates, nicotine, amphetamines and cocaine, cannabis, and hallucinogens

5. Know the classification system that DSM-IV uses to differentiate between substance abuse and substance dependence.

6. Describe the typical course and outcome of alcoholism according to the findings of Vaillant.

7. Know the epidemiology, including gender differences, of alcoholism and controlled substances.

8. Explain how social factors influence the initial experimentation with drugs and alcohol.

9. State some of the basic findings regarding the genetics of alcoholism--from twin and adoption studies.

10. Explain the endorphin hypothesis and the serotonin hypothesis.

11. Understand the importance of cognitive expectations in the effects of alcohol.

12. Delineate the attention allocation model and how it explains the typical functioning of inebriated people.

13. Understand the integrated systems approach to substance use and abuse.

14. Describe the following treatment programs: detoxification, self-help groups, controlled drinking training, and relapse prevention training.

Key Terms - Matching #1

The following terms related to substance use disorders are important to know. To test your knowledge, match the following terms with their definitions. Answers are listed at the end of the chapter.

a.	Substance dependence	n.	Alcohol withdrawal delirium
b.	Substance abuse	o.	Delirium tremens
c.	Polysubstance abuse	p.	Tranquilizers
d.	Addiction	q.	Barbiturates
e.	Psychoactive substance	r.	Benzodiazepines
f.	Hypnotics	s.	Delirium
g.	Sedatives (anxiolytics)	t.	Opiates
h.	Narcotic analgesics	u.	Morphine
i.	Craving	v.	Codeine
j.	Psychological dependence	w.	Heroin
k.	Physiological dependence	x.	Methadone
l.	Tolerance	y.	Psychomotor stimulants
m.	Withdrawal	z.	Cocaine

1. _____ CNS depressants that are used for relieving anxiety
2. _____ a less severe pattern of drug use defined in terms of interference with a person's ability to fulfill major role obligations, the recurrent use of a drug in dangerous situations, or the experience of legal problems associated with the drug use
3. _____ drugs with properties similar to opium, often used to relieve pain
4. _____ convulsions, hallucinations, and a sudden disturbance of consciousness with changes in cognitive processes during withdrawal from alcohol
5. _____ the process through which the nervous system becomes less sensitive to the effects of a substance with repeated exposure to that substance
6. _____ a synthetic opiate often injected, inhaled, or smoked
7. _____ physical symptoms related to drug use, including tolerance and withdrawal
8. _____ a class of drugs, discovered in the early twentieth century, used widely for many years to treat anxiety, prevent seizures, and relieve pain

9. _____ drugs which produce their effects by simulating the actions of certain neurotransmitters
10. _____ also known as drug of abuse; a chemical substance that alters mood, level of perception, or brain functioning
11. _____ a synthetic opiate sometimes used therapeutically as an alternative to heroin
12. _____ used to decrease anxiety or agitation
13. _____ CNS depressants that are used to help people sleep
14. _____ the abuse of several types of drugs
15. _____ opiates that can be used clinically to decrease pain
16. _____ a cognitive disorder characterized by impairment in consciousness, attention, and other cognitive abilities
17. _____ symptoms experienced when a person stops using a drug
18. _____ a more severe pattern of repeated self-administration often resulting in tolerance, withdrawal, or compulsive drug-taking behavior
19. _____ one of the active ingredients of opium, very similar to heroin
20. _____ one of the active ingredients of opium, available in small quantities in Canada in over-the-counter medications
21. _____ an older term used to describe substance use problems such as alcoholism, characterized by craving and lack of control
22. _____ feeling compelled to use a drug to control one's feelings or to prepare for certain activities
23. _____ an older term for alcohol withdrawal delirium
24. _____ synthetic drugs whose therapeutic effects were discovered in the 1950s which have largely replaced barbiturates in medical practice
25. _____ a naturally occuring stimulant drug extracted from the leaf of a small tree that grows at high elevations
26. _____ a forceful urge to use drugs

Key Terms - Matching #2

The following terms related to substance use disorders are important to know. To test your knowledge, match the following terms with their definitions. Answers are listed at the end of the chapter.

1.	Amphetamines	14.	Pencyclidine (PCP)
2.	Crack	15.	Psychedelic
3.	Amphetamine psychosis	16.	Flashbacks
4.	Cannabis	17.	Endorphins
5.	Marijuana	18.	Balanced placebo design
6.	Hashish	19.	Risk
7.	Temporal disintegration	20.	Relative risk
8.	Reverse tolerance	21.	High-risk research design
9.	Hallucinogens	22.	Vulnerability indicators
10.	LSD	23.	Alcohol myopia
11.	Psilocybin	24.	Detoxification
12.	Mescaline	25.	Antabuse
13.	Peyote	26.	Abstinence violation effect

a. _____ the dried leaves and flowers of the hemp plant
b. _____ a form of cocaine that is smoked, leading to more rapid absorption and a much stronger drug effect
c. _____ "mind-expanding," or having deep insights into thoughts or feelings
d. _____ synthetically produced psychomotor stimulants such as dexedrine or methamphetamine
e. _____ a procedure that allows the investigator to separate the direct, biological effects of the drug from the subjects' expectations about how the drug should affect their behavior
f. _____ drugs that cause people to experience hallucinations at relatively low doses
g. _____ a drug that can block the chemical breakdown of alcohol which will make the person taking it violently ill if he or she consumes alcohol
h. _____ brief visual aftereffects that can occur at unpredictable intervals long after a hallucinogen has cleared the body
i. _____ a technique where subjects are selected from the general population based on some identified risk factor that has a fairly high risk ratio
j. _____ auditory or visual hallucinations as well as delusions of persecution or grandeur that can occur with high doses of amphetamines or cocaine and usually disappears after the drug is metabolized
k. _____ manifestations of the genotype associated with a mental disorder
l. _____ a hallucinogen found in certain mushrooms which bears a chemical resemblance to serotonin
m. _____ a synthetic hallucinogen which bears a strong chemical resemblance to serotonin
n. _____ a condition often accompanying cannabis intoxication in which people have trouble retaining and organizing information
o. _____ becoming more sensitive to a drug with prolonged use; reported by users but not yet documented in laboratory studies
p. _____ a synthetic drug that can induce psychotic behavior at high doses
q. _____ the probability that a certain outcome will occur
r. _____ the probability that someone with a certain characteristic will develop a disorder divided by the probability that someone without the same characteristic will develop the same disorder
s. _____ the guilt and perceived loss of control that a person feels whenever he or she slips and takes a drug after an extended period of abstinence
t. _____ the removal of a drug on which a person has become dependent
u. _____ a drug with the active ingredient called THC, derived from the hemp plant
v. _____ a type of hallucinogen that resembles norepinephrine
w. _____ the dried resin from the top of the female hemp plant
x. _____ a marked tendency to engage in shortsighted information processing when intoxicated
y. _____ a cactus that contains mescaline
z. _____ endogenous opioids that are naturally synthesized in the brain and are closely related to morphine

Names You Should Know - Matching

The following people have played an important role in research and theory of substance use disorders. To test your knowledge, match the following names with the descriptions of their contributions to the study of abnormal psychology. Answers are listed at the end of the chapter.

a. George Vaillant   c. Robert Cloninger
b. Alan Marlatt   d. Linda and Mark Sobell

1. _____ proposed that there were two types of alcoholism, Type I, which has a later onset, psychological dependence, and the absence of antisocial personality traits, and Type II, which is predominantly among men, has an earlier onset, and co-occurs with antisocial behaviors
2. _____ conducted a longitudinal study of alcoholism among inner-city adolescents and college students
3. _____ developed a cognitive behavioral view of the relapse process and a relapse prevention model for treament of substance use
4. _____ developed a treatment for alcoholism known as Individualized Behavior Therapy for Alcoholics (IBTA) which was controversial because it included as a goal controlled drinking rather than lifelong abstinence

Review of Concepts - Fill in the Blank and True/False

This section will help focus your studying by testing whether you understand the concepts presented in the text. After you have read and reviewed the material, test your comprehension and memory by filling in the following blanks or circling the right answer. Answers are listed at the end of the chapter.

1. Most researchers have moved toward a view of substance abuse that emphasizes common causes, behaviors, and consequences of using the substance rather than a focus on the particular drug used: **true**   **false**

2. One of the best indices for defining alcoholism is the amount of alcohol a person consumes: **true**   **false**

3. A crucial feature of alcoholism is diminished _____.

4. The most substantial tolerance effects are found among people who use which drugs? _____

   _____

5. What drugs have not been shown to have tolerance effects? _____

6. _____ is the most widely used psychoactive substance in the world.

7. What organ metabolizes alcohol? _____

8. Blood alcohol levels are only weakly correlated with intoxicating effects:

   true   **false**

9. When blood alcohol levels go too high, the person will become unconscious and can always sleep off the effects of the alcohol with no acute dangers:

    true   **false**

10. There is a strong correlation between crime and alcohol: **true**   **false**

11. The abuse of alcohol has more negative health consequences over an extended period of time than any other drug: **true**   **false**

12. Sedatives and hypnotics can lead to a state of arousal similar to that of cocaine:

    true   **false**

13. Barbiturates and benzodiazepines seem to work by enhancing the effects of which neurotransmitter? _____

14. Barbiturates are dangerous because they can cause death by accidental or intentional overdose by stopping a person's _____.

15. Opiates produce _____.

16. Heroin withdrawal is much more severe than withdrawal from alcohol or barbiturates: **true**   **false**

17. Nicotine may mimic the effects of _____ drugs.

18. Nicotine produces CNS   **arousal** or **depression**.

19. The FDA decided to regulate cigarettes as a   **drug** or **medical device**.

20. At what age does addiction to nicotine almost always begin? _____

21. From a psychological point of view, withdrawal from nicotine is just as difficult as withdrawal from _____.

22. Cocaine and amphetamines activate the sympathetic nervous system:

    true   **false**

23. Amphetamine psychosis is a permanent condition: **true**   **false**

24. The most common reaction to discontinuing stimulant drugs is _____

25. Marijuana and hashish show strong tolerance effects: **true**   **false**

26. Hallucinogens may trigger persistent psychosis is people vulnerable to that type of disorder: **true**   **false**

27. A typical American during colonial times never consumed alcohol: **true false**

28. Most alcoholics go through repeated periods of _____.

29. In Vaillant's study, relapse to alcohol abuse was unlikely if the period of abstinence was how many years? _____

30. What three types of disorders are commonly associated with alcohol abuse?

    _____, _____,

    and _____

31. Cannabis is used almost exclusively in North America: **true**   **false**

32. Among all men and women who have ever used alcohol, about _____ percent will develop serious problems with drinking sometime during their lives.

33. Men outnumber women in chronic abuse of alcohol by a ratio of about:

          3 to 1   **5 to 1**   **10 to 1**

34. Women who drink experience more social _____ than men.

35. Women metabolize alcohol more slowly than men, even when differences in body weight are controlled: **true**   **false**

36. The lifetime prevalence for addiction to nicotine is:

          4 percent   **14 percent**   **24 percent**

37. The lifetime prevalence for addiction to drugs (illegal and prescription) other than nicotine or alcohol is: **4.5 percent**   **7.5 percent**   **14.5 percent**

38. The elderly are more likely to be addicted to alcohol than are younger people:

                     true   **false**

39. Parents have a greater influence over their children's decision to use _____ and peers seem to play a more important role in the decision to use

_____.

40. Adolescents with alcoholic parents are less likely to drink than those whose parents are not alcoholic: **true**   **false**

41. A flushing response to even a small amount of alcohol, including flushed skin, nausea, and an abnormal heartbeat occurs in 30-50 percent of people of what racial ancestry? _____

42. There is an elevated risk for alcoholism among first-degree relatives of alcoholics:

                   true   **false**

43. Twin studies indicate that genetic factors alone are responsible for the increased risk for alcoholism among relatives of alcoholics: **true**   **false**

44. In one study, there were stronger twin concordance rates for alcoholism among **men** or **women**.

45. In an adoption study, alcoholism was linked to genes in _____ but not in

_____.

46. There is evidence that a deficiency in the activity of what type of neurotransmitter is related to vulnerability to alcoholism? _____

47. The tension-reduction hypothesis suggests that people drink alcohol in an effort to reduce the impact of a _____ environment.

48. In one study, people who believed they consumed alcohol but really did not showed increased _____ and _____ arousal.

49. _____ expectancies about effects of alcohol predict drinking problems.

50. Detoxification from alcohol is typically accomplished by abruptly discontinuing consumption of alcohol: **true** **false**

51. Many patients using Antabuse have poor compliance with treatment, that is they stop taking the Antabuse: **true** **false**

52. There is no research evidence that Alcoholics Anonymous is an effective form of treatment: **true** **false**

53. Most mental health professionals see controlled drinking as the goal of treatment for alcoholism: **true** **false**

54. The relapse prevention model of treatment teaches patients to interpret slips in abstinence as _____.

55. Research suggests that a person's coping skills, social support, and stress are **better** or **worse** predictors of successfully stopping drinking than the particular type of treatment received.

Multiple Choice Questions

The following multiple choice questions will test your comprehension of the material presented in the chapter. Answers are listed at the end of the chapter.

1) The two terms included in the DSM-IV to describe substance use disorders are:

   a. substance dependence and substance abuse
   b. substance abuse and addiction
   c. tolerance and addiction
   d. substance abuse and polysubstance abuse

2) Although disulfiram (Antabuse) can effectively block the chemical breakdown of alcohol, people resist using this drug because:

   a. it is an extremely expensive drug to administer
   b. the effect of the drug is very short-lived; that is, it reduces alcohol intake for only a few hours after its ingestion
   c. individuals who use this drug have to monitor their dietary intake
   d. use of the drug produces a dramatically adverse physical reaction

3) Because alcoholism is associated with many diverse problems, distinguishing between people who are dependent on alcohol and those who are not is often determined by which of the following?

   a. the presence of legal problems (e.g., driving under the influence)
   b. whether or not the person reports tolerance to alcohol
   c. the number of problems that the person experiences
   d. the presence of medical problems

4) Research on the long term course of alcohol suggests that:

    a. the typical individual is able to successfully stop drinking only after hospitalization

    b. the typical individual cycles through periods of alcohol consumption, cessation, and relapse

    c. the typical individual rarely experiences relapse after making the decision to stop drinking

    d. the typical individual spends approximately 10 years in the alcohol consumption period before making the decision to quit

5) Which of the following is an example of a CNS stimulant?

    a. alcohol   c. morphine
    b. cocaine   d. hashish

6) Results from adoption studies focusing on the genetic transmission of alcohol indicate that:

    a. the familial nature of alcoholism appears to be at least partially determined by genes; that is, having an alcoholic biological parent increases risk for alcoholism

    b. if a person does not have a alcoholic biological parent, having an adopted parent with alcohol problems greatly increases risk for alcoholism

    c. having the personality trait of "behavioral overcontrol" increases risk for alcoholism

    d. only people with at least one alcoholic biological parent are at risk for alcoholism

7) John currently drinks large amounts of alcohol on a daily basis. He plans his day around when alcohol will be available to him. He drives a certain route home from work that passes two liquor stores in order to ensure that liquor will be available each evening. His weekend activities are planned around the availability of alcohol, and he will not attend social functions where alcohol is absent. Which term best describes John's condition?

    a. binge drinker   c. psychological dependence
    b. controlled drinker   d. prealcoholic drinker

8) In most states, the current legal limit of alcohol concentration for driving is:

    a. 50 mg percent   c. 150 mg percent
    b. 100 mg percent   d. 200 mg percent

9) A person who has a compelling need to use a drug and cannot control or regulate his/her drug use is commonly described as:

    a. in withdrawal   c. intoxicated
    b. a recreational drug user   d. addicted

10) One reason that risk for substance dependence is increased in elderly people is:

    a. the elderly demonstrate a reduced sensitivity to drug toxicity and therefore require higher drug dosages
    b. adult children often encourage their elderly parents to use drugs to control their nerves
    c. the elderly use prescribed psychoactive drugs more frequently than compared to other age groups
    d. in fact, there is little risk for substance dependence in the elderly (less than 1 percent of the population)

11) A principal assumption of Alcohlics Anonymous (AA) is:

    a. people need to relapse several times before they will learn to take their alcohol problem seriously
    b. individuals cannot recover on their own
    c. individuals need to remove themselves from the stressful situations that trigger alcohol use
    d. with enough help, people can develop effective methods of controlled drinking

12) Which of the following statements is accurate regarding the definition of substance dependence in the DSM-IV?

    a. evidence of tolerance and withdrawal is required
    b. the individual must exhibit several characteristics that describe a pattern of compulsive use
    c. the person must exhibit characteristics of problematic substance use for at least two years
    d. a prior diagnosis of substance abuse is required before the diagnosis of substance dependence may be considered

13) Which would NOT be considered an example of a common alcohol expectancy?

    a. alcohol decreases power and aggression
    b. alcohol enhances social and physical pleasure
    c. alcohol enhances sexual performance
    d. alcohol increases social assertiveness

14) Aerosol spray, glue, and paint thinner are all examples of which class of psychoactive drugs?

    a. CNS depressants   c. solvents
    b. over-the-counter drugs   d. hallucinogens

15) What percentage of MEN in the United States develop problems resulting from prolonged alcohol consumption?

    a. 10 percent   c. 30 percent
    b. 20 percent   d. 40 percent

16) Which of the following statements is TRUE regarding alcohol expectancies?

    a. negative expectancies appear to be less powerful than positive expectancies in influencing alcohol use
    b. adolescents do not appear to have strong beliefs about alcohol prior to taking their first drink
    c. expectations regarding alcohol do not predict drinking behaviors
    d. portrayal of alcohol in the mass media does not appear to influence individuals' alcohol expectancies

17) Which of the following statements regarding tolerance is TRUE?

    a. individuals can develop tolerance to all psychoactive drugs over time
    b. certain hallucinogens may not lead to the development of tolerance
    c. the most substantial tolerance effects are found among cannabis users
    d. heroin and CNS stimulants do not lead to the development of tolerance

18) The most controversial aspect of Individualized Behavior Therapy for Alcoholics (IBTA) is its:

    a. exclusion of group meetings for alcoholics
    b. inclusion of problem-solving techniques that enable the drinker to identify situations which may potentially trigger heavy drinking
    c. assumption that controlled drinking is a plausible goal for alcoholics
    d. inclusion of aversive therapy techniques in which the use of alcohol is paired with an aversive stimulus

19) Which of the following statements is TRUE regarding the presence of alcohol dependence over a long period of time?

    a. alcohol dependence always results in Korsakoff's psychosis
    b. alcohol dependence follows opiate dependence and cocaine dependence in terms of potential negative health consequences
    c. nutritional disturbances caused by alcohol dependence can be controlled through appropriate medication
    d. alcohol dependence has more negative health consequences than does abuse of any other substance

20) Which of the following symptoms are side effects of alcohol withdrawal?

    a. hand tremors, sweating, and nausea
    b. anxiety and insomnia
    c. convulsions and hallucinations
    d. all of the above

21) The most promising neurochemical explanation of alcoholism currently focuses on which of the following neurotransmitters?

    a. serotonin
    b. dopamine
    c. epinephrine
    d. norepinephrine

22) Considering all the direct and indirect ways that alcohol use contributes to death (e.g., suicides, accidents, medical disorders), alcohol is considered:

    a. the first leading cause of death in this country
    b. the second leading cause of death in this country
    c. the third leading cause of death in this country
    d. the fourth leading cause of death in this country

23) Which of the following statements reflects a difference between men and women in their use of alcohol?

    a. the average age of onset for alcoholism is higher among men
    b. women are less likely to develop hepatic disorders even after drinking heavily for many years
    c. women are more likely to report additional symptoms of depression and anxiety, while antisocial personality traits are more likely to be displayed in men
    d. men are more likely to drink if their partners drink

24) Which of the following factors is a predictor of long-term successful treatment outcome for alcoholism?

    a. the availability of residential alcohol treatment programs in the area
    b. the alcoholic's participation in AA
    c. the presence of environmental stress
    d. the availability of social support

25) Which class of drugs is LEAST associated with severe withdrawal effects?

    a. stimulants   c. sedatives and anxiolytics
    b. alcohol   d. opiates

26) One reason that it is difficult to gather epidemiological information on substance use is that:

    a. the definition of substance abuse and dependence has been clearly restricted in the past
    b. this type of research is expensive and therefore has not been adequately funded
    c. drug users are often reluctant to accurately report their drug use because of the illegal status of many drugs
    d. all of the above

Understanding Research - Fill in the Blank

The Swedish Adoption Studies: The text presents a detailed description of a study by Cloninger, Bohman, and Sigvardsson in the Research Close-Up on pp. 411-412. Finding the answers to these questions will help you get a good understanding of this study and why it is important. It is not necessary to memorize the answers; the process of finding them in the textbook will help you learn the material you need to know.

1. What are the two types of alcoholism that were evaluated in this study? _____ and _____. What were the two cities where subjects were collected? _____ and _____.   Did the findings from the two sites agree? _____   How old were the men at the time of the study? Between the ages of _____ and _____. How were these men selected? _____

_____

2. The information was gathered from the records of local _____ boards, hospital and _____ records, and the national _____ register.   It was felt that this approach would identify _____ percent of those who had a serious drinking problem. What two types of background were evaluated? _____ and _____.   Which type of alcoholism is characterized by criminal activity and an early age of onset?   Type _____.

3. For those with a genetic background of Type 1 alcoholism, a significant increase in the risk of alcoholism was evident in those people with what type of genetic and environmental background? _____

_____.

For those with a genetic background of Type 2 alcoholism, which was a stronger predictor of alcoholism, environmental factors or genetic factors? _____ Females with a genetic predisposition to Type 1 alcoholism were _____ times more likely to abuse alcohol. Females with a genetic predisposition to Type 2 alcoholism _____ more likely to abuse alcohol. What is one criticism of this study? _____

_____.

Risk, Risk Factors, and Studies of High-Risk Samples: The text discusses this type of research in the Research Methods section on pp. 415-416. Finding the answers to these questions will help you get a good understanding of these issues.

4.   What is the risk that a person in the U.S. will develop alcoholism at some point in their lives? _____   What is the risk for all other types of illegal and controlled substances? _____   Risk implies _____, not certainty. What does a relative risk of 3 mean? _____

_____

5. Does risk imply causality? _____ What benefit do longitudinal studies of risk provide? _____

Why aren't they used all the time? _____

What is one technique used to increase the productivity of longitudinal research? _____ How are subjects selected for this type of

research? _____

What is a vulnerability indicator? _____

_____

Brief Essay

As a final exercise, write out answers to the following brief essay questions. Then compare your answers with the material presented in the text.

After you have answered these questions, review the "critical thinking" questions that are presented at the end of the text chapter. Answering these questions will help you integrate important issues and themes that have been featured throughout the chapter.

1. Explain Robert Cloninger and Michael Bohman's theory of Type 1 and Type 2 alcoholism. What do you think are possible weaknesses of their model? What further type of research is necessary to support or disconfirm such a theory?

2. Describe the balanced placebo design. Why is it a useful research design for the study of the effects of alcohol on behavior?

3. Review the attention-allocation model of alcohol as proposed by Claude Steele and Robert Josephs. What are the two general factors on which this model is based? How does the theory predict such behaviors as drunken excess, drunken self-inflation, and drunken relief?

Answers to the exercises are listed below; page numbers where the information is referenced in the textbook are given in parentheses.

Key Terms - Matching #1   **Names You Should Know**

1. g (387)   10. e (387)   19. u (394)   1. c (403, 411-2)
2. b (387)   11. x (394)   20. v (394)   2. a (403)
3. t (394)   12. p (393)   21. d (387)   3. b (420)
4. n (391)   13. f (387)   22. j (390)   4. d (419-20)
5. l (390)   14. c (387)   23. o (391)
6. w (394)   15. h (387)   24. r (393)
7. k (390)   16. s (393)   25. z (397)
8. q (393)   17. m (391)   26. i (390)
9. y (397)   18. a (386)

Key Terms - Matching #2

a. 5 (398)   h. 16 (400)   o. 8 (399)   v. 12 (399)
b. 2 (397)   i. 21 (416)   p. 14 (399)   w. 6 (398)
c. 15 (400)   j. 3 (398)   q. 19 (415)   x. 23 (416)
d. 1 (397)   k. 22 (416)   r. 20 (415)   y. 13 (399)
e. 18 (414)   l. 11 (399)   s. 26 (420)   z. 17 (413)
f. 9 (399)   m. 10 (399)   t. 24 (418)
g. 25 (418)   n. 7 (399)   u. 4 (398)

Multiple Choice

1. a   6. a   11. b   16. a   21. a   26. c
2. d   7. c   12. b   17. b   22. d
3. c   8. b   13. a   18. c   23. c
4. b   9. d   14. c   19. d   24. d
5. b   10. c   15. a   20. d   25. a

Understanding Research

1. Type 1; Type 2; Stockholm; Gothenburg; yes; 23; 43; They were born out of wedlock and adopted away at a young age.

2. temperance; insurance; criminal; 70; genetic; environmental; two

3. Both genetic and environmental predispositions to alcoholism were necessary; genetic; three; were not; the measure of environmental factors was limited to social class, which is a crude measure

4. 14 in 10; 8 in 100; probability; the risk for a person with that characteristic is three times higher than the risk for a person without that characteristic

5. No; They can determine causality; They are expensive and time-consuming; High-risk research design; by a risk factor with a high risk ratio; manifestation of the genotype associated with a mental disorder in the absence of the full-blown disorder

Review of Concepts

1. true (388)
2. false (390)
3. control over drinking (390)
4. alcohol, nicotine, heroin, cocaine, amphetamines (390)
5. hallucinogens (391)
6. caffeine (391)
7. the liver (392)
8. false (392)
9. false (392)
10. true (392)
11. true (393)
12. false (393)
13. GABA (393)
14. breathing (393)
15. euphoria (394)
16. false (394)
17. antidepressant (395)
18. arousal (395)
19. medical device (396)
20. adolescence (396)
21. heroin (397)
22. true (397)
23. false (398)
24. depression (398)
25. false (399)
26. true (400)
27. false (401)
28. abstinence (403)
29. six (404)
30. antisocial personality disorder, mood disorder, and anxiety disorder (404)
31. false (405)
32. 20 percent (405)
33. 5 to 1 (406)
34. disapproval (406)
35. true (406)
36. 24 percent (406)
37. 7.5 percent (406)
38. false (407)
39. alcohol; marijuana (409)
40. false (409)
41. Asian (409)
42. true (410)
43. false (410)
44. men (410)
45. men; women (410)
46. serotonin (413)
47. stressful (414)
48. aggression; sexual (414)
49. positive (416)
50. false (418)
51. true (418)
52. false (419)
53. false (420)
54. temporary (420)
55. better (421)

CHAPTER 12 - SEXUAL AND GENDER IDENTITY DISORDERS

Chapter Outline

I. Overview
    A. Brief Historical Perspective
    B. Orgasm and Emotional Satisfaction

II. Sexual Dysfunctions
    A. Typical Symptoms and Associated Features
        1. Hypoactive Sexual Desire Disorder
        2. Sexual Aversion Disorder
        3. Male Erectile Disorder
        4. Female Sexual Arousal Disorder
        5. Premature Ejaculation
        6. Female Orgasmic Disorder
        7. Pain During Sex
    B. Epidemiology
        1. Sexual Behavior Across the Lifespan
    C. Etiology
        1. Biological Factors
        2. Social Factors
        3. Psychological Factors
    D. Treatment
        1. Psychological Procedures
        2. Biological Treatments

III. Paraphilias
    A. Typical Symptoms and Associated Features
    B. Classification of Paraphilias
        1. Fetishism
        2. Transvestic Fetishism
        3. Sexual Masochism
        4. Sexual Sadism
        5. Exhibitionism
        6. Voyeurism
        7. Frotteurism
        8. Pedophilia
        9. Rape and Sexual Assault
    C. Epidemiology
    D. Etiology
        1. Biological Factors
        2. Social Factors
        3. Psychological Factors
    E. Treatment
        1. Aversion Therapy
        2. Cognitive-Behavioral Treatment
        3. Hormones and Medication
        4. Legal Issues

IV. Gender Identity Disorders
    A. Typical Symptoms and Associated Features
    B. Epidemiology
    C. Etiology
    D. Treatment

Learning Objectives

After reviewing the material presented in this chapter, you should be able to:

1. Understand that a great deal of our thinking about sexual disorders is a result of cultural and religious values.

2. Know the role of Freud, Ellis, Kinsey, and Masters and Johnson in the study of human sexuality.

3. Distinguish hypoactive sexual desire from sexual aversion disorder.

4. Define male erectile disorder, female arousal disorder, premature ejaculation, dyspareunia, and female orgasmic disorder.

5. Know which sexual disorders are the most common.

6. List some of the biological and psychological causes of hypoactive sexual desire, disorder of sexual arousal, premature ejaculation, and inhibited orgasm.

7. Describe sensate focus as a treatment technique for sexual disorders.

8. Identify the major forms of paraphilias.

9. Describe some of the causes of paraphilias, including faulty lovemaps, imprinting, courtship disorders, and intimacy deficits.

10. Distinguish disorders of gender identity from disorders of sexual disorder (e.g., transvestic fetishism).

Key Terms - Matching #1

The following terms related to sexual and gender identity disorders are important to know. To test your knowledge, match the following terms with their definitions. Answers are listed at the end of the chapter.

a.	Sexual dysfunctions	k.	Hypoactive sexual desire disorder
b.	Paraphilias	l.	Sexual aversion disorder
c.	Gender identity	m.	Erectile dysfunction
d.	Gender identity disorder	n.	Impotence
e.	Excitement	o.	Female sexual arousal disorder

f.	Orgasm
g.	Resolution
h.	Refractory period
i.	Probability sampling
j.	Convenience sampling

p.	Male erectile disorder
q.	Inhibited sexual arousal
r.	Hypothetical construct
s.	Operational definition

1. _____ sudden intensely pleasurable release of sexual tension
2. _____ a strong and persistent identification with the opposite sex coupled with a sense of discomfort with one's anatomical sex
3. _____ a disorder in which a person has an extreme aversion to and avoidance of genital sexual contact with a partner
4. _____ persistent or recurrent erectile dysfunction
5. _____ sampling in which every member of a clearly specified population has a known probability of selection
6. _____ forms of sexual disorder that involve inhibitions of sexual desire or interference with the physiological responses leading to orgasm
7. _____ a procedure used to measure a theoretical construct
8. _____ sampling from a readily available group of participants
9. _____ forms of sexual disorder that involve sexual arousal in association with unusual objects and situations
10. _____ persistent or recurrent inability to attain or maintain an adequate lubrication-swelling response of sexual excitement even in the presence of sexual desire
11. _____ a person's sense of being male or female
12. _____ third stage of Masters and Johnson's human sexual response cycle where the body returns to its resting state
13. _____ disorder characterized by diminished desire for sexual activity and reduced frequency of sexual fantasies
14. _____ first stage of Masters and Johnson's human sexual response cycle involving physiological responses and subjective feelings
15. _____ inability to attain or maintain an adequate lubrication-swelling response of sexual excitement
16. _____ an older term for erectile dysfunction that is no longer used because of its negative implications
17. _____ events or states that reside within a person and are proposed to explain that person's behavior
18. _____ difficulty in obtaining an erection that is sufficient to accomplish intercourse or to satisfy self or partner during intercourse
19. _____ period of time after orgasm the person is unresponsive to further sexual stimulation

Key Terms - Matching #2

The following terms related to sexual and gender identity disorders are important to know. To test your knowledge, match the following terms with their definitions. Answers are listed at the end of the chapter.

1. Penile plethysmograph
2. Vaginal photometer
3. Construct validity
4. Premature ejaculation
5. Female orgasmic disorder
6. Genital anesthesia
7. Dyspareunia
8. Vaginismus
9. Anorgasmic
10. Performance anxiety
11. Sensate focus
12. Scheduling
13. Fetishism
14. Partialism
15. Transvestite
16. Transvestic fetishism
17. Drag queens
18. Transvestic fetishism with gender dysphoria
19. Sexual masochism
20. Sexual sadism

a. _____ the extent that a measure produces results consistent with the theoretical construct it is purported to assess
b. _____ a procedure for measuring male sexual arousal
c. _____ inhibited orgasm
d. _____ a person who dresses in the clothing of the other gender
e. _____ a paraphilia in which sexual arousal is associated with the actual act of being humiliated, beaten, bound, or otherwise made to suffer
f. _____ cross-dressing for sexual arousal with eventual persistent discomfort with gender identity
g. _____ involuntary muscular spasm preventing sexual intercourse
h. _____ setting aside specific time for sexual activity
i. _____ a treatment for sexual dysfunction that involves a series of simple exercises in which the couple spends time in a quiet, relaxed setting, learning to touch each other
j. _____ a paraphilia in which sexual arousal is associated with desires to inflict physical or psychological suffering or humiliation on another person
k. _____ absense of genital sensations during sexual activity
l. _____ a procedure for measuring female sexual arousal
m. _____ association of sexual arousal with nonliving objects
n. _____ persistent genital pain during or after intercourse
o. _____ gay men who engage in cross-dressing for reasons other than sexual arousal
p. _____ inability to achieve orgasm even though a person experiences uninhibited sexual arousal
q. _____ intense sexual attraction to specific, nonsexual body parts
r. _____ fear of failure
s. _____ cross-dressing for the purpose of sexual arousal
t. _____ a disorder in which a man is unable to delay ejaculation long enough to accomplish intercourse

Key Terms - Matching #3

The following terms related to sexual and gender identity disorders are important to know. To test your knowledge, match the following terms with their definitions. Answers are listed at the end of the chapter.

a. Exhibitionism
b. Voyeurism
c. Frotteurism
d. Pedophilia
e. Incest
f. Rape
g. Acquaintance rape
h. Sadistic rapists
i. Nonsadistic rapists
j. Vindictive rapists

k. Opportunistic rapists
l. Lovemap
m. Aversion therapy
n. Community notification laws
o. Sexual predator laws
p. Sex roles
q. Transsexualism (gender dysphoria)
r. Pseudohermaphroditism
s. Sex-reassignment surgery

1. _____ a paraphilia characterized by distress over, or acting on, urges to expose one's genitals to an unsuspecting stranger

2. _____ rape committed by someone known to the victim

3. _____ sexual activity between close blood relatives (or between stepparents and stepchildren)

4. _____ a category of rapist who is preoccupied with sadistic sexual fantasies whose actions are brutal and violent

5. _____ a paraphilia characterized by distress over or acting on urges involving sexual activity with a prepubescent child

6. _____ discomfort with one's anatomical sex

7. _____ characteristics, behaviors, and skills that are defined within a culture as being either masculine or feminine

8. _____ surgery in which the person's genitals are changed to match his or her gender identity

9. _____ a category of rapist whose actions are intended to degrade and humiliate the victim

10. _____ being genetically male but lacking a hormone responsible for shaping the penis and scrotum, resulting in ambiguous external genitalia

11. _____ a paraphilia characterized by recurrent, intense sexual urges involving touching and rubbing against a nonconsenting person

12. _____ a paraphilia in whic a person becomes sexually aroused by observing unsuspecting people while they are undressing or involved in sexual activity

13. _____ a category of rapist with distorted views of sexuality and women, feelings of inferiority, and poor social skills

14. _____ a treatment where the therapist repeatedly presents the stimulus that elicits inappropriate sexual arousal in association with an aversive stimulus

15. _____ acts involving nonconsensual sexual penetration obtained by physical force, threat of bodily harm, or when the victim is incapable of giving consent

16. _____ a mental picture representing a person's ideal sexual relationship

17. _____ laws designed to keep some criminals in custody indefinitely

18. _____ a category of rapist with impulsive, unplanned actions who seeks immediate gratification

19. _____ laws which require the distribution of information to the public regarding the presence of child molesters and sexually violent offenders when they are released from prison

Names You Should Know - Matching

The following people have played an important role in research and theory of sexual and gender identity disorders. To test your knowledge, match the following names with the descriptions of their contributions to the study of abnormal psychology. Answers are listed at the end of the chapter.

a. Richard von Krafft-Ebing
b. Alfred Kinsey
c. William Masters and Virginia Johnson
d. John Money

1. _____ proposed a system of sexual perversions
2. _____ proposed a model of the human sexual response cycle and developed treatments for sexual dysfunctions
3. _____ applied scientific methods to the study of sexuality
4. _____ studied the etiology of paraphilias; developed the concept of lovemaps

Review of Concepts - Fill in the Blank and True/False

This section will help focus your studying by testing whether you understand the concepts presented in the text. After you have read and reviewed the material, test your comprehension and memory by filling in the following blanks or circling the right answer. Answers are listed at the end of the chapter.

1. Male and female orgasm have different numbers of stages: **true**   **false**
2. Women typically have a longer refractory period than men: **true**   **false**
3. Women are capable of multiple orgasms while men are typically not: **true false**
4. Sexual problems are best seen as problems of the individual: **true**   **false**
5. Early scientific approaches to sexual behavior were strongly influenced by the idea that the exclusive goal of sexuality was _____.
6. Victorian society dictated that   **men** or **women**   were supposed to be asexual.
7. Kinsey rejected the distinction between _____ and _____ sexual behavior and saw differences as quantitative rather than qualitative.
8. Men report that their sexual partners have orgasms more often than women report having orgasms: **true**   **false**
9. The only factor important to sexual satisfaction, especially among women, is experiencing an orgasm: **true**   **false**
10. Failure to reach orgasm is not considered a disorder unless it is _____ and results in _____.
11. What are the two types of patterns of onset of sexual dysfunction?
    _____ or _____

12. What are the two types of patterns of context of occurrence?
    _____ or _____

13. Hypoactive Sexual Desire Disorder can be diagnosed by comparing a person's interest level with a chart of normal levels of sexual interest: **true**   **false**

14. People with low sexual desire often have _____ disorders.

15. What proportion of men have experienced problems achieving an erection at some point in their lives: **a quarter**   **a third**   **half**

16. There are high correlations between subjective and physiological measures of arousal in normal women: **true**   **false**

17. Almost all clinicians will identify the response of ejaculating before or upon _____ or after _____ thrusts as premature ejaculation.

18. Dyspareunia is more common in   **men** or **women**.

19. What is the most frequent form of male sexual dysfunction? _____

20. There is a cultural prejudice against sexual activity among older _____.

21. Older men achieve erections   **more quickly** or **more slowly**.

22. The subjective experience of the intensity of orgasm   **increases** or **decreases**   with age.

23. Frequency of sexual dysfunction among men typically   **increases** or **decreases**   with age.

24. Frequency of sexual dysfunction among women typically   **increases** or **decreases**   with age.

25. The influence of male sex hormones on sexual behavior is thought to be on sexual _____ rather than on sexual _____.

26. Men who smoke cigarettes are more likely to have problems with _____.

27. Antidepressants can include the side-effect of orgasm problems: **true false**

28. Women born in more recent decades are less likely to be orgasmic: **true false**

29. Changing the way people think about sex is a major aspect of sex therapy: **true**   **false**

30. Research shows that therapy for sexual dysfunction is ineffective: **true**   **false**

31. Paraphilias are only diagnosed if the person has _____ the urges or is _____ by them.

32. Most of the people in treatment for sexual disorders are people with paraphilias: **true**   **false**

33. The central feature of paraphilia is that sexual arousal is dependent on images that are detached from _____ relationships with another adult.

34. Paraphilias are similar to the _____.

35. Masochists tend to be disproportionately represented among poorer groups of people: **true**   **false**

36. Most exhibitionists are women: **true**   **false**

37. A voyeur is not aroused by watching people who know they are being observed: **true**   **false**

38. Most pedophiles are homosexual: **true**   **false**

39. Rape is not included as a paraphilia because it is not always motivated by _____.

40. Many rapists in one study had a history of paraphilias: **true**   **false**

41. Most people with a paraphilia exhibit other paraphilias as well: **true false**

42. About what percent of people with paraphilias are men?
60 percent   **75 percent**   **95 percent**

43. Damage to what part of the brain can lead to unusual sexual behaviors?
_____

44. _____ skills may play as important a role in paraphilias as sexual arousal.

45. A surprising number of people involved in masochism had what type of experience as children? _____

46. Most people in treatment for paraphilias are there _____.

47. Cognitive-behavioral treatment was found to be   **more** or **less** effective than aversion therapy in treating paraphilia.

48. Gender identity disorders are relatively   **rare** or **common**.

49. Pseudohermaphrodites typically make a quick and fairly easy transition from a childhood female to an adult male gender identity: **true**   **false**

50. Results of sex-reassignment surgery have mostly been negative: **true**   **false**

Multiple Choice Questions

The following multiple choice questions will test your comprehension of the material presented in the chapter. Answers are listed at the end of the chapter.

1) All of the following types of medication have been used to treat paraphilias EXCEPT:

a. antipsychotic medications
b. antidepressants

c. antianxiety medications
d. all of the above have been used

2) According to Freund and Blanchard, all of the following factors may increase the probability that a person might experiment with unusual types of sexual stimulation or employ maladaptive sexual behaviors EXCEPT:

a. ignorance and poor understanding of human sexuality
b. lack of diverse sexual experiences
c. lack of self-esteem
d. lack of confidence and ability in social interactions

3) With regard to the context of occurrence, which of the following terms indicates that the sexual dysfunction is not limited only to certain situations or partners:

a. situational
b. lifelong
c. acquired
d. generalized

4) Recent revisions of the DSM reflect the following important changes in society's attitudes toward sexual behavior EXCEPT:

a. growing acceptance of women of their own sexuality
b. tolerance for greater variety in human sexuality
c. society's complete acceptance of organized groups that represent specific forms of sexual orientation and expression
d. increased recognition that the main purpose of sexual behavior need not be reproduction

5) _____ disorders are more common among women while _____ disorders are more common among men.

a. Orgasm; arousal
b. Arousal; orgasm
c. Aversion; desire
d. Desire; aversion

6) Studies show that most women seeking treatment for hypoactive sexual desire report all of the following EXCEPT:

a. negative perceptions of their parents' attitudes regarding sexual behavior
b. a history of physical and sexual abuse
c. negative perceptions of their parents' demonstration of affection
d. feeling less close to their husbands and having fewer romantic feelings

7) This involves the use of nonliving objects for the purpose of sexual arousal.

a. frotteurism
b. pedophilia
c. fetishism
d. sexual masochism

8) Sex-reassignment surgery is the process whereby a person's genitals are changed to match his or her:

a. gender identity
b. sex role
c. sexual identity
d. gender role

9) According to your text, _____ may be the most common neurologically-based cause of impaired erectile responsiveness among men.

   a. depression
   b. coronary heart disease
   c. diabetes
   d. cancer

10) All of the following are treatment options for sexual dysfunctions EXCEPT:

   a. sensate focus
   b. cognitive restructuring
   c. communication training
   d. aversion therapy

11) _____ of the people who seek treatment for paraphilia disorders are men.

   a. 40 percent
   b. 60 percent
   c. 75 percent
   d. 95 percent

12) _____ and _____ have undoubtedly been the best-known sex therapists and researchers in the United States since the late 1960s.

   a. William Masters; Virginia Johnson
   b. Alfred Kinsey; Havelock Ellis
   c. Sigmund Freud; Richard von Krafft-Ebing
   d. Robert Spitzer; Helen Singer Kaplan

13) The sense of ourselves as being either male or female is known as:

   a. sexual identity
   b. gender dysphoria
   c. gender identity
   d. sex roles

14) Premature ejaculation may be the most frequent form of sexual dysfunction, affecting nearly 1 in every:

   a. 5 adult men
   b. 10 adult men
   c. 15 adult men
   d. 20 adult men

15) The treatment approach used for paraphilias in which the therapist repeatedly presents a stimulus eliciting inappropriate sexual arousal in association with an aversive stimulus is called:

   a. counterconditioning
   b. aversion therapy
   c. flooding
   d. systematic desensitization

16) Research on sexual behavior across the life span shows that:

   a. younger men have difficulty regaining an erection if it is lost before orgasm, while older men can only maintain erections for a short period of time
   b. older adults are not as interested in, or capable of, performing sexual behaviors as younger adults
   c. differences between younger and older people are mostly a matter of degree
   d. as women get older, the clitoris becomes more responsive

17) Men with this problem may report feeling subjectively aroused, but the vascular reflex mechanism fails, and sufficient blood is not pumped to the penis.

    a. sexual aversion disorder   c. male orgasmic disorder
    b. premature ejaculation   d. erectile dysfunction

18) In order to meet diagnostic criteria, all categories of sexual dysfunction require all of the following EXCEPT:

    a. the sexual dysfunction is associated with atypical stimuli and the person is preoccupied with, or consumed by, these activities
    b. the disturbance causes marked distress or interpersonal difficulty
    c. the sexual dysfunction is not better accounted for by another Axis I disorder (such as major depression)
    d. the sexual dysfunction is not due to direct physiological effects of a substance or a general medical condition

19) Perhaps as many as _____ of females seeking treatment for hypoactive sexual desire report other forms of sexual dysfunction.

    a. 25 percent   c. 60 percent
    b. 40 percent   d. 75 percent

20) According to your text, sexual desire remains a controversial topic because:

    a. it is so difficult to define
    b. there is very little empirical research on sexual desire
    c. it is a different construct for men than it is for women
    d. all of the above

21) The unresponsiveness of men to further engage in sexual stimulation for a period of time after reaching orgasm is called:

    a. sensation of suspension   c. sexual aversion
    b. pulsation   d. refractory period

22) Premature ejaculation might be present if a man is unable to delay ejaculation until his partner reaches orgasm at least _____ of the time.

    a. 25 percent   c. 75 percent
    b. 50 percent   d. 100 percent

23) Studies have shown that all of the following are important factors contributing to failure to reach orgasm among anorgasmic women EXCEPT:

    a. failure to engage in effective behaviors during foreplay
    b. negative attitudes toward masturbation
    c. feelings of guilt about sex
    d. failure to communicate effectively with their partner about sexual activities involving direct stimulation of the clitoris

24) All of the following refer to a sense of discomfort with one's anatomical sex EXCEPT:

a. gender identity disorder
b. transvestic fetishism
c. gender dysphoria
d. transsexualism

25) Research suggests that _____ of men over age 75 report experiencing erectile dysfunction.

a. 30 percent
b. 40 percent
c. 50 percent
d. 60 percent

26) This involves the act of observing an unsuspecting person who is naked, in the process of disrobing, or engaging in sexual activity:

a. sexual sadism
b. voyeurism
c. exhibitionism
d. fetishism

27) Which of the following characterizes an individual who is genetically male, but is unable to produce a hormone that is responsible for shaping the penis and scrotum in the fetus, and is therefore born with external genitalia that are ambiguous in appearance?

a. transsexualism
b. secondary sexual characteristic disorder
c. transvestic fetishism
d. pseudohermaphroditism

Understanding Research - Fill in the Blank

Sexual Activity in the General Population: The text presents a detailed description of a study by Michael, Laumann, and Gagnon in the Research Close-Up on pp. 430-431. Finding the answers to these questions will help you get a good understanding of this study and why it is important. It is not necessary to memorize the answers; the process of finding them in the textbook will help you learn the material you need to know.

1. This study was the first large-scale followup to the _____ reports. How many men and women participated? _____ What ages were the subjects? _____ to _____. What was the most important element of the research design? The study used _____. Most of the existing research on normal sexual activities used _____. During the year of the survey, _____ percent of the participants had more than one sexual partner, and _____ percent had no partner. What percent of people born between 1963 and 1974 have had premarital sex? _____ percent of men and _____ percent of women.

2. People without _____ affiliation felt less guilty about masturbating. Which was more prevalent, masturbation or anal sex? _____ Younger, better-educated people were more likely to use _____. When were people most reluctant to use condoms? _____

Hypothetical Constructs and Construct Validity: The text discusses these research issues in the Research Methods section on pp. 435-436. Finding the answers to these questions will help you get a good understanding of these issues.

3. Why is sexual arousal a hypothetical construct? _____
_____

Why is an erect penis not the same as sexual arousal? _____
_____

Sexual arousal is _____ than the sum of feelings and responses that can be measured directly.

4. The penile plethysmograph records changes in penile _____.
The vaginal photometer is probably most useful in measuring _____
to _____ levels of sexual arousal. These research devices are merely reflections of the construct of sexual arousal that has many _____.

Brief Essay

As a final exercise, write out answers to the following brief essay questions. Then compare your answers with the material presented in the text.

After you have answered these questions, review the "critical thinking" questions that are presented at the end of the text chapter. Answering these questions will help you integrate important issues and themes that have been featured throughout the chapter.

1. Compare and contrast the treatment of paraphilias with the treatment of sexual dysfunction. Choose two types of paraphilias and two types of sexual dysfunctions and discuss which type of treatment would be most effective for each of them.

2. Discuss David Barlow's series of studies comparing sexually dysfunctional men with control subjects in laboratory settings. What were his findings? What are some of the possible limitations to these studies? What are the applications of his findings?

3. Compare and contrast the different proposals regarding the etiology of paraphilias as presented in your text. Which proposal(s) do you believe best explains the etiology of paraphilias? Why?

ANSWER KEY

Answers to the exercises are listed below; page numbers where the information is referenced in the textbook are given in parentheses.

Key Terms - Matching #1

1. f (426)	8. j (430)
2. d (426)	9. b (426)
3. l (434)	10. o (435)
4. p (435)	11. c (426)
5. i (430)	12. g (427)
6. a (426)	13. k (432)
7. s (436)	14. e (426)

15. q (435)	
16. n (435)	
17. r (435)	
18. m (435)	
19. h (427)	

Names You Should Know

1. a (428)
2. c (426)
3. b (429)
4. d (452)

Key Terms - Matching #2

a. 3 (436)	k. 6 (437)
b. 1 (436)	l. 2 (436)
c. 9 (440)	m. 13 (444)
d. 15 (444)	n. 7 (437)
e. 19 (445)	o. 17 (445)
f. 18 (445)	p. 5 (437)
g. 8 (437)	q. 14 (444)
h. 12 (441)	r. 10 (440)
i. 11 (441)	s. 16 (444)
j. 20 (446)	t. 4 (436)

Key Terms - Matching #3

1. a (446)	11. c (446)
2. g (448)	12. b (446)
3. e (447)	13. i (449)
4. h (449)	14. m (453)
5. d (447)	15. f (447)
6. q (454)	16. l (452)
7. p (454)	17. o (454)
8. s (456)	18. k (449)
9. j (449)	19. n (454)
10. r (455)	

Multiple Choice

1. a	6. b	11. d	16. c	21. d	26. b
2. b	7. c	12. a	17. d	22. b	27. d
3. d	8. a	13. c	18. a	23. a	
4. c	9. c	14. a	19. d	24. b	
5. a	10. d	15. b	20. a	25. c	

Review of Concepts

1. true (427)
2. false (427)
3. true (427)
4. false (428)
5. reproduction (428)
6. women (428)
7. normal and abnormal (429)
8. true (429)
9. false (430)
10. persistent; distress (432)
11. lifelong; acquired (432)
12. generalized; situational (432)
13. false (432)
14. mood (433)
15. half (435)
16. false (435)
17. insertion; 3-4 (436)
18. women (437)
19. premature ejaculation (438)
20. women (438)
21. more slowly (438)
22. decreases (439)
23. increases (439)
24. decreases (439)
25. appetite; performance (439)
26. erection (439)
27. true (440)
28. false (440)
29. true (441)
30. false (442)
31. acted on; distressed (443)
32. false (443)
33. loving (443)
34. addictions (443)
35. false (445)
36. false (446)
37. true (446)
38. false (447)
39. sexual arousal (448)
40. true (448)
41. true (448)
42. 95 percent (448)
43. temporal lobe (451)
44. Interpersonal (451)
45. traumatic disease and painful medical procedures (452)
46. involuntarily (452)
47. more (453)
48. rare (455)
49. true (455)
50. false (456)

Understanding Research

1. Kinsey; 3,500; 18 to 59; probability sampling; convenience sampling; 16 percent; 11 percent; 84 percent; 80 percent

2. religious; masturbation; condoms; in new sexual relationships

3. because it cannot be observed directly; it is not always accompanied by subjective arousal; more

4. tumescence; moderate; low; dimensions

CHAPTER 13 - SCHIZOPHRENIC DISORDERS

Chapter Outline

I. Overview

II. Typical Symptoms and Associated Features
    A. Hallucinations
    B. Delusional Beliefs
    C. Disorganized Speech
    D. Motor Disturbances
    E. Affective and Emotional Disturbances
    F. Social Withdrawal and Avolition

III. Classification
    A. Brief Historical Perspective
    B. DSM-IV
    C. Subtypes
        1. DSM-IV Subcategories
        2. Evaluation of Traditional Subtypes
    D. Related Disorders
    E. Course and Outcome

IV. Epidemiology
    A. Gender Differences
    B. Cross-Cultural Comparisons

V. Etiological Considerations and Research
    A. Biological Factors
        1. Genetics
            a. Family Studies
            b. Twin Studies
            c. Adoption Studies
            d. The Spectrum of Schizophrenic Disorders
            e. Linkage Studies
        2. Pregnancy and Birth Complications
        3. Viral Infections
        4. Neuropathology
            a. Structural Brain Imaging
            b. Functional Brain Imaging
            c. General Conclusions
        5. Neurochemistry
            a. The Dopamine Hypothesis of Schizophrenia
            b. Current Neurochemical Models
    B. Social Factors
        1. Social Class
    C. Psychological Factors
        1. Family Interaction
        2. Expressed Emotion

D. Integrated Systems and Multiple Pathways
E. The Search for Markers of Vulnerability
    1. Attention and Cognition
    2. Eye-Tracking Dysfunction

VI. Treatment
  A. Neuroleptic Medication
    1. Side Effects
    2. Maintenance Medication
    3. Atypical Antipsychotics
  B. Psychosocial Treatment
    1. Family-Oriented Aftercare
    2. Social Skills Training
    3. Institutional Programs

Learning Objectives

After reviewing the material presented in this chapter, you should be able to:

1. Distinguish between positive symptoms, negative symptoms, and disorganization.

2. Distinguish the prodromal, active, and residual phases of schizophrenia.

3. Define and describe hallucinations, delusional beliefs, and disorganized speech.

4. Provide examples of typical motor disturbances, affective and emotional disturbances, and avolition.

5. Know the contributions of Kraepelin, Bleuler, and Schneider in defining schizophrenia.

6. Distinguish disorganized, catatonic, paranoid, undifferentiated, and residual types of schizophrenia using DSM IV criteria.

7. Describe the following related disorders: schizoaffective disorders, delusional disorder, brief psychotic disorders.

8. Know the basic epidemiological statistics for incidence and prevalence of the disorder, as well as gender differences in age of onset.

9. Understand the genetic evidence for schizophrenia, which leads to a diathesis-stress model of etiology.

10. Describe some of the research that has discovered structural brain abnormalities for schizophrenics.

11. Explain the dopamine hypothesis and current beliefs about the role of dopamine in schizophrenia.

12. Identify some social and psychological factors that may contribute to the development and/or maintenance of schizophrenia.

13. Understand the significance of research that has identified attentional, cognitive, and eye-tracking dysfunctions in schizophrenics and their biological relatives.

14. Describe the effectiveness of neuroleptic medication and atypical antipsychotic medications and the relevant side effects that are involved in such treatments.

15. Provide a description of family-oriented aftercare programs, social skills training, and institutional programs in which token economy systems may be used.

Key Terms - Matching #1

The following terms related to schizophrenia are important to know. To test your knowledge, match the following terms with their definitions. Answers are listed at the end of the chapter.

a.	Negative symptoms	n.	Perseveration
b.	Positive symptoms	o.	Alogia
c.	Disorganization	p.	Poverty of speech
d.	Schizophreniform disorder	q.	Thought blocking
e.	Active phase	r.	Catatonia
f.	Prodromal phase	s.	Delusions
g.	Residual phase	t.	Blunted affect
h.	Hallucinations	u.	Anhedonia
i.	Disorganized speech	v.	Inappropriate affect
j.	Stuporous state	w.	Avolition
k.	Incoherent	x.	Dementia praecox
l.	Loose associations	y.	Catatonic type
m.	Tangentiality	z.	Disorganized type

1. _____ the patient's train of speech is interrupted before a thought is completed
2. _____ when hallucinations, delusions, and disorganized speech are evident
3. _____ after positive symptoms; continued deterioration of role functioning
4. _____ reflect loss of normal functions
5. _____ immobility and marked muscular rigidity, or excitement and overactivity
6. _____ extremely disorganized speech which conveys little meaning
7. _____ an early grouping of several types of psychosis now seen as schizophrenia
8. _____ reflect a distortion of normal functions, like psychosis
9. _____ inability to experience pleasure

10. ____ remarkable reductions in the amount of speech
11. ____ schizophrenia characterized by disorganized speech, disorganized behavior, and flat or inappropriate affect
12. ____ shifting topics too abruptly
13. ____ schizophrenia characterized by symptoms of motor immobility or excessive and purposeless motor activity
14. ____ psychotic symptoms lasting between 1 and 6 months
15. ____ idiosyncratic beliefs that are rigidly held despite their preposterous nature
16. ____ indecisiveness, ambivalence, and loss of willpower
17. ____ generally reduced responsiveness
18. ____ persistently repeating the same word or phrase over and over again
19. ____ prior to positive symptoms, marked by deterioration in role functioning
20. ____ a flattening or restriction of a person's nonverbal display of emotion
21. ____ incongruity and lack of adaptability in emotional expression
22. ____ severe disruptions of verbal communication involving the form of speech
23. ____ replying to a question with an irrelevant response
24. ____ impoverished thinking marked by nonfluent or barren speech
25. ____ verbal communication problems and bizarre behavior
26. ____ sensory experiences not caused by actual external stimuli

Key Terms - Matching #2

The following terms related to schizophrenia are important to know. To test your knowledge, match the following terms with their definitions. Answers are listed at the end of the chapter.

1. Paranoid type
2. Undifferentiated type
3. Residual type
4. Schizoaffective disorder
5. Delusional disorder
6. Brief psychotic disorder
7. Lifetime morbid risk
8. Lateral ventricles
9. Magnetic resonance imaging
10. Hemispheric asymmetry
11. Regional cerebral blood flow
12. Hypofrontality
13. Positron emission tomography

14. Dopamine hypothesis
15. Social causation hypothesis
16. Social selection hypothesis
17. Communication deviance
18. Expressed emotion
19. Case control design
20. Schizotaxia
21. Threshold model
22. Vulnerability marker
23. Neuroleptic drugs
24. Extrapyramidal symptoms
25. Tardive dyskinesia
26. Atypical antipsychotics

a. ____ harmful events associated with membership in lowest social classes play a causal role in the development of schizophrenia
b. ____ subtle neurological defect in people predisposed to schizophrenia
c. ____ an imaging technique that allows identification of specific, small brain structures
d. ____ comparisons between groups of people with a disorder and groups of people who do not have the disorder

e. _____ side effects including muscular rigidity, tremors, restless agitation, peculiar involuntary postures, and motor inertia

f. _____ the cavities on each side of the brain that are filled with cerebrospinal fluid

g. _____ an imaging technique that reflects changes in brain activity as the person performs various tasks

h. _____ focuses on the function of specific dopamine pathways in the limbic area of the brain as having a role in the etiology of schizophrenia

i. _____ schizophrenia characterized by psychotic symptoms but that does not fit any one subtype

j. _____ antipsychotic medications that induce side effects that resemble the motor symptoms of Parkinson's disease

k. _____ a decrease in frontal lobe activity

l. _____ schizophrenia characterized by systematic delusions with persecutory or grandiose content

m. _____ a specific measure that might be useful in identifying people who are vulnerable to a disorder

n. _____ an episode of symptoms of both schizophrenia and a mood disorder

o. _____ people with schizophrenia experience downward social mobility

p. _____ peculiar statements, difficulty in completing answers, and other types of disruptive verbal behavior in parents of schizophrenics

q. _____ does not meet the criteria of schizophrenia but are preoccupied for at least one month with delusions that are not bizarre

r. _____ the proportion of a specific population that wll be affected by a disorder at some point during their lives

s. _____ negative or intrusive attitudes displayed by relatives of schizophrenics

t. _____ a syndrome caused by prolonged treatment with neuroleptic drugs consisting of involuntary movements of the mouth and face as well as spasmodic movements of the limbs and trunk of the body

u. _____ people who exhibit psychotic symptoms for at least a day but less than a month

v. _____ new forms of antipsychotic medication that do not produce extra-pyramidal symptoms or tardive dyskinesia

w. _____ a structure being larger in one hemisphere of the brain than the other

x. _____ liability to have a disorder lies along a continuum, but the probability that certain symptoms will be present changes dramatically as the person crosses a certain point on the continuum

y. _____ an imaging technique that evaluates blood flow patterns in the brain when a person is at rest or performing a specific task

z. _____ schizophrenia in partial remission, with no active phase symptoms

Names You Should Know - Matching

The following people have played an important role in research and theory of schizophrenic disorders. To test your knowledge, match the following names with the descriptions of their contributions to the study of abnormal psychology. Answers are listed at the end of the chapter.

a. Emil Kraeplin
b. Eugen Bleuler
c. Lyman Wynne & Margaret Singer
d. Kurt Schneider
e. Irving Gottesman
f. Leonard Heston
g. Paul Meehl

1. ____ one of the world's leading experts on genetic factors and schizophrenia; described hypothetical pathways showing interactions between genetic and environmental factors
2. ____ grouped together several psychotic disorders into the category of dementia praecox, an early term for schizophrenia
3. ____ proposed a theory of schizophrenia involving schizotaxia
4. ____ conducted the first adoption study of schizophrenia
5. ____ developed a diagnostic system for schizophrenia which emphasized first-rank symptoms
6. ____ coined the term schizophrenia, which means splitting of mental associations
7. ____ explored communication deviance among parents of schizophrenics

Review of Concepts - Fill in the Blank and True/False

This section will help focus your studying by testing whether you understand the concepts presented in the text. After you have read and reviewed the material, test your comprehension and memory by filling in the following blanks or circling the right answer. Answers are listed at the end of the chapter.

1. What are the three categories of symptoms of schizophrenia? _____
   _____ and _____
2. What is the period of risk for the development of a first episode of schizophrenia?
   _____ years old to _____ years old
3. After the onset of schizophrenia, most people return to their previous levels of
   functioning: **true**   **false**
4. What is the most common type of hallucination? _____
5. Delusions are typically shared by the patient's family: **true**   **false**
6. Disorganized speech breaks all the rules of grammar: **true**   **false**
7. During a stuporous state, schizophrenic patients remain aware of what is
   happening around them: **true**   **false**
8. Many people with schizophrenia evidence social withdrawal: **true**   **false**
9. Schizophrenia is a sort of multiple personality disorder: **true**   **false**
10. Schizophrenia follows a predictable course among most patients: **true**   **false**
11. What is the lifetime morbid risk of schizophrenia?   _____ percent
12. Women typically have an earlier age of onset than men: **true**   **false**
13. Men typically have more negative symptoms than women: **true**   **false**

14. Women typically respond better to treatment than men: **true   false**

15. Schizophrenia is very rare in nonindustrialized countries: **true   false**

16. People with schizophrenia have a better outcome if they live in a developing country rather than a developed country: **true   false**

17. What is the lifetime risk of developing schizophrenia if your identical twin has the disorder? _____ percent

18. What is the lifetime risk of developing schizophrenia if your fraternal twin has the disorder? _____ percent

19. Genetic factors do not play a role in the etiology of schizophrenia: **true   false**

20. Adoption studies indicate that environmental factors cause schizophrenia:
    true   false

21. The data suggest that multiple genes are responsible for vulnerability to schizophrenia: **true   false**

22. People with schizophrenia are more likely to have experienced difficulties during and prior to their birth: **true   false**

23. Severe _____ of the mother during the early part of pregnancy increases the child's later risk for schizophrenia.

24. People with schizophrenia were more likely to be born during what season?

    _____

25. People with schizophrenia have been found to have _____ lateral ventricles in the brain.

26. People with schizophrenia are more likely to show a decrease in the size of what brain structure? _____

27. Patients with schizophrenia show a _____ in frontal lobe activity.

28. One MZ twin pair discordant for schizophrenia involved one brother who was a successful businessman and another who was severely impaired with schizophrenia. Whose lateral ventricles were five times larger?

    _____

29. The original dopamine hypothesis was too _____.

30. What other neurotransmitter besides dopamine may be involved in schizo-phrenia? _____

31. Which hypothesis has received support in the research literature, the social causation hypothesis or the social selection hypothesis? _____

32. Parents of schizophrenic children who show communication deviance in their conversations with their ill children   **do** or **do not**   show CD in their conversations with their well children.

33. Men with schizophrenia were   **more** or **less**   likely to return to the hospital if they were discharged to live with their wives or parents rather than their siblings or strangers.

34. What seems to be the important component of expressed emotion? _____

35. Lots of contact with relatives high on EE   **helps** or **hurts**   patients with schizophrenia; and lots of contact with relatives low on EE   **helps** or **hurts**   patients with schizophrenia.

36. High EE is   **more** or **less**   common in Western countries.

37. Schizophrenic patients are   **more** or **less**   accurate than normal people in the Continuous Performance Task.

38. Relatives of schizophrenic patients are   **more** or **less**   accurate than normal people in the Continuous Performance Task.

39. _____ - tracking performance may be associated with a predisposition to schizophrenia.

40. Neuroleptic medications take _____ to have an effect.

41. All people with schizophrenia respond to neuroleptic medications given in the correct dose: **true**   **false**

42. What percent of patients develop tardive dyskinesia after long-term treatment with neuroleptic drugs? _____ percent

43. Continued maintenance on neuroleptic drugs after recovery significantly reduces relapse: **true**   **false**

44. Why is Clozaril not used with all schizophrenic patients? _____
_____

45. Patients who do not respond to neuroleptic medication do not improve with any type of treatment: **true**   **false**

Multiple Choice Questions

The following multiple choice questions will test your comprehension of the material presented in the chapter. Answers are listed at the end of the chapter.

1) Research on the relationship between expressed emotion (EE) and schizophrenia supports which of the following?

   a. the presence of expressed emotion is only associated with the onset of an individual's initial episode of schizophrenia
   b. among the various types of comments that contribute to a high EE rating, criticism is typically most associated with the likelihood of relapse
   c. the influence of expressed emotions is unique to schizophrenia
   d. all of the above

2) The trend in the DSM diagnosis of schizophrenia over time has been which of the following?

    a. include more affective symptoms
    b. omit subtyping of the disorder
    c. move from a broader to narrower definition of schizophrenia
    d. move from a more restrictive to less restrictive duration criterion

3) Which of the following would NOT be considered a positive symptom of schizophrenia?

    a. hallucinations
    b. blunted affect
    c. delusions
    d. disorganized speech

4) The distribution of schizophrenia within families is probably best explained by which of the following genetic models?

    a. polygenic
    b. single dominant gene
    c. single recessive gene
    d. linked genes

5) A difference between schizophrenia and delusional disorder is that:

    a. patients with schizophrenia display less impairment in their daily functioning than patients with delusional disorder
    b. patients with delusional disorder display more negative symptoms during the active phase of their illness
    c. the behavior of patients with schizophrenia is considerably less bizarre
    d. patients with delusional disorder are preoccupied with delusions that are not necessarily considered bizarre

6) In the search to identify people who are vulnerable to schizophrenia, several potential vulnerability markers have been considered. Which of the following would NOT be considered a good criterion for a vulnerability marker?

    a. the marker should be able to distinguish between people who are already schizophrenic and people who are not
    b. the marker should be a characteristic which is stable over time
    c. the marker should be able to identify more people who are relatives of schizophrenics than people in the general population
    d. the marker should be able to predict the likelihood of relapse for people who have already experienced their first episode of schizophrenia

7) Individuals who exhibit psychotic symptoms for no more than a month and that cannot be attributed to other disorders such as substance abuse or mood disorder usually receive the diagnosis of:

    a. delusional disorder
    b. schizophreniform disorder
    c. brief psychotic disorder
    d. schizoaffective disorder

8) Tangentiality is an example of which type of disturbance?

    a. motor disturbance
    b. affective disturbance
    c. disorganized speech
    d. delusional belief

9) Which of the following statements is TRUE regarding the use of neuroleptic medication?

    a. beneficial effects are noticed within 24 hours after beginning the medication
    b. they appear to be particularly effective for relief of the positive symptoms associated with schizophrenia
    c. almost all schizophrenic patients are considered to be complete responders to this type of medication
    d. schizophrenic patients with the most severe symptoms respond best to them

10) Research on schizophrenic twins and adopted-away offspring of schizophrenics suggests which of the following?

    a. vulnerability to schizophrenia is consistently manifested by the same symptoms of this disorder across relatives
    b. vulnerability to schizophrenia is expressed through a variety of different symptom patterns, including depressive and anxiety syndromes
    c. vulnerability to schizophrenia is consistently manifested by the same symptoms of this disorder only when male relatives are affected
    d. vulnerability to schizophrenia is sometimes manifested by schizophrenialike personality traits and non-schizophrenic psychotic disorders

11) Which of the following is NOT a possible explanation for the relationship between the presence of familial communication problems and schizophrenia?

    a. parental communication problems may cause the child's disorder
    b. the child's adjustment problems may cause the parents' problems
    c. both the child's disorder and the parent communication problems reflect a common genetic influence
    d. all of the above are possible explanations for the presence of this relationship

12) Which of the following reflects a change in the DSM-IV definition of schizophrenia:

    a. negative symptoms assume a more prominent role
    b. positive symptoms assume a more prominent role
    c. the person must display active symptoms of the illness for at least one year
    d. a decline in the person's functioning is no longer required

13) A restriction of an individual's nonverbal display of his or her emotional responses is referred to as:

    a. blunted affect
    b. affective loosening
    c. anhedonia
    d. inappropriate affect

14) An interesting and consistent result across numerous CT scan studies is that some people with schizophrenia have:

a. an enlarged hypothalamus
b. enlarged lateral ventricles

c. enlarged temporal lobes
d. less cerebrospinal fluid

15) Studies investigating the relationship between social class and schizophrenia support that risk for the disorder:

a. is associated with adverse social and economic circumstances
b. is not associated by circumstances most likely to be present in the lives of people who are economically disadvantaged
c. is associated with the unique types of circumstances most frequently affiliated with high social class
d. is most associated with recent immigration to a country

16) Which statement about the course of schizophrenia is TRUE?

a. a significant amount of individuals experience their first episode between 35-50 years of age
b. the onset of the disorder typically occurs during adolescence or early adulthood
c. the active phase of illness is always the longest of the three phases
d. the premorbid phase of illness usually lasts no longer than six months

17) Inconsistencies associated with the dopamine model of schizophrenia include which of the following?

a. dopamine blockage begins immediately when medication is administered but the drugs often take several days to become effective
b. some patients do not respond positively to drugs that block dopamine receptors
c. studies investigating the byproducts of dopamine in cerebrospinal fluid are inconsisent and inconclusive
d. all of the above

18) Which of the following is NOT included in the DSM-IV as a subtype of schizophrenia?

a. paranoid
b. residual

c. undifferentiated
d. negative

19) Joshua's behavior has been observed on the hospital ward for several hours. He has been sitting perfectly still in one position. Furthermore, he has been completely mute (has not spoken a single word) since admission. Which subtype of schizophrenia best represents Joshua's behavior?

a. disorganized
b. paranoid

c. catatonic
d. undifferentiated

20) The Danish high-risk for schizophrenia project has supported which of the following hypotheses?

   a. families with individuals who develop the positive symptoms of the disorder appear to be at higher genetic risk
   b. children who experience head injuries before age five appear to be at greater risk for schizophrenia
   c. neurodevelopmental problems in schizophrenia are antecedents rather than consequences of the disorder
   d. problems in delivery at birth do not appear to be associated with vulnerability to schizophrenia

21) A criticism of twin studies and their persuasive evidence for the role of genetic factors in schizophrenia is that:

   a. DZ and MZ twin concordance rates are approximately equal, suggesting that genetic factors are less important than environmental factors
   b. MZ twins, because of their physical similarity, are probably treated more similarly by their parents than even DZ twins, which confounds environmental with genetic factors
   c. the studies determining concordance rates are flawed because they do not take into account the birth order of the MZ twins
   d. the concordance rates for MZ twins for schizophrenia has fluctuated dramatically across studies

22) The potentially exciting part of eye-tracking dysfunction and the possibility of this characteristic being a vulnerability marker for schizophrenia is that:

   a. eye-tracking dysfunction appears to be influenced by genetic factors and is apparently a stable trait
   b. eye-tracking dysfunction appears to be present only in patients with schizophrenia
   c. approximately 90 percent of the first-degree relatives of schizophrenic individuals show this characteristic
   d. the eye-tracking dysfunction only appears during episodes of schizophrenia

23) Research suggests that the outcome of schizophrenia may be best described by which of the following statements?

   a. 50 percent of the individuals continue to deteriorate after their first episode, 10 percent completely recover, and 40 percent experience intermittent episodes
   b. 30 percent of the individuals recover fairly well after their initial episode, 30 percent continue to deteriorate, and 40 percent continue to experience intermittent episodes
   c. approximately 60 percent of the individuals recover fairly well after their initial episode, while 40 percent continue to deteriorate
   d. approximately 60 percent of the individuals continue to deteriorate after their initial episode, while 40 percent continue to experience intermittent episodes

24) When Samuel grins as he talks about the loss of his father in a traumatic accident, he is displaying:

a. disorganized affect
b. avolition
c. catatonia
d. inappropriate affect

25) The theory that harmful events associated with being a member of the lowest social class (e.g., poor nutrition, social isolation) is called:

a. the social class hypothesis
b. the social causation hypothesis
c. the social impairment hypothesis
d. the social selection hypothesis

26) The usefulness of subtyping schizophrenia has been criticized because:

a. some individuals do not fit the traditional subtype descriptions
b. some individuals display the symptoms of more than one subtype simultaneously
c. the symptoms of some individuals change from one episode to the next, reflecting subtype instability
d. all of the above

27) The average concordance rate for monozygotic twins for schizophrenia is:

a. 22 percent
b. 36 percent
c. 48 percent
d. 72 percent

28) Perhaps the most unpleasant side effect of neuroleptics is:

a. the fact that the drugs must be taken for two to four months before the patient experiences relief from symptoms
b. potentially toxic reactions to the drugs if the patient's diet is not carefully monitored
c. the presence of extrapyramidal symptoms
d. acute gastrointestinal symptoms (e.g., nausea, vomiting) during the first few weeks of use

29) Research on gender differences in schizophrenia supports that:

a. men experience their first episode of schizophrenia about five years later than women
b. women typically display better premorbid social competence prior to their first episode of schizophrenia
c. men typically display a less chronic course compared to women
d. women display more negative symptoms

30) Bleuler's definition of schizophrenia emphasized which of the following?

    a. signs and symptoms of the disorder
    b. course and outcome
    c. genetic vulnerability markers
    d. impairment in social roles

Understanding Research - Fill in the Blank

The Danish High-Risk Project: The text presents a detailed description of a study by Mednick and Schulsinger in the Research Close-Up on p. 479. Finding the answers to these questions will help you get a good understanding of this study and why it is important. It is not necessary to memorize the answers; the process of finding them in the textbook will help you learn the material you need to know.

1. What was the high-risk group used in this study? _____
_____ What percent of the sample was expected to develop schizophrenia? _____ percent How many subjects were there all together? _____ The children in the comparison group came from families that had been free of mental illness for at least _____ generations. Data came from _____ records at the time of birth, structured _____ interviews, and _____ scans.

2. How many of the high-risk offspring have developed schizophrenia? _____ What percent of the high-risk offspring have developed schizotypal personality disorder? _____ percent Rates of mood disorders were _____ in the high-risk and the control groups. Delivery complications and enlarged ventricles were _____ in the high-risk but not the low-risk group. The members of the high-risk group who did develop schizophrenia had _____ pregnancy and birth complications that those who did not develop the disorder.

Comparison Groups in Psychopathology Research: The text discusses this research issue in the Research Methods section on pp. 487-488. Finding the answers to these questions will help you get a good understanding of these issues.

3. A case control design depends on comparisons between _____ and _____. How much finding a difference between these groups indicates that difference is causally related to the disorder depends on whether the _____ was appropriate. What are two types of comparison groups? _____ and _____ _____.

4. Lack of specificity of a particular variable to a particular disorder may suggest that the variable is not a cause of the disorder but a _____ of being mentally ill or being treated in a psychiatric hospital. Expressed emotion predicts relapse among schizophrenic patients and also among _____ _____. However, expressed emotion is clearly still an _____ variable.

Brief Essay

As a final exercise, write out answers to the following brief essay questions. Then compare your answers with the material presented in the text.

After you have answered these questions, review the "critical thinking" questions that are presented at the end of the text chapter. Answering these questions will help you integrate important issues and themes that have been featured throughout the chapter.

1. Pretend that you are on the committee that will be responsible for developing the definition for schizophrenia (i.e., the diagnostic criteria) for DSM-V. Signs and symptoms, duration of episodes, degree of impairment, familial, biological, genetic data, etc.-- what would you consider to be the most appropriate criteria to be included in your definition and why?

2. Explain what is meant by the diathesis-stress model of schizophrenia. Which factors reviewed in your text would represent the diathesis? Which factors would represent stress?

3. Review the questions and considerations that an investigator must address as she designs a research project in psychopathology, comparing patients with a certain diagnosis with a comparison group. What are the issues involved in the selection of a meaningful comparison group?

4. Briefly describe and compare the three forms of psychosocial treatment reviewed in your textbook that have been shown to be effective for schizophrenia. What are their advantages and disadvantages as treatment programs?

ANSWER KEY

Answers to the exercises are listed below; page numbers where the information is referenced in the textbook are given in parentheses.

Key Terms - Matching #1

1. q (466)	10. p (466)	19. f (461)	
2. e (461)	11. z (471)	20. t (466)	
3. g (462)	12. l (465)	21. v (466)	
4. a (460)	13. y (471)	22. i (464)	
5. r (466)	14. d (460)	23. m (465)	
6. k (465)	15. s (463)	24. o (466)	
7. x (467)	16. w (467)	25. c (460)	
8. b (460)	17. j (466)	26. h (463)	
9. u (466)	18. n (465)		

Names You Should Know

1. e (475, 489)
2. a (467)
3. g (489)
4. f (476-7)
5. d (468)
6. b (467)
7. c (484)

Key Terms - Matching #2

a. 15 (483)	h. 14 (482)	o. 16 (483)	v. 26 (495)
b. 20 (489)	i. 2 (471)	p. 17 (484)	w. 10 (480)
c. 9 (480)	j. 23 (493)	q. 5 (472)	x. 21 (489)
d. 19 (487)	k. 12 (480)	r. 7 (473)	y. 11 (480)
e. 24 (493)	l. 1 (471)	s. 18 (486)	z. 3 (471)
f. 8 (478)	m. 22 (490)	t. 25 (494)	
g. 13 (480)	n. 4 (472)	u. 6 (472)	

Multiple Choice

1. b	6. d	11. d	16. b	21. b	26. d
2. c	7. c	12. a	17. d	22. a	27. c
3. b	8. c	13. a	18. d	23. b	28. c
4. a	9. b	14. b	19. c	24. d	29. b
5. d	10. d	15. a	20. c	25. b	30. a

Review of Concepts

1. positive symptoms; negative symptoms; and disorganization (460)
2. 15; 35 (461)
3. false (462)
4. auditory (463)
5. false (464)
6. false (465)
7. true (466)
8. true (467)
9. false (467)
10. false (473)
11. 1 percent (473)
12. false (474)
13. true (474)
14. true (474)
15. false (474)
16. true (475)
17. 48 percent (476)
18. 17 percent (476)
19. false (476)
20. false (476)
21. true (477)
22. true (477)
23. malnutrition (478)
24. winter (478)
25. larger (478)
26. left temporal lobe (480)
27. decrease (480)
28. the businessman (481)
29. simplified (482)
30. serotonin (483)
31. both (483)
32. do not (484)
33. more (486)
34. criticism (486)
35. hurts; helps (486)
36. more (488)
37. less (491)
38. less (491)
39. Eye (492)
40. several weeks (493)
41. true (493)
42. 20 percent (494)
43. true (494)
44. causes fatal agranulocytosis in 1 percent of patients (495)
45. false (496)

Understanding Research

1. children of schizophrenic patients; 13 percent; 311; three; hospital; diagnostic; CT

2. 31; 18 percent; similar; correlated; more

3. cases and a control group; comparison; normal participants and patient controls

4. consequence; patients with mood disorders; important

CHAPTER 14 - DEMENTIA, DELIRIUM, AND AMNESTIC DISORDERS

Chapter Outline

I. Overview

II. Delirium: Typical Symptoms and Associated Features

III. Dementia: Typical Symptoms and Associated Features
   A. Cognitive Symptoms
      1. Memory and Learning
      2. Verbal Communication
      3. Perception
      4. Abstract Thinking
      5. Judgment and Social Behavior
   B. Assessment of Cognitive Impairment
   C. Associated Features
      1. Emotion
      2. Motor Behavior
      3. Psychotic Symptoms

IV. Amnestic Disorder: Typical Symptoms and Associated Features

V. Classification
   A. Brief Historical Perspective
   B. DSM-IV
   C. Specific Disorders
      1. Dementia of the Alzheimer's Type
      2. Pick's Disease
      3. Huntington's Disease
      4. Parkinson's Disease
      5. Vascular Dementia
      6. Dementia versus Depression

VI. Epidemiology of Dementia
   A. Incidence and Prevalence by Age Group
   B. Prevalence by Subtypes

VII. Dementia: Etiological Considerations and Research
   A. Genetic Factors
   B. Neurotransmitters
   C. Viral Infections
   D. Immune System Dysfunction
   E. Environmental Factors

VIII. Treatment and Management
   A. Medication
   B. Environmental and Behavioral Management
   C. Support for Caregivers

Learning Objectives

After reviewing the material presented in this chapter, you should be able to:

1. Define and distinguish dementia, delirium, and amnestic disorders.

2. Provide the basic symptoms of delirium.

3. Distinguish retrograde from anterograde amnesia.

4. Describe the primary symptoms of aphasia, apraxia, and agnosia.

5. Identify the functions of neuropsychological assessment in diagnosis of dementia.

6. Describe some of the primary features of amnestic disorder and distinguish them from dementia.

7. Identify the key contributions of Pinel, Broca, Wernicke, Korsakoff, Alzheimer, and Kraepelin in the diagnosis of cognitive disorders.

8. Distinguish primary from secondary dementia--and differentiated from undifferentiated primary dementia.

9. Describe some of the features of Alzheimer's, Pick's, Huntington's, Parkinson's, and vascular diseases.

10. Describe the role of genetics, neurotransmitters, viral infections, and environmental factors in the development of cognitive disorders.

11. Know the importance of accurate diagnosis in the treatment of dementia.

12. Discuss the importance of environmental and behavioral management as well as caregiver support and respite programs in treatment of the patient suffering from a cognitive disorder.

Key Terms - Matching #1

The following terms related to dementia, delirium, and amnestic disorders are important to know. To test your knowledge, match the following terms with their definitions. Answers are listed at the end of the chapter.

a.	Dementia	j.	Aphasia
b.	Delirium	k.	Apraxia
c.	Amnestic disorders	l.	Agnosia
d.	Neurologists	m.	Neuropsychological assessment
e.	Neuropsychologists	n.	Dyskinesia
f.	Mechanics	o.	Korsakoff's syndrome
g.	Pragmatics	p.	Primary dementia

h. Retrograde amnesia q. Secondary dementia
i. Anterograde amnesia

1. _____ a gradually worsening loss of memory and related cognitive functions
2. _____ inability to learn or remember new material after a particular point in time
3. _____ a disorder caused by chronic alcoholism characterized by memory impairment
4. _____ problems identifying stimuli in the environment
5. _____ cognitive impairment is produced by the direct effect of a disease on brain tissue
6. _____ a confusional state that develops over a short period of time and is often associated with agitation and hyperactivity
7. _____ involuntary movements such as tics and tremors
8. _____ fluid intelligence, the "hardware" of the mind
9. _____ psychologists with expertise in the assessment of specific types of cognitive impairment
10. _____ various types of loss or impairment in language caused by brain damage
11. _____ evaluation of performance on psychological tests to indicate whether a person has a brain disorder
12. _____ physicians who deal primarily with diseases of the brain and nervous system
13. _____ a cognitive disorder characterized by limited memory impairments
14. _____ difficulty performing purposeful movements in response to verbal commands
15. _____ cognitive impairment is a by-product or side effect of some other type of biological or psychological dysfunction
16. _____ loss of memory for events prior to the onset of an illness or traumatic event
17. _____ crystallized intelligence, the "software" of the mind

Key Terms - Matching #2

The following terms related to dementia, delirium, and amnestic disorders are important to know. To test your knowledge, match the following terms with their definitions. Answers are listed at the end of the chapter.

1. Alzheimer's disease
2. Neurofibrils
3. Neurofibrillary tangles
4. Senile plaques
5. Beta-amyloid
6. Pick's disease
7. Pick's bodies
8. Huntington's disease
9. Chorea
10. Parkinson's disease
11. Infarct
12. Vascular dementia
13. Pseudodementia
14. Autosomal dominant trait
15. Genetic linkage
16. Creutzfeldt-Jakob disease
17. Respite programs

a. _____ a protein material
b. _____ caused by a dominant gene not located on one of the sex chromosomes
c. _____ a lesion consisting of a central core of homogenous protein material surrounded by clumps of debris left over from destroyed neurons
d. _____ a distinctive ballooning of nerve cells
e. _____ provide structural support for the cell and help transport chemical used in the production of neurotransmitters
f. _____ a form of dementia associated with atrophy in the frontal and temporal lobes of the brain
g. _____ a close association between two genes on a chromosome
h. _____ disorder of the motor system caused by a degeneration of the substantia nigra and loss of dopamine but rarely including dementia
i. _____ provide caregivers with temporary periods of relief from caring for a demented patient
j. _____ symptoms of dementia actually produced by a major depressive disorder
k. _____ a form of dementia characterized by the presence of unusual involuntary muscle movements, as well as personality changes
l. _____ a form of dementia in which cognitive impairment appears gradually and deterioration is progressive
m. _____ a form of dementia produced by a slow-acting virus
n. _____ the area of dead tissue produced by a stroke
o. _____ a form of dementia associated with strokes
p. _____ when the structural network of some neurofibrils becomes highly disorganized
q. _____ unusual involuntary muscle movements

Review of Concepts - Fill in the Blank and True/False

This section will help focus your studying by testing whether you understand the concepts presented in the text. After you have read and reviewed the material, test your comprehension and memory by filling in the following blanks or circling the right answer. Answers are listed at the end of the chapter.

1. Delirium can fluctuate throughout the day: **true**   **false**
2. Delirium is less common among the elderly: **true**   **false**
3. Dementia can be cured: **true**   **false**
4. Changes in cognitive processes are not a normal part of aging: **true**   **false**
5. Which of the following typically show a decline with age:
    mechanics   **pragmatics**
6. Neuropsychological tests can sometimes be used to infer the location of a brain lesion: **true**   **false**
7. Hallucinations and delusions are seen in what percent of dementia cases: _____
8. Korsakoff's syndrome may be caused in part by a _____ deficiency.
9. Which types of dementias are most common:
    differentiated   **undifferentiated**

10. A definitive diagnosis of Alzheimer's disease can only be made after _____.

11. Huntington's disease is caused by _____.

12. Vascular dementia often results in **unilateral** or **bilateral** impairment.

13. Almost _____ percent of people over 90 years of age exhibit symptoms of moderate or severe dementia: **20**   **40**   **60**

14. Average time between the onset of Alzheimer's disease and death is _____ years.

15. Genetic factors have been shown to play a role in dementia: **true**   **false**

16. Alzheimer's disease has been linked to what birth defect? _____

17. Alzheimer's disease may involve dysfunction of the _____ system.

18. There is a controversial link between Alzheimer's disease and levels of what metal in the water system? _____

19. People who smoke cigarettes are **more** or **less** likely to develop Alzheimer's disease.

20. People with higher educational levels are less likely to develop Alzheimer's disease: **true**   **false**

21. Patients with dementia benefit from _____ environments.

22. Patients with dementia who remain active have less _____.

Multiple Choice Questions

The following multiple choice questions will test your comprehension of the material presented in the chapter. Answers are listed at the end of the chapter.

1) All of the following are goals in designing an environment conducive to demented patients EXCEPT:

    a. keep the patients relatively inactive in order to prevent them from hurting themselves

    b. facilitate the patients knowledge of the environment through labeled rooms, hallways, etc.

    c. keep the environment negotiable (i.e., keep areas that a person will use often visible from their room if they cannot be remembered)

    d. stay abreast of safety and health issues

2) The _____ is probably the best known neuropsychological assessment procedure that involves the examination of performance on psychological tests to indicate whether a person has a brain disorder.

    a. Halstead-Reitan

    b. Weschler

    c. Symptoms Checklist-90 (SCL-90)

    d. Minnesota Multiphasic Personality Inventory-2 (MMPI-2)

3) _____ is a type of motor dysfunction that involves jerky, semi-purposeful movements of the person's face and limbs.

    a. Anoxia   c. Chorea
    b. Myotonia   d. Lipofuscin

4) Which of the following appears to be the most common type of dementia?

    a. Pick's disease   c. Alzheimer's disease
    b. Huntington's disease   d. vascular dementia

5) All of the following are typical symptoms of Parkinson's disease EXCEPT:

    a. tremors   c. gradual dementia
    b. postural abnormalities   d. reduction in voluntary movements

6) A _____ deals primarily with diseases of the brain and the nervous system.

    a. neurologist   c. psychologist
    b. psychiatrist   d. cardiologist

7) Which of the following diagnoses depends on the presence of a positive family history for the disorder?

    a. Parkinson's disease   c. Pick's disease
    b. Alzheimer's disease   d. Huntington's disease

8) According to Baltes, _____ is to fluid intelligence as _____ is to crystallized intelligence.

    a. wisdom; knowledge
    b. knowledge; wisdom
    c. cognitive mechanics; cognitive pragmatics
    d. cognitive pragmatics; cognitive mechanics

9) The DSM-IV currently classifies dementia and related clinical phenomena as:

    a. organic mental disorders
    b. biological mental disorders
    c. psychological disorders with organic etiology
    d. cognitive disorders

10) Betty's physician handed her a hairbrush and said, "Show me what you do with this object." She took the brush and brushed her hair with it, but was unable to name the object. She is most likely suffering from which of the following?

    a. agnosia   c. apraxia
    b. aphasia   d. ataxia

11) Hallucinations and delusions are seen in about _____ of dementia cases.

    a. 10 percent   c. 30 percent
    b. 20 percent   d. 40 percent

12) The most effective form of treatment for improving cognitive functioning in dementia of the Alzheimer's type is:

    a. cognitive therapy
    b. cognitive-behavioral therapy
    c. rational-emotive therapy (RET)
    d. no form of treatment is presently capable of improving cognitive functioning in dementia of the Alzheimer's type

13) One theory regarding Korsakoff's syndrome suggests that lack of _____ leads to atrophy of the medial thalamus.

    a. zinc   c. vitamin B1 (thiamin)
    b. vitamin C   d. potassium

14) Which of the following is a confusional state that develops over a short period of time and is often associated with agitation and hyperactivity:

    a. delirium   c. dementia
    b. amnesia   d. Alzheimer's disease

15) All of the following are frequently associated with dementia EXCEPT:

    a. personality changes   c. high frequency of drug abuse
    b. emotional difficulties   d. motivational problems

16) A definite diagnosis of Alzheimer's disease requires the observation of:

    a. neurofibrillary tangles and senile plaques
    b. degeneration of the substantia nigra
    c. enlargement of the hypothalamus
    d. all of the above

17) Which of the following neurotransmitters has been shown to have reduced levels in Alzheimer's patients?

    a. acetylcholine (Ach)   c. norepinephrine
    b. serotonin   d. dopamine

18) In order to qualify for a diagnosis of dementia, the person must exhibit memory impairment and which of the following?

    a. aggressive behavior   c. a previous episode of delirium
    b. problems in abstract thinking   d. age of at least 65 years

19) All of the following are true of delirium EXCEPT:

    a. it usually has a rapid onset
    b. speech is typically confused
    c. the person usually remains alert and responsive to the environment
    d. it can be resolved

20) Parkinson's disease is primarily a disorder of the motor system that is caused by a loss of the neurotransmitter dopamine and a degeneration of this specific area of the brain stem:

    a. substantia nigra   c. fornix
    b. thalamus   d. superior colliculi

21) Although controversial, epidemiologic investigations have discovered that some types of dementia, especially Alzheimer's disease, may be related to all of the following EXCEPT:

    a. aluminum   c. level of educational experience
    b. cigarette smoking   d. lead

22) The incidence of dementia will be much greater in the near future because:

    a. diagnostic criteria are more loosely defined
    b. the average age of the population is increasing steadily
    c. more people are being exposed to the environmental factors that have been shown to cause dementia
    d. dementia is now striking people at a much earlier age

23) Which of the following can be distinguished from other types of dementia listed in the DSM-IV on the basis of speed of onset (i.e., cognitive impairment appears gradually, and the person's cognitive deterioration is progressive)?

    a. vascular dementia
    b. Huntington's disease
    c. Alzheimer's disease
    d. substance-induced persisting dementia

24) Which of the following is an example of a differentiated dementia?

    a. Huntington's disease   c. vascular dementia
    b. Alzheimer's disease   d. HIV disease

25) Some studies have confirmed an association between Alzheimer's disease and which of the following:

    a. dependent personality disorder   c. Korsakoff's syndrome
    b. vascular dementia   d. Down syndrome

26) _____ is a disorder that is frequently associated with dementia.

    a. Bipolar disorder   c. Schizophrenia
    b. Depression   d. Multiple personality disorder

27) Which of the following is/are treatment options for demented patients?

    a. behavioral strategies   c. insight-oriented strategies
    b. cognitive strategies   d. all of the above

28) Almost _____ of people over 90 years of age exhibit symptoms of moderate or severe dementia.

    a. 25 percent   c. 65 percent
    b. 40 percent   d. 80 percent

29) All of the following are true of delirium EXCEPT:

    a. it typically fluctuates throughout the day and is usually worse at night
    b. the delirious person loses the ability to learn new information or becomes unable to recall previously learned information
    c. the delirious person is likely to be disoriented with relation to time or place
    d. the primary symptom is clouding of consciousness, which might also be described as a person's reduced awareness of his or her surroundings

Understanding Research - Fill in the Blank

Memory Differences in Alzheimer's Disease and Huntington's Disease: The text presents a detailed description of a focus of research in the Research Close-Up on pp. 518-519. Finding the answers to these questions will help you get a good understanding of this study and why it is important. It is not necessary to memorize the answers; the process of finding them in the textbook will help you learn the material you need to know.

1. What would the uses be for laboratory tests that identify specific types of cognitive impairment? as _____ of the onset of dementia, as diagnostic tools to help distinguish the various types of _____, and as measures of _____ to mark the progression of the disorder or the response to _____. What part of the brain was damaged in the man who had problems during heart surgery and developed severe amnesia? _____. What type of memory is the hippocampus essential for? _____

2. How many patient groups were compared in the study? _____ Each subject performed two _____ memory tasks. The motor task involved keeping a stylus on a rotating metalic _____. The lexical priming task

involved being shown a sequence of _____ words that subjects rated in terms of how well they _____ the words. Later the subjects were asked to complete a word stem to make the first word that came to their minds. The index of implicit memory was the percentage of word stems completed with words they had been asked to _____. The Alzheimer's patients were impaired on the _____ _____ task and the Huntington's patients were impaired on the _____ task.

<u>Genetic Linkage Analysis</u>: The text discusses this type of research in the Research Methods section on pp. 522-523. Finding the answers to these questions will help you get a good understanding of these issues.

3. Huntington's disease is considered an_____ because exactly _____ percent of an affected person's first-degree relatives will develop the disorder. Genetic linkage is shown between the gene causing the disorder and the locus for a _____ gene that is very close to it. Research was slow until the discovery of _____. What country did the family come from that had abnormally high levels of Huntington's disease and researchers studying them discovered a marker for the disease? _____

Brief Essay

As a final exercise, write out answers to the following brief essay questions. Then compare your answers with the material presented in the text.

After you have answered these questions, review the "critical thinking" questions that are presented at the end of the text chapter. Answering these questions will help you integrate important issues and themes that have been featured throughout the chapter.

1. Briefly discuss how the behavioral effects of a stroke are different from those of dementia.

2. Discuss the environmental factors that have been shown to be possibly linked to some types of dementia. What do you see as being problematic with these findings? What must we be cautious of when interpreting this data?

3. Briefly discuss the similarities and differences between dementia and depression. Discuss a case where it might be difficult to distinguish them apart. How could this be done?

4. Briefly review the defining characteristics of delirium, Korsakoff's syndrome, Alzheimer's disease, and Huntington's disease.

ANSWER KEY

Answers to the exercises are listed below; page numbers where the information is referenced in the textbook are given in parentheses.

Key Terms - Matching #1

1. a (502)	10. j (509)
2. i (509)	11. m (511)
3. o (514)	12. d (503)
4. l (510)	13. c (502)
5. p (515)	14. k (509)
6. b (502)	15. q (515)
7. n (512)	16. h (509)
8. f (508)	17. g (508)
9. e (503)	

Key Terms - Matching #2

a. 5 (516)	j. 13 (520)
b. 14 (522)	k. 8 (517)
c. 4 (516)	l. 1 (516)
d. 7 (516)	m. 16 (523)
e. 2 (516)	n. 11 (519)
f. 6 (516)	o. 12 (519)
g. 15 (523)	p. 3 (516)
h. 10 (517)	q. 9 (517)
i. 17 (527)	

Review of Concepts

1. true (506)	12. unilateral (519)
2. false (507)	13. 40 percent (521)
3. false (507)	14. eight (521)
4. false (508)	15. true (522)
5. mechanics (508)	16. Down Syndrome (522)
6. true (511)	17. immune (524)
7. 20 percent (512)	18. aluminum (524)
8. vitamin (514)	19. less (524)
9. undifferentiated (515)	20. true (524)
10. death (516)	21. structured (526)
11. a gene (517)	22. depression (526)

Multiple Choice

1. a	6. a	11. b	16. d	21. d	26. b
2. a	7. d	12. d	17. a	22. b	27. d
3. c	8. c	13. c	18. b	23. c	28. b
4. c	9. d	14. a	19. c	24. a	29. b
5. c	10. b	15. c	20. a	25. d	

Understanding Research

1. early signs; dementias; adjustment; treatment; hippocampus; explicit

2. three; implicit; disk; 10; liked; rate; lexical priming; motor learning

3. autosomal dominant trait; 50 percent; known; RFLPs; Venezuela

CHAPTER 15 - MENTAL RETARDATION AND PERVASIVE DEVELOPMENTAL DISORDERS

Chapter Outline

I. Overview

II. Mental Retardation
- A. Typical Symptoms and Associated Features
    - 1. Significantly Subaverage IQ
        - a. Measurement of Intelligence
        - b. Controversies About Intelligence Tests
    - 2. Limitations in Adaptive Skills
    - 3. Onset Before Age 18 Years
- B. Classification
    - 1. Brief Historical Perspective
    - 2. Contemporary Classification
- C. Epidemiology
- D. Etiological Considerations and Research
    - 1. Biological Factors
        - a. Chromosomal Disorders
        - b. Genetic Disorders
        - c. Infectious Diseases
        - d. Toxins
        - e. Other Biological Abnormalities
        - f. Normal Genetic Variation
    - 2. Psychological Factors
    - 3. Social Factors
- E. Treatment: Primary, Secondary, and Tertiary Prevention and Normalization
    - 1. Primary Prevention
    - 2. Secondary Prevention
    - 3. Tertiary Prevention
    - 4. Normalization

III. Autistic Disorder and Pervasive Developmental Disorders
- A. Typical Symptoms and Associated Features
    - 1. Impaired Social Interaction
    - 2. Impaired Communication
    - 3. Stereotyped Behavior, Interests, and Activities
    - 4. Apparent Sensory Deficits
    - 5. Self-Injury
    - 6. Savant Performance
- B. Classification
    - 1. Brief Historical Perspective
    - 2. Contemporary Classification
- C. Epidemiology
- D. Etiological Considerations and Research
    - 1. Psychological and Social Factors
    - 2. Biological Factors

    a. Autism as a Consequence of Known Biological Disorders
    b. A Strongly Genetic Disorder?
    c. Integration: Multiple Pathways to a Brain Disorder
    d. Neurophysiology and Autism
    e. Neuroanatomy and Autism
    f. A Disorder of Brain Development
  E. Treatment
      1. Course and Outcome
      2. Medication
      3. Psychotherapy: Intensive Behavior Modification

Learning Objectives

After reviewing the material presented in this chapter, you should be able to:

1. Know the basic defining characteristics of mental retardation and autism.

2. Distinguish between practical intelligence and social intelligence.

3. Identify the four levels of mental retardation that DSM IV delineates: mild, moderate, severe, and profound.

4. Appreciate that mental retardation can be caused by a variety of biological factors: chromosomal disorders, genetic disorders, infectious diseases, and environmental or chemical toxins.

5. Distinguish between primary, secondary, and tertiary prevention in treatment of mental retardation.

6. Describe the types of difficulties autistic children have with social interactions.

7. Define: dysprosody, echolalia, and pronoun rehearsal as they apply to impaired communication in autism.

8. Know the basic epidemiological statistics for autism.

9. Provide five reasons that we now believe autism is a biologically-based disorder.

10. Understand the advantages and disadvantages of intensive behavior modification treatment for autism.

Key Terms - Matching #1

The following terms related to mental retardation and pervasive developmental disorders are important to know. To test your knowledge, match the following terms with their definitions. Answers are listed at the end of the chapter.

a. Mental retardation
b. Intelligence quotient (IQ)
c. Normal distribution
d. Standard deviation
e. Mild mental retardation
f. Moderate mental retardation
g. Severe mental retardation
h. Profound mental retardation
i. Down syndrome
j. Fragile-X syndrome
k. Klinefelter syndrome
l. XYY syndrome
m. Turner syndrome

n. Phenylketonuria (PKU)
o. Tuberous sclerosis
p. Tay-Sachs disease
q. Hurler syndrome
r. Lesch-Nyhan syndrome
s. Cytomegalovirus
t. Toxoplasmosis
u. Rubella
v. Syphilis
w. Genital herpes
x. Encephalitis
y. Meningitis
z. Fetal alcohol syndrome

1. _____ an infection of the membranes that line the brain which can lead to inflammation that can damage the brain
2. _____ a relatively common and usually harmless infection that can be passed to the fetus that can cause mental retardation
3. _____ a chromosomal abnormality transmitted genetically which sometimes leads to mental retardation or learning disabilities
4. _____ characterized by mental retardation and self-mutilation
5. _____ substantial limitations in present functioning characterized by significantly subaverage intellectual functioning, concurrent limitations in adaptive skills, and an onset before age 18
6. _____ motor skills, communication, and self-care are severely limited; constant supervision required
7. _____ a bacterial sexually transmitted disease which, if untreated, can be passed to the fetus and can result in physical and sensory handicaps in the fetus, including mental retardation
8. _____ a protozoan infection caused by ingestion of infected raw meats or from contact with infected cat feces which can cause brain damage to a fetus
9. _____ an intelligence test's rating of an individual's intellectual ability
10. _____ can generally function at the second grade level academically, require close training and supervision in work activities, and need family or group home supervision
11. _____ a very rare dominant-gene disorder characterized by white growths in the ventricles of the brain
12. _____ also called German measles, a viral infection that can cause severe mental retardation or death in a fetus
13. _____ caused by a recessive gene, this disorder involves the absence of an enzyme that metabolizes phenylalanine, an amino acid in certain foods, which leads to brain damage that results in mental retardation
14. _____ once thought to increase criminality but now recognized to be linked with minor social deviance and a mean IQ 10 points lower than average
15. _____ a measure of dispersion of scores around the mean
16. _____ an extra X chromosome in males that leads to low normal to mildly mentally retarded intellectual functioning
17. _____ results in gross physical abnormalities, including dwarfism, humpback, bulging head, and clawlike hands

18. _____ a bell-shaped frequency distribution
19. _____ a rare recessive-gene disorder that eventually results in death during the infant or preschool years which is particularly common among Jews of Eastern European heritage
20. _____ can be transmitted to the baby at birth and cause mental retardation, blindness, or death
21. _____ a missing X chromosome in females that leads to failure to develop sexually and intelligence near or within the normal range
22. _____ a disorder characterized by retarded physical development, a small head, narrow eyes, cardiac defects, and cognitive impairment
23. _____ can generally function at the sixth grade level academically, acquire vocational skills, and live in the community without special supports
24. _____ typically have abnormal motor development, sharply limited communicative speech, and require close supervision for community living
25. _____ a brain infection that can cause permanent brain damage in about 20 percent of cases
26. _____ a chromosomal disorder characterized by a distinctively abnormal physical appearance and mental retardation typically in the moderate to severe range

Key Terms - Matching #2

The following terms related to mental retardation and pervasive developmental disorders are important to know. To test your knowledge, match the following terms with their definitions. Answers are listed at the end of the chapter.

1. Mercury poisoning
2. Lead poisoning
3. Rh incompatibility
4. Premature birth
5. Anoxia
6. Epilepsy
7. Cultural-familial retardation
8. Heritability ratios
9. Reaction range
10. Amniocentesis
11. Normalization
12. Mainstreaming
13. Pervasive developmental disorders
14. Autism
15. Gaze aversion
16. Dysprosody
17. Echolalia
18. Pronoun reversal
19. Self-stimulation
20. Apparent sensory deficit
21. Self-injurious behavior
22. Savant performance
23. Asperger's disorder
24. Childhood disintegrative disorder
25. Rett's disorder
26. Developmental aphasia

a. _____ a diagnostic procedure in which fluid is extracted from the amniotic sac that protects the fetus during pregnancy and genetic tests are run on the fluid to identify genetic abnormalities
b. _____ proposes that heredity determines the upper and lower limits of IQ, and experience determines the extent to which people fulfill their genetic potential
c. _____ a person's repetition of phrases that are spoken to them

d. _____ a disorder characterized by delayed or absent speech
e. _____ can produce severe physical, emotional, and intellectual impairments
f. _____ disturbance in rate, rhythm, and intonation of speech production
g. _____ indices to measure the extent of genetic contribution to a characteristic
h. _____ a disorder similar to autism but which does not involve language delay
i. _____ at least five months of normal development followed by a deceleration in head growth, loss of purposeful hand movements, loss of social engagement, poor coordination, and language delay
j. _____ profound problems in social interaction, communication, and stereotyped behavior, interests, and activities
k. _____ confusion of pronouns, such as between "you" and "I"
l. _____ active avoidance of eye contact
m. _____ an exceptional ability in a highly specialized area of functioning
n. _____ cases of mental retardation with no known etiology that run in families and is linked with poverty
o. _____ seizure disorder that can result in mental retardation
p. _____ at toxic levels can produce behavioral and cognitive impairments, including mental retardation
q. _____ means that people with mental retardation are entitled to live as much as possible like other members of society
r. _____ unresponsiveness to auditory, tactile, or visual sensations even though there is no impairment in the sensory organ
s. _____ unusual psychological problems that begin early in life and involve severe impairments in a number of areas of functioning
t. _____ keeping mentally retarded children in regular classrooms as much as possible
u. _____ problems in social interaction and communication, as well as stereotyped behavior, with an onset following at least two years of normal development
v. _____ poses a risk for subsequent pregnancies because the mother's body produces antibodies which attack the developing fetus unless treated with an antibiotic
w. _____ ritual actions such as flapping a string or spinning a top that seem to serve no other purpose that to provide sensory feedback
x. _____ can result in sensory impairments, poor physical development, and mental retardation; worse outcomes are typically associated with lower birth weights
y. _____ often repeated head-banging or biting of fingers
z. _____ oxygen deprivation that can lead to brain damage

Names You Should Know - Matching

The following people have played an important role in research and theory of mental retardation and pervasive developmental disorders. To test your knowledge, match the following names with the descriptions of their contributions to the study of abnormal psychology. Answers are listed at the end of the chapter.

a. Alfred Binet   c. Langdon Down   e. Hans Asperger
b. Jean Marc Itard   d. Leo Kanner   f. O. Ivar Lovaas

1. _____ first described autism
2. _____ first described a subgroup of children with a chromosomal disorder later named after him
3. _____ described a subgroup of people with a disorder similar to autism but not involving mental retardation
4. _____ worked extensively with a feral child found living in the woods
5. _____ developed the first successful IQ test
6. _____ applied behavioral techniques to the management of people with autism

Review of Concepts - Fill in the Blank and True/False

This section will help focus your studying by testing whether you understand the concepts presented in the text. After you have read and reviewed the material, test your comprehension and memory by filling in the following blanks or circling the right answer. Answers are listed at the end of the chapter.

1. Which type of disorder is more common:

   mental retardation   **pervasive developmental disorders**

2. Intelligence is _____ distributed in the general population.

3. Intelligence tests have a mean of _____ and a standard deviation of _____.

4. The IQ of a particular person changes a lot over time: **true   false**

5. IQ tests measure potential for _____.

6. Adaptive skills include both _____ and _____
   intelligence.

7. The physician who worked with Victor, the feral child of Aveyron, France, had
   great success in educating and socializing him: **true   false**

8. More people fall into the   **lower** or **upper**   range of the curve of IQs
   than would be predicted by a normal distribution.

9. What are the two categories of etiology of mental retardation?
   _____ and _____

10. The incidence of Down syndrome is related to maternal and paternal _____.

11. Intensive intervention with people with Down syndrome has been shown to be
    beneficial to their achievement: **true   false**

12. People with Down syndrome typically die in their forties: **true   false**

13. Fragile-X syndrome is more likely to lead to mental retardation in boys than in
    girls: **true   false**

14. There is no known treatment for phenylketonuria: **true   false**

15. Pregnant women who drink one ounce of alcohol per day or less are not putting
    their fetus at risk for fetal alcohol syndrome: **true   false**

16. Crack babies are more likely to be born _____.

17. Children living in dilapidated housing are at increased risk for ingesting paint chips containing _____.

18. Rh incompatibility is only a potential danger to children of mothers who are Rh **negative** or **positive**.

19. The IQs of adopted children are more highly correlated to the IQs of their **adoptive** or **biological** parents.

20. What is the most impoverished age group in the United States? _____

21. Environment has been shown to have little effect on IQ: **true**   **false**

22. Children who participate in Head Start are less likely to _____.

23. The use of neuroleptics to manage aggression and uncontrolled behavior among mentally retarded patients in institutions is recommended: **true**   **false**

24. People with autism have unusual physical appearances: **true**   **false**

25. Autism is not usually identified until the child reaches kindergarten: **true**   **false**

26. Children with autism tend to be very affectionate: **true**   **false**

27. Many children with autism remain mute: **true**   **false**

28. People with autism have problems in their capacity for social _____.

29. People with autism **resist** or **require** routine.

30. People with autism have superior intelligence: **true**   **false**

31. Some brain injured patients demonstrate savant abilities: **true**   **false**

32. Autism is more common among the upper social classes: **true**   **false**

33. Autism is more common among **boys** or **girls**.

34. Siblings of people with autism are more likely to have autism: **true**   **false**

35. Autism is likely caused by some combination of poor parenting and biological factors: **true**   **false**

36. MZ twins show higher concordance for autism than DZ twins: **true**   **false**

37. Most people grow out of autism: **true**   **false**

38. A number of teens with autism develop _____ disorders.

39. A number of medications show promise in improving functioning of autistic patients: **true**   **false**

40. Behavioral treatments to reduce self-injurious behavior in autistic patients are controversial because they involve _____.

41. The only form of treatment found to be effective in increasing the functioning of autistic patients is _____ operant behavior therapy.

Multiple Choice Questions

The following multiple choice questions will test your comprehension of the material presented in the chapter. Answers are listed at the end of the chapter.

1) Which of the following toxins presents the greatest threat to a fetus?

   a. cigarettes
   b. alcohol
   c. lead
   d. mercury

2) All of the following are central symptoms of autism EXCEPT:

   a. impaired communication abilities
   b. impairments in social interaction
   c. abnormalities of the eyes, nose, and ears
   d. stereotyped patterns of behavior, interests, and activities

3) Mild mental retardation is designated for individuals with IQ scores between which of the following?

   a. 20-25 and 40
   b. 35-40 and 50
   c. 50-55 and 70
   d. 65-70 and 90

4) As outlined in your text, which of the following has been suggested as an interpretation for pronoun reversal as documented in some cases of autism?

   a. pronoun reversal demonstrates a lack of understanding of speech
   b. pronoun reversal is a result of faulty neurotransmitters
   c. pronoun reversal results from damage to specific areas in the frontal lobe
   d. pronoun reversal is due to the autistic child's disinterest in other people

5) Autism is considered to be a _____ disorder, with approximately _____ out of every 10,000 children qualifying for the diagnosis.

   a. rare; 4-5
   b. rare; 20-25
   c. common; 1,000-1,500
   d. common; 3,000-3,500

6) Which of the following is one of the most important current secondary prevention efforts in preventing cultural-familial retardation?

   a. amniocentesis
   b. prenatal care
   c. Head Start
   d. respite care

7) Treatment for self-injurious behavior that is sometimes seen in autistic children is controversial because:

   a. there is no empirical support to back up the treatment
   b. the treatment typically involves punishment (e.g., slap or mild electric shock)
   c. the treatment has been relatively ineffective
   d. the treatment has been used without guardian consent

8) The reaction range concept of IQ proposed that (the) _____ determines the upper and lower limits of IQ, and (the) _____ determines the extent to which people fulfill their genetic potential.

   a. heredity; experience
   b. experience; heredity
   c. parents' IQ; age
   d. age; parents' IQ

9) Mental retardation with a specific, known organic cause:

   a. is typically more common among families living in poverty
   b. generally is more common among Hispanics and African-Americans
   c. is most prevalent among the upper class
   d. generally has an equal prevalence among all social classes

10) Which of the following was the original developer of IQ tests?

   a. Douglas Biklen
   b. Alfred Binet
   c. Leo Kanner
   d. O. Ivan Lovaas

11) All of the following are true of autistic children EXCEPT:

   a. most are normal in physical appearance
   b. physical growth and development is generally normal
   c. their body movements are typically grossly uncoordinated
   d. they sometimes have unusual actions and postures

12) Premature birth is defined either as a birth weight of less than 5 1/2 pounds or as birth before _____ weeks of gestation.

   a. 35
   b. 36
   c. 37
   d. 38

13) The most common form of self-injury that can accompany autism and other pervasive developmental disorders is:

   a. head-banging
   b. repetitive hitting of objects with one's fists
   c. dare-devil behaviors (i.e., skydiving, bungee jumping, etc.)
   d. cutting of oneself with sharp objects

14) All of the following are diagnostic criteria for autism EXCEPT:

   a. lack of social or emotional reciprocity
   b. a prior diagnosis of Rett's disorder
   c. apparently compulsive adherence to specific, nonfunctional routines or rituals
   d. lack of varied spontaneous make-believe play or social imitative play appropriate to developmental level

15) Autism is believed to be caused by:

   a. poor parenting
   b. an abusive environment
   c. neurological abnormalities
   d. there is no known etiology for autism

16) Almost _____ of all children in the United States are born to teenage mothers.

   a. 8 percent   c. 16 percent
   b. 12 percent   d. 20 percent

17) Savant performance is NOT typical in which of the following areas:

   a. artistic   c. musical
   b. mathematical   d. athletic

18) Which of the following interpretations of self-stimulation is most plausible according to your text?

   a. it is a way for the autistic child to feel like he or she is similar to others
   b. it serves the purpose of increasing stimulation to the autistic child who
         receives too little sensory input
   c. it serves the function of making a terrifying world more constant and
         predictable and therefore less frightening
   d. it is merely a repetitive behavior that serves no function

19) According to the American Association on Mental Retardation's (AAMR) definition, mental retardation manifests before age:

   a. 5   c. 13
   b. 8   d. 18

20) Which of the following is an infectious disease that is the result of infection of the brain and produces inflammation and permanent damage in approximately 20 percent of all cases?

   a. meningitis   c. encephalitis
   b. rubella   d. cytomegalovirus

21) Which of the following is caused by the presence of an extra chromosome and is characterized by a distinctively abnormal physical appearance, which includes slanting eyes, small head and stature, protruding tongue, and a variety of organ, muscle, and skeletal abnormalities?

   a. Down syndrome   c. Phenylketonuria (PKU)
   b. Fetal Alcohol syndrome d. Tuberous sclerosis

22) Severe mental retardation accounts for approximately _____ of the mentally retarded.

a. 1-2 percent
b. 3-4 percent
c. 8-10 percent
d. 12-15 percent

23) Which of the following is the most promising approach to treating autism?

a. intensive behavior modification using operant conditioning techniques
b. antidepressant medication
c. psychodynamic therapy that focuses on providing a nurturing, supportive environment
d. none of the above have been effective in treating autism

24) Both mental retardation and pervasive developmental disorders include all of the following EXCEPT:

a. either are present at birth or begin early in life
b. serious disruptions in many areas of functioning, often including an inability to care for oneself independently
c. gross physical abnormalities
d. often, but not always, associated with a below-average IQ

25) Autism is usually first noticed:

a. early in life
b. during the teenage years
c. in adulthood
d. late in life

26) Which of the following terms was used for several years to classify autism together with other severe forms of childhood psychopathology?

a. childhood dissociation
b. disruptive childhood behaviors
c. psychopathology first evident in childhood
d. childhood schizophrenia

27) Which of the following developmental periods is particularly important to the course of autism?

a. birth to 6 months
b. 6 - 36 months
c. early school years
d. early adulthood

28) Allen is a six-year-old boy who has been diagnosed with autism. Frequently, when asked "would you like a drink," Allen will repeat the question over and over again. This is an example of:

a. pronoun reversal
b. dysprosody
c. echolalia
d. self-stimulation

Understanding Research - Fill in the Blank

A Study of Facilitated Communication: The text presents a detailed description of a technique developed and advocated by Crossley and Biklen in the Research Close-Up on pp. 562-564. Finding the answers to these questions will help you get a good understanding of this study and why it is important. It is not necessary to memorize the answers; the process of finding them in the textbook will help you learn the material you need to know.

1. Facilitated communication involves a "facilitator" who supports the hand and arm of a disabled person to allow them to _____. The technique was hailed as a _____, and purported to allow people with autism who never had communicated to express themselves and display insight and awareness.   Biklin advocated a _____ approach to evaluating the technique. One systematic study was conducted with _____ adolescents with autism and _____ adult facilitators who were _____ about the technique.

2. There were four procedures in this study. The first, the _____ condition, involved asking the autistic adolescent questions and letting them type or communicate to the best of their abilities.   The second, the pretest, the adolescents answered the same questions with the aid of the _____, who was _____ from hearing or seeing the questions being asked. The third, the _____, involved the adolescents answering with the full help of the facilitator after 20 hours of training. In the fourth, the _____, the adolescents were asked to respond to the identical questions as in the first and second conditions with the aid of the facilitator, who was again _____.

3. Results indicated that the responses during the pretest were _____ than during the baseline. The answers were phenomenal during the free response, with adolescents typing things like "EMOTION ZOMETHIN _____ EXPREZ." However, during the posttest, when the facilitators couldn't _____ or _____ again, they again did _____ than on baseline.

Central Tendency, Variability, and Standard Scores: The text discusses these statistical issues in the Research Methods section on pp. 536-537. Finding the answers to these questions will help you get a good understanding of these issues.

4.   A frequency distribution is _____

The mean is the _____ of a distribution of scores, a measure of central _____. The median is the _____ of a frequency distribution. The mode is _____ in a distribution.

5. The range is a simple measure of _____. Variability gives an indication of how much the scores vary, or are dispersed, around the mean. Why are the differences from the mean squared when calculating the variance?

_____

Why is the standard deviation used more often than the variance?

_____

Z-scores have a mean of _____ and a standard deviation of _____.

Brief Essay

As a final exercise, write out answers to the following brief essay questions. Then compare your answers with the material presented in the text.

After you have answered these questions, review the "critical thinking" questions that are presented at the end of the text chapter. Answering these questions will help you integrate important issues and themes that have been featured throughout the chapter.

1. Despite the value of IQ tests in predicting academic performance, one controversial question is whether intelligence tests are "culture fair." Briefly discuss your views on this topic, including material from your chapter to support your ideas.

2. Currently, mental retardation can be classified according to the American Association on Mental Retardation (AAMR) and by the DSM-IV. Briefly discuss the similarities and differences in classification according to these two approaches.

3. Briefly discuss the various etiological considerations regarding autism. Which hypotheses seem most plausible to you and why? What research supports these hypotheses?

4. Briefly discuss the ethical debate regarding behavior modification treatments for decreasing potentially dangerous behaviors in autistic children. Do you believe these treatments to be unethical? If so, what do you believe are some viable options?

Answers to the exercises are listed below; page numbers where the information is referenced in the textbook are given in parentheses.

Key Terms - Matching #1

1. y (544)
2. s (544)
3. j (542)
4. r (544)
5. a (535)
6. h (541)
7. v (544)
8. t (544)
9. b (535)
10. f (540)
11. o (543)
12. u (544)
13. n (543)
14. l (543)
15. d (536)
16. k (543)
17. q (543)
18. c (536)
19. p (543)
20. w (544)
21. m (543)
22. z (544)
23. e (540)
24. g (541)
25. x (544)
26. i (542)

Names You Should Know

1. j (557)
2. c (539)
3. e (558)
4. b (539)
5. a (539)
6. f (567)

Key Terms - Matching #2

a. 10 (548)
b. 9 (546)
c. 17 (554)
d. 26 (558)
e. 1 (545)
f. 16 (554)
g. 8 (546)
h. 23 (558)
i. 25 (558)
j. 14 (550)
k. 18 (554)
l. 15 (552)
m. 22 (556)
n. 7 (545)
o. 6 (545)
p. 2 (545)
q. 11 (549)
r. 20 (555)
s. 13 (550)
t. 12 (549)
u. 24 (558)
v. 3 (545)
w. 19 (555)
x. 4 (545)
y. 21 (556)
z. 5 (545)

Multiple Choice

1. b
2. c
3. c
4. a
5. a
6. c
7. b
8. a
9. d
10. b
11. c
12. d
13. a
14. b
15. c
16. a
17. d
18. c
19. d
20. c
21. a
22. b
23. a
24. c
25. a
26. d
27. c
28. c

Review of Concepts

1. mental retardation (532)
2. normally (536)
3. 100; 15 (536)
4. false (536)
5. school achievement (538)
6. practical; social (538)
7. false (539)
8. lower (541)
9. organic; familial (541)
10. age (542)
11. true (542)
12. true (542)
13. true (542)
14. false (543)
15. false (544)
16. premature (544)
17. lead (545)
18. negative (545)
19. biological (546)
20. children (547)
21. false (547)
22. repeat a grade (548)
23. false (549)
24. false (551)
25. false (551)
26. false (552)
27. true (554)
28. imitation (554)
29. require (555)
30. false (556)
31. true (557)
32. false (559)
33. boys (559)
34. true (559)
35. false (560)
36. true (561)
37. false (564)
38. seizure (564)
39. false (565)
40. punishment (566)
41. intensive (567)

Understanding Research

1. type on a keyboard; breakthrough; case study; 21; 10; enthusiastic

2. baseline; facilitator; screened; free response; posttest; screened

3. worse; FEEL; see; hear; worse

4. a way of arranging data according to the frequencies of different possible scores; arithmetic average; tendency; midpoint; the most frequent score

5. variability; to keep them from summing to zero; because it is in the original units of measurement; zero; one

CHAPTER 16 - PSYCHOLOGICAL DISORDERS OF CHILDHOOD

Chapter Outline

I. Overview

II. Typical Symptoms: Externalizing Disorders
    A. Rule Violations
        1. Seriousness of Children's Rule Violations
        2. Children's Age and Rule Violations
        3. Adolescence-Limited Versus Life-Course-Persistent Externalizing Behavior
    B. Negativity, Anger, and Aggression
    C. Impulsivity
    D. Hyperactivity
        1. Attention Deficits

III. Typical Symptoms: Internalizing Disorders
    A. Internalizing Symptoms and Normal Development: A Challenge for Research
    B. Children's Fears in Developmental Perspective
    C. Separation Anxiety Disorder and School Refusal

IV. Additional Symptoms of Childhood Disorders
    A. Troubled Peer Relationships
    B. Specific Delays or Deviations in Development

V. Classification of Psychological Disorders of Childhood
    A. Brief Historical Perspective
    B. Contemporary Classification: Some Strengths and Weaknesses in DSM-IV
        1. Overinclusive Listing of Disorders
        2. Subclassification of Externalizing Disorders
            a. Attention-Deficit/Hyperactivity Disorder
            b. Oppositional Defiant Disorder
            c. ADHD Versus ODD
            d. ADHD with and without Hyperactivity
            e. Conduct Disorder
    C. Contextual Classifications for Abnormal Child Behavior?

VI. Epidemiology of Psychological Disorders of Childhood
    A. Gender Differences in Externalizing and Internalizing Problems
    B. Family Risk Factors
    C. Suicide Among Children and Adolescents

VII. Etiological Considerations and Research
    A. Social Factors
        1. Attachment Relationships
            a. Reactive Attachment Disorder

           b. Insecure Attachments
           c. Separation and Loss
        2. Socialization
           a. Ineffective Discipline and Parenting Styles
           b. Coercion
           c. The Importance of Parental Love
           d. Conflict and Inconsistent Discipline
           e. Broader Social Influences: Peers, Neighborhoods, Television,
              and Society
           f. Social Factors in Attention-Deficit/Hyperactivity Disorder
     B. Biological Factors
        1. Temperament
        2. Behavior Genetic Research
        3. Neuropsychological Abnormalities
        4. Food Additives and Sugar
     C. Psychological Factors
        1. Self-Control and Externalizing Disorders
        2. Emotion Regulation and Internalizing Behavior
     D. Integration and Alternative Pathways

VIII. Treatment
     A. Treatment of Internalizing Disorders
     B. Treatment of Externalizing Disorders
        1. Psychostimulants and ADHD
           a. The "Paradoxical Effect" Paradox
           b. Usage and Effects
           c. Side Effects
           d. Antidepressant Medication for ADHD
        2. Behavioral Family Therapy
        3. Treatment of Conduct Disorders and Juvenile Delinquency
           a. Residential Programs and Juvenile Courts
     C. Course and Outcome

Learning Objectives

After reviewing the material presented in this chapter, you should be able to:

1.   Distinguish between externalizing and internalizing disorders of childhood.

2.   State some of the primary factors considered in the evaluation of
      externalizing symptoms.

3.   Compare separation anxiety with separation anxiety disorder.

4.   Understand that children's psychological problems are not simply miniature
      versions of adult disorders.

5. Describe some of the rare childhood disorders: pica, rumination disorder, Tourette's disorder, selective mutism, reactive attachment disorder, stereotypic movement disorder, encopresis, and enuresis.

6. Give the defining characteristics of conduct disorder, oppositional defiant disorder, and attention-deficit/hyperactivity disorder.

7. Understand how attachment theory attempts to explain disorders of childhood.

8. State and describe the four parenting styles and explain how inconsistent parenting leads to externalizing symptoms in children.

9. List and describe some of the genetic and biological evidence, both positive and negative, concerning the etiology of childhood disorders.

10. Describe the ways in which behavioral family therapy is utilized in the treatment of externalizing disorders.

11. Identify the common course and outcome of the primary childhood disorders.

Key Terms - Matching #1

The following terms related to psychological disorders of childhood are important to know. To test your knowledge, match the following terms with their definitions. Answers are listed at the end of the chapter.

a. Externalizing disorders
b. Attention-deficit/hyperactivity disorder
c. Oppositional defiant disorder
d. Conduct disorder
e. Internalizing disorders
f. Learning disorders
g. Continuous performance test
h. Separation anxiety
i. Separation anxiety disorder
j. School refusal
k. Peer sociometrics
l. Pica
m. Rumination disorder

n. Tourette's disorder
o. Stereotypic movement disorder
p. Selective mutism
q. Reactive attachment disorder
r. Encopresis
s. Enuresis
t. Hyperkinesis
u. Index offenses
v. Juvenile delinquency
w. Status offenses
x. Representative sample
y. Attachment theory
z. Anaclitic depression

1. _____ crimes against people or property that are illegal at any age
2. _____ consistent failure to speak in certain social situations, while speech is unrestricted in other situations
3. _____ a set of proposals about the normal development of attachments and the adverse consequences of troubled attachment relationships
4. _____ a legal classification determined by a judge

5. _____ a disorder of childhood characterized by persistent and excessive worry for the safety of an attachment figure, fears of separation, nightmares with separation themes, and refusal to be alone
6. _____ an outdated term for hyperactivity
7. _____ the lack of social responsiveness found among infants who do not have a consistent attachment figure
8. _____ normal distress following separation from an attachment figure which peaks at about 15 months of age
9. _____ repeated motor and verbal tics
10. _____ acts that are illegal only becuase of the youth's status as a minor
11. _____ an empirically derived category of disruptive child behavior problems that create problems for the external world
12. _____ the repeated regurgitation and rechewing of food
13. _____ a disorder defined primarily by behavior that is illegal as well as antisocial
14. _____ characterized by severely disturbed and developmentally inappropriate social relationships
15. _____ a sample that accurately represents some larger group of people
16. _____ an extreme reluctance to go to school, accompanied by symptoms of anxiety
17. _____ a laboratory task that requires the subject to monitor and respond to numbers or letters presented on a computer screen
18. _____ a group of educational problems characterized by academic performance that is notably below academic aptitude
19. _____ a method of assessing children's social relationships and categorizing children's social standing by obtaining information on who is "liked most" and who is "liked least" from a group of children who know each other
20. _____ self-stimulation or self-injurious behavior that is serious enough to require treatment
21. _____ inappropriately controlled defecation
22. _____ a disorder characterized by hyperactivity, inattention, and impulsivity
23. _____ the persistent eating of nonnutritive substances
24. _____ inappropriately controlled urination
25. _____ a disorder characterized by negative, hostile, and defiant behavior
26. _____ an empirically derived category of psychological problems of childhood that affect the child more than the external world

Key Terms - Matching #2

The following terms related to psychological disorders of childhood are important to know. To test your knowledge, match the following terms with their definitions. Answers are listed at the end of the chapter.

1. Secure attachments
2. Anxious attachments
3. Anxious avoidant attachments
4. Anxious resistant attachments
5. Disorganized attachments
6. Resilience

14. Salicylates
15. Delay of gratification
16. Emotion regulation
17. Psychostimulants
18. Dose-response effects
19. Behavioral family therapy

7. Authoritative parenting
8. Authoritarian parenting
9. Indulgent parenting
10. Neglectful parenting
11. Coercion
12. Time-out
13. Temperament

20. Parent training
21. Negotiation
22. Multisystemic therapy
23. Recidivism
24. Rehabilitation
25. Parens patriae
26. Diversion

a. _____ an anxious attachment where the infant is wary of exploration, not easily soothed by the attachment figure, and angry or ambivalent about contact

b. _____ an anxious attachment where the infant responds inconsistently because of conflicting feelings toward an inconsistent caregiver who is the potential source of either reassurance or fear

c. _____ a food additive that was thought to be related to ADHD but which controlled research has found to be unrelated

d. _____ the response to different dosages of medications

e. _____ parenting that is unconcerned with both the child's emotional needs and needs for discipline

f. _____ repeat offending

g. _____ learning to identify, evaluate, and control one's feelings based on the reactions, attitudes, and advice of others in the social world

h. _____ combines family treatment with coordinated interventions in other important contexts of the troubled child's life

i. _____ teaching parents discipline strategies

j. _____ parenting that is affectionate but lax in discipline

k. _____ parenting that is strict, often harsh and undemocratic, as well as lacking in warmth

l. _____ keeping problem youths out of the juvenile justice system

m. _____ a technique of briefly isolating a child following misbehavior

n. _____ infants with these attachments are fearful about exploration and are not easily comforted by their attachment figures, who respond inadequately or inconsistently to the child's needs

o. _____ infants with these attachments separate easily and explore away from their attachment figure but seek comfort when threatened

p. _____ a child's inborn behavioral characteristics, such as activity level, emotionality, and sociability

q. _____ a form of family treatment which trains parents to use the principles of operant conditioning to improve child discipline

r. _____ a system of interaction in which parents and children reciprocally reinforce child misbehavior and parent capitulation

s. _____ an anxious attachment where the infant is generally unwary of strange situations and shows little preference for the attachment figure over others

t. _____ the adaptive ability to defer smaller but immediate rewards for larger long-term benefits

u. _____ the goal of treatment for delinquent youths

v. _____ a process in which young people are actively involved in defining rules

w. _____ the ability to bounce back from adversity

x. _____ the state as parent

y. _____ medications used to treat children with ADHD
z. _____ parenting that is both loving and firm

Names You Should Know - Matching

The following people have played an important role in research and theory of psychological disorders of childhood. To test your knowledge, match the following names with the descriptions of their contributions to the study of abnormal psychology. Answers are listed at the end of the chapter.

a. Mary Ainsworth   c. John Bowlby   e. Gerald Patterson
b. Michael Rutter   d. Lawrence Kohlberg   f. Benjamin Feingold

1. _____ developed the family adversity index
2. _____ conducted many empirical studies on attachment theory
3. _____ developed the concept of coercion
4. _____ proposed that food additives caused hyperactivity
5. _____ studied moral development in children
6. _____ developed attachment theory

Review of Concepts - Fill in the Blank and True/False

This section will help focus your studying by testing whether you understand the concepts presented in the text. After you have read and reviewed the material, test your comprehension and memory by filling in the following blanks or circling the right answer. Answers are listed at the end of the chapter.

1. Which of the following disorders involves violations of laws?
   oppositional defiant disorder   **conduct disorder**
2. What percent of arrests for index offenses are of juveniles under 18 years of age?
   7 percent   **29 percent**   **63 percent**
3. Adult antisocial behavior is better predicted by information about the person during
   childhood or **adolescence**.
4. In adolescence, violations of rules is _____.
5. Impulsivity is acting before _____.
6. Where is hyperactivity often first noticed? _____
7. The behavioral problems that characterize ADHD are largely
   intentional or **unintentional**.
8. Assessment of children's feelings is   **straightforward** or **difficult**.
9. Parents are very good at detecting their children's depression: **true**   **false**
10. If in error, parents are likely to   **overestimate** or **underestimate**   their

children's depression.

11. Fears in children are a symptom of some emotional disorder: **true** **false**

12. School refusal often indicates a child's fear of _____.

13. Which category of peer ratings is the most correlated with psychological disorders? _____

14. What type of norms are essential in assessing abnormal behavior in children? _____ norms

15. A learning disorder is defined as one or two standard deviations between _____ and _____.

16. There is a high degree of comorbidity between learning disorders and which two psychological disorders? _____ and _____

    _____

17. Learning disorders are easily treated: **true** **false**

18. Encopresis and enuresis are usually **causes of** or **reactions to** psychological distress.

19. The bell and pad is a device that is effective in treating _____.

20. The current DSM-IV is probably **overinclusive** or **underinclusive** in its listing of childhood psychological disorders.

21. Hyperactivity is the result of inattention: **true** **false**

22. ADHD and oppositional defiant disorder are separate but _____ disorders.

23. More **boys** or **girls** are treated for psychological disorders; more **men** or **women** enter into therapy.

24. Girls are more likely to have _____ problems, and boys are more likely to have _____ problems.

25. Risk for _____ problems increase substantially when more than one family adversity risk factor is present.

26. What is the third leading cause of death among teenagers? _____

27. Picking up a crying infant makes it **easier** or **more difficult** to manage.

28. Children with serious conduct problems often have parents who use what type of parenting? _____

29. Negative attention is sometimes _____ to children.

30. Crime rates are about the same in the United States and in Europe: **true** **false**

31. Research has shown that critical and demanding parenting is the **cause** or **result** of hyperactive child behavior.

32. A certain temperamental style has been linked to _____ disorders in adulthood.

33. Genetic factors appear to be moderately linked to ADHD: **true** **false**

34. Children with externalizing disorders may be less _____ reactive than other children.

35. Research has shown that sugar increases hyperactive behavior: **true** **false**

36. Children with externalizing disorder have problems with _____ control.

37. Aggressive children demonstrate immaturity in moral development: **true** **false**

38. Children with mothers who are depressed are more likely to develop _____.

39. Children usually grow out of internalizing disorders: **true** **false**

40. Antidepressants are effective in treating children with depression: **true** **false**

41. Psychostimulants are effective in treating children with ADHD: **true** **false**

42. Psychostimulants have a paradoxical effect on children with ADHD, which demonstrates the biological underpinnings of the disorder: **true** **false**

43. Psychostimulants are taken for a couple of weeks and their effects last for several months at a time: **true** **false**

44. Psychostimulants given at high doses provide maximum _____ _____ but interfere with _____.

45. Medication is more helpful in the treatment of ADHD than behavioral family therapy: **true** **false**

46. When juveniles are diverted from the juvenile justice system, they show higher rates of recidivism: **true** **false**

Multiple Choice Questions

The following multiple choice questions will test your comprehension of the material presented in the chapter. Answers are listed at the end of the chapter.

1) In his study on family adversity, Michael Rutter found that all of the following were predictors of behavior problems among children EXCEPT:

a. low income
b. overcrowding in the home
c. conflict between parents
d. paternal depression

2) All of the following are major problems in evaluating children's internalizing symptoms EXCEPT:

   a. there are insufficient self-report measures to assess internalizing symptoms in children
   b. it is much more difficult for adults to assess children's inner experiences than it is to observe children's behavior
   c. children often are not reliable or valid informants about their internal life
   d. children's capacity to recognize emotions in themselves emerges slowly over the course of development and therefore they may not be aware of their own emotional turmoil

3) Reactive attachment disorder is most likely caused by which of the following?

   a. it appears to have genetic origins
   b. an unstable home environment in which caregivers are frequently changing
   c. extremely neglectful parenting
   d. its etiology is unknown

4) All of the following are major subtypes of externalizing disorders EXCEPT:

   a. attention-deficit/hyperactivity disorder
   b. conduct disorder
   c. depression
   d. oppositional defiant disorder

5) Which of the following is the most helpful information for scientists to have for predicting adult antisocial behavior?

   a. information obtained during birth and infancy
   b. information obtained during childhood
   c. information obtained during adolescence
   d. information obtained during adulthood

6) According to a panel of experts assembled by the National Academy of Sciences, at least _____ percent of the 63 million children living in the United States suffer from a mental disorder:

   a. 5   c. 17
   b. 12   d. 23

7) Which of the following is a sample that accurately depicts a larger group of people?

   a. representative sample   c. convenience sample
   b. random sample   d. heterogeneous sample

8) _____ implies that an externalizing problem has environmental origins, while _____ implies problems with some sort of biological cause.

   a. Attention-deficit/hyperactivity disorder; oppositional defiant disorder
   b. Oppositional defiant disorder; attention-deficit/hyperactivity disorder
   c. Conduct disorder; oppositional defiant disorder
   d. Oppositional defiant disorder; conduct disorder

9) Separation anxiety disorder is typically associated with all of the following EXCEPT:

   a. fears of getting lost or being kidnapped
   b. refusal to be alone
   c. persistent and excessive worry for the safety of an attachment figure
   d. refusal to interact with others when the attachment figure is not present

10) Typically, the attachment figure for an infant with an anxious attachment responds to the infant in which of the following ways?

   a. appropriately attends to the infant's needs
   b. inadequately or inconsistently attends to the infant's needs
   c. immediately attends to the infant's needs
   d. is completely unresponsive to the infant's needs

11) The FBI reports that about _____ percent of arrests for major crimes including murder, forcible rape, and robbery are of juveniles under the age of 18.

   a. 10   c. 30
   b. 20   d. 40

12) Which of the following is a well-known treatment device that awakens children with enuresis by setting off an alarm as they begin to wet the bed?

   a. bell and pad   c. sensitive signal seat
   b. light and alarm   d. responsive wetting device

13) Which of the following is characterized by self-stimulation or self-injurious behavior?

   a. conduct disorder
   b. developmental coordination disorder
   c. Tourette's disorder
   d. stereotypic movement disorder

14) ADHD is characterized by all of the following symptoms EXCEPT:

   a. impulsivity   c. aggression
   b. hyperactivity   d. inattention

15) Treatment with children often begins with which of the following?

    a. an attempt to get the adults (i.e., parents, teachers) to agree as to what the problem really is
    b. identifying a disorder and then building hypotheses to either prove or disprove it
    c. helping the child to identify his or her problems
    d. an attempt to treat the family, independent of the child, in order to facilitate change in the child's environment

16) Which of the following gender differences is NOT TRUE in respect to internalizing and externalizing problems?

    a. more adult men enter into therapy than do adult women
    b. boys are treated more for psychological problems than are girls
    c. by early adult life, more females report psychological problems than males
    d. boys have far more externalizing disorders than girls

17) According to the "peer sociometric method" of assessing children's relationships, which of the following groups is characterized by a high frequency of "liked least" ratings and a low frequency of "liked most" ratings?

    a. average   c. rejected
    b. neglected   d. controversial

18) All of the following are internalizing symptoms EXCEPT:

    a. somatic complaints   c. aggressive behavior
    b. fears   d. sadness

19) All of the following factors influence how adults evaluate children's rule violations EXCEPT:

    a. frequency of the child's behavior   c. intensity of the child's behavior
    b. duration of the child's behavior   d. all of the above

20) Brandon is a three-year-old who frequently throws a tantrum when in the grocery store if he does not get what he wants. Because this is such an embarrassing situation for his mother, she will give Brandon whatever he desires in order to get his cooperation. In this case, Brandon is being _____ while his mother is being _____.

    a. positively reinforced; negatively reinforced
    b. negatively reinforced; positively reinforced
    c. classically conditioned; punished
    d. positively reinforced; punished

21) Infants typically develop a fear of _____ around the age of seven to eight months.

   a. strangers
   b. the dark
   c. monsters
   d. unfamiliar environments

22) Which of the following is the process of shaping children's behavior and attitudes to conform to the expectations of parents, teachers, and society as a whole?

   a. modeling
   b. socialization
   c. conditioning
   d. vicarious learning

Understanding Research - Fill in the Blank

Family Treatment of Childhood Anxiety: The text presents a detailed description of a study by Barrett, Dadds, and Rapee in the Research Close-Up on p. 601. Finding the answers to these questions will help you get a good understanding of this study and why it is important. It is not necessary to memorize the answers; the process of finding them in the textbook will help you learn the material you need to know.

1. There is _____ research on treatment of children's anxiety disorders. In the only other existing study, cognitive behavior therapy was found to produce significant _____ among children with an anxiety disorder. The family treatment developed by the authors of this study involved teaching parents to _____ their children's courageous behavior and _____ excessive _____ or fearful behavior. Parents were taught to become more aware of their _____ anxiety and _____ coping with fear. Parents were taught _____ and problem-solving skills. How many children were in the study? _____ The children were assigned to CBT, _____, or a waiting list.

2. There were follow-ups immediately after treatment, _____ months after treatment, and _____ months after treatment. They found that CBT+FAM was _____ than just CBT. These improvement rates are _____ than those for the treatment of adult anxiety disorders. What percent of the children on the waiting list improved with no treatment? _____ percent

<u>Samples and Sampling</u>: The text discusses this research issue in the Research Methods section on pp. 589-590. Finding the answers to these questions will help you get a good understanding of these issues.

3.   Instead of representative samples, researchers often use _____ samples in their research. Representative samples are essential only when trying to determine questions such as whether single parenting causes _____ _____. What type of sample can be used to generalize to a larger sample?   _____

In one of the most famous examples of sampling errors, newspaper headlines stated that _____ beat _____ in the presidential elections.

4. In a survey of _____ children that constituted a _____ sample, _____ percent of children had a learning, behavioral, or developmental disorder. _____ percent had significant emotional or behavioral problems. More than _____ percent had received treatment for psychological problems. These problems were associated, but only modestly, with family _____. Black and Latino parents reported _____ problems than white parents, but when _____ records were examined, they had more problems.

Brief Essay

As a final exercise, write out answers to the following brief essay questions. Then compare your answers with the material presented in the text.

After you have answered these questions, review the "critical thinking" questions that are presented at the end of the text chapter. Answering these questions will help you integrate important issues and themes that have been featured throughout the chapter.

1. Discuss the challenges of identifying internalizing problems in children. How do different sources of information vary on their estimation of internalizing problems (e.g., children, parents, teachers, self-report inventories)? What is the best course of action for psychologists and researchers studying these problems?

2. Your text discusses classifying children's psychological problems in the context of key interpersonal relationships rather than using the current method of classification. Briefly discuss the strengths and weaknesses of each approach.

3. Compare and contrast the following disorders: attention-deficit/hyperactivity disorder, oppositional defiant disorder, and conduct disorder. Include a brief discussion on the overlap between these disorders.

ANSWER KEY

Answers to the exercises are listed below; page numbers where the information is referenced in the textbook are given in parentheses.

Key Terms - Matching #1

1. u (587)	14. q (582)
2. p (582)	15. x (589)
3. y (592)	16. j (579)
4. v (587)	17. g (577)
5. i (579)	18. f (573)
6. t (584)	19. k (580)
7. z (592)	20. o (582)
8. h (579)	21. r (583)
9. n (582)	22. b (572)
10. w (587)	23. l (582)
11. a (572)	24. s (583)
12. m (582)	25. c (572)
13. d (572)	26. e (573)

Names You Should Know

1. b (591)
2. a (592)
3. e (594)
4. f (598)
5. d (599)
6. c (593)

Key Terms - Matching #2

a. 4 (593)	n. 2 (592)
b. 5 (593)	o. 1 (592)
c. 14 (598)	p. 13 (597)
d. 18 (603)	q. 19 (604)
e. 10 (594)	r. 11 (594)
f. 23 (605)	s. 3 (592)
g. 16 (599)	t. 15 (599)
h. 22 (604)	u. 24 (605)
i. 20 (604)	v. 21 (604)
j. 9 (594)	w. 6 (593)
k. 8 (593)	x. 25 (605)
l. 26 (605)	y. 17 (602)
m. 12 (594)	z. 7 (593)

Multiple Choice

1. d	6. b	11. c	16. a	21. a
2. a	7. a	12. a	17. c	22. b
3. c	8. b	13. d	18. c	
4. c	9. d	14. c	19. d	
5. b	10. b	15. a	20. a	

Review of Concepts

1. conduct disorder (572)
2. 29 percent (575)
3. childhood (576)
4. normative (576)
5. thinking (576)
6. in the classroom (577)
7. unintentional (577)
8. difficult (578)
9. false (578)
10. underestimate (578)
11. false (579)
12. leaving a parent (579)
13. rejected (580)
14. developmental (582)
15. aptitude; achievement (581)
16. ADHD; oppositional defiant disorder (581)
17. false (581)
18. causes of (584)
19. enuresis (584)
20. overinclusive (584)
21. false (584)
22. overlapping (586)
23. boys; women (590)
24. internalizing; externalizing (591)
25. externalizing (591)
26. suicide (591)
27. easier (593)
28. neglectful (594)
29. reinforcing (595)
30. false (595)
31. result (596)
32. anxiety (597)
33. true (597)
34. emotionally (598)
35. false (599)
36. self (599)
37. true (599)
38. depression (599)
39. false (600)
40. false (600)
41. true (602)
42. false (602)
43. false (602)
44. behavioral control; learning (603)
45. true (604)
46. false (605)

Understanding Research

1. little; improvements; reward; ignore; complaining; own; model; communication; 79; CBT+FAM

2. six; 12; better; better; 26 percent

3. convenience; children's psychological problems; A sample that is representative of the population that will be generalized to; Dewey; Truman

4. 17; 110; representative; 20; 13.4; 10; income; fewer; school

CHAPTER 17 - ADJUSTMENT DISORDERS AND DIFFICULT LIFE EVENTS: LIFE-CYCLE TRANSITIONS

Chapter Outline

I. Overview
    A. Typical Symptoms and Associated Features of Life-Cycle Transitions
    B. Classification of Life-Cycle Transitions
        1. Brief Historical Perspective
        2. Contemporary Classification of Life-Cycle Transitions

II. The Transition to Adulthood
    A. Typical Symptoms and Associated Features of the Adult Transition
        1. Identity Crisis
        2. Changes in Roles and Relationships
        3. Emotional Turmoil
    B. Classification of Identity Conflicts
    C. Epidemiology of Identity Conflicts
    D. Etiological Considerations and Research on the Adult Transition
    E. Treatment During the Transition to Adult Life

III. Family Transitions
    A. Typical Symptoms and Associated Features of Family Transitions
        1. Family Conflict
        2. Emotional Distress
        3. Cognitive Conflicts
    B. Classification of Troubled Family Relationships
    C. Epidemiology of Family Transitions
    D. Etiological Considerations and Research on Family Transitions
        1. Psychological Factors
            a. Communication Problems
            b. Family Roles
        2. Social Factors
        3. Biological Factors
    E. Treatment During Family Transitions
        1. Prevention Programs
        2. Couples Therapy and Family Therapy
            a. Behavioral Marital Therapy
            b. Treating Individual Problems with Couples Therapy or Family Therapy

IV. Aging and the Transition to Later Life
    A. Ageism
    B. Typical Symptoms and Associated Features of the Transition to Later Life
        1. Physical Functioning and Health
            a. Menopause
            b. Sensation and Physical Movement
        2. Life Satisfaction, Work, and Relationships
            a. Integrity versus Despair

      b. Relationships
    3. Grief and Bereavement
    4. Mental Health
C. Classification of Aging
D. Epidemiology of Aging
E. Etiological Considerations and Research on the Aging Transition
F. Treatment of Psychological Problems in Later Life

Learning Objectives

After reviewing the material presented in this chapter, you should be able to:

1.   Define life-cycle transition.

2.   Understand that life-cycle transitions may play a role in the development of psychopathology.

3.   Describe Erikson's psychosocial moratorium and identity crisis.

4.   Define Marcia's four identity statuses.

5.   Describe some common gender differences that occur in the transition to adulthood.

6.   Identify ways in which power struggles, intimacy struggles, affiliation, interdependence, and scapegoating impact upon the family structure.

7.   Describe Gottman's four communication problems, giving examples for each type of problem.

8.   Describe some premarital and marital therapy treatment programs.

9.   Compare Bowlby's and Kubler-Ross's model of grieving in bereavement

10.   Identify typical psychological and physiological processes in young-old, old-old, and oldest-old adults.

11.   Describe some gender differences in adults in later life in terms of relationships.

Key Terms - Matching #1

The following terms related to adjustment disorders and difficult life events are important to know. To test your knowledge, match the following terms with their definitions. Answers are listed at the end of the chapter.

    a. Adjustment disorders   k. Identity crisis
    b. Life-span development   l. Intimacy versus self-absorption

c. Life-cycle transitions
d. Transition to adult life
e. Family transitions
f. Transition to later life
g. Interpersonal diagnoses
h. Crisis of the healthy personality
i. Identity
j. Identity versus role confusion

m. Generativity versus stagnation
n. Integrity and despair
o. Family life cycle
p. Early adult transition
q. Midlife transition
r. Late adult transition
s. Social clocks

1. _____ the challenge in establishing intimate relationships, balanced between closeness and independence
2. _____ clinically significant symptoms in response to stress that are not severe enought to warrant classification as another mental disorder
3. _____ career and family accomplishments with purpose or direction versus lacking purpose or direction
4. _____ struggles in the process of moving from one social or psychological stage of adult development into a new one
5. _____ a series of normal conflicts related to change as the comfortable and predictable conflicts with the fearsome but exciting unknown
6. _____ becoming less driven by internal and external demands and developing more compassion for ourselves and others
7. _____ classification of psychological problems that reside within the context of human relationships rather than within an individual
8. _____ age-related goals for ourselves
9. _____ a period of basic uncertainty about self
10. _____ the challenge of adolescence and young adulthood, this stage involves integrating various role identities into a global sense of self
11. _____ continuities and changes in behavior from infancy through the last years of life
12. _____ looking back on one's life with either a sense of acceptance and pride or anger and despair
13. _____ global sense of self
14. _____ the changing roles and relationships of later life
15. _____ the developmental course of family relationships throughout life
16. _____ in the middle years of life; includes birth of first child and divorce
17. _____ in the late teens and early twenties; struggling with identity, career, and relationship issues
18. _____ moving away from family and assuming adult roles
19. _____ major changes in life roles like retirement, grief over death of loved ones, and aging and facing mortality

Key Terms - Matching #2

The following terms related to adjustment disorders and difficult life events are important to know. To test your knowledge, match the following terms with their definitions. Answers are listed at the end of the chapter.

1. Moratorium
2. Identity diffusion
3. Identity foreclosure
4. Identity moratorium
5. Identity achievement
6. Alienated identity achievement
7. Empty nest
8. Power struggles
9. Intimacy struggles
10. Boundaries
11. Reciprocity
12. Demand and withdrawal pattern
13. Affiliation
14. Interdependence
15. Scapegoat
16. Heritability
17. Heritability ratio
18. Criticism
19. Contempt
20. Defensiveness
21. Stonewalling
22. Androgynous couples
23. Behavioral marital therapy

a. _____ a dimension with control on one end and emancipation at the other
b. _____ couples in which both husbands and wives have high levels of masculinity and femininity
c. _____ the adjustment that occurs when adult children leave the family home
d. _____ a new identity status common in the 1960s, where one's definition of self is alienated from many values held by the larger society
e. _____ attacking someone's personality rather than his or her actions
f. _____ emphasizes the couple's moment-to-moment interaction, focusing on exchange of positive and negative behaviors, style of communication, and strategies for problem-solving
g. _____ where the wife becomes increasingly demanding and the husband withdraws further and further as time passes
h. _____ a statistic used for summarizing the genetic contributions to behavioral characteristics; equal to the variance due to genetic factors divided by the total variance in a behavioral characteristic
i. _____ the category of being in the middle of an identity crisis and actively searching for adult roles
j. _____ a form of self-justification, such as denying responsibility or blaming the other person
k. _____ social exchange of cooperation and conflict
l. _____ a pattern of isolation and withdrawal
m. _____ attempts to change dominance relations
n. _____ a time of uncertainty about self and goals
o. _____ a family member who is held to blame for all of a family's troubles
p. _____ attempts to alter the degree of closeness in a relationship
q. _____ the category of having questioned childhood identity but not actively searching for new adult roles
r. _____ a continuum anchored by active love at one end and attack at the other
s. _____ the category of having questioned one's identity and having successfully decided on long-term goals
t. _____ an insult motivated by anger and intended to hurt the other person
u. _____ the rules of a relationship
v. _____ the relative contribution of genes to behavioral characteristics
w. _____ the category of having never questioned oneself or one's goals but instead proceeding along the predetermined course of one's childhood commitments

Key Terms - Matching #3

The following terms related to adjustment disorders and difficult life events are important to know. To test your knowledge, match the following terms with their definitions. Answers are listed at the end of the chapter.

a. Ageism
b. Menopause
c. Estrogen
d. Hormone replacement therapy
e. Reminiscence
f. Integrative reminiscence
g. Instrumental reminiscence
h. Transitive reminiscence
i. Escapist reminiscence
j. Obsessive reminiscence
k. Narrative reminiscence
l. Grief
m. Bereavement
n. Gerontology
o. Young-old adults
p. Old-old adults
q. Oldest-old adults
r. Behavioral gerontology

1. _____ the cessation of menstruation
2. _____ descriptive rather than interpretive
3. _____ misconceptions and prejudices about aging
4. _____ the recounting of personal memories of the distant past
5. _____ the multidisciplinary study of aging
6. _____ a female sex hormone that fluctuates during menopause
7. _____ the emotional and social process of coping with a separation or loss
8. _____ adults ages 85 and older
9. _____ an attempt to achieve a sense of self-worth, coherence, and reconciliation with the past
10. _____ preoccupation with failure; full of guilt, bitterness, and despair
11. _____ adults roughly between the ages of 65 and 75; those in good health and active in their communities
12. _____ a subdiscipline of health psychology and behavioral medicine which focuses on the study and treatment of behavioral components of health and illness among older adults
13. _____ a specific form of grieving in response to the death of a loved one
14. _____ the administration of artifical estrogen
15. _____ full of glorification of the past and deprecation of the present
16. _____ includes both direct moral instruction and storytelling with clear moral implications; serves the function of passing on cultural heritage and personal legacy
17. _____ adults roughly between the ages of 75 and 85; those who suffer from major physical, psychological, or social problems and require some routine assistance in living
18. _____ the review of goal-directed activities and attainments reflecting a sense of control and success in overcoming life's obstacles

Names You Should Know - Matching

The following people have played an important role in research and theory of adjustment disorders and difficult life transitions. To test your knowledge, match the following names with the descriptions of their contributions to the study of abnormal psychology. Answers are listed at the end of the chapter.

a. Erik Erikson
b. Daniel Levinson
c. Karen Horney
d. Lorna Benjamin
e. John Gottman
f. Elisabeth Kubler-Ross

1. ____ argues that there are two key dimensions of relationships, an affiliation dimension and an interdependence dimension
2. ____ widened the emphasis of adult development to social as well as psychological tasks
3. ____ developed a stage theory of grieving in bereavement
4. ____ developed a stage theory of psychosocial development from birth to death
5. ____ focused on communication patterns in marital interaction
6. ____ theorized that people have competing needs to move toward, to move away from, and to move against others

Review of Concepts - Fill in the Blank and True/False

This section will help focus your studying by testing whether you understand the concepts presented in the text. After you have read and reviewed the material, test your comprehension and memory by filling in the following blanks or circling the right answer. Answers are listed at the end of the chapter.

1. The DSM-IV has a comprehensive, detailed section on adjustment disorders and other conditions besides mental disorders that may be the focus of psycho-therapy: **true**   **false**
2. Erikson focused more on the _____ side of "psychosocial" development, while Levinson focused more on the _____ aspects.
3. Research has shown that   **adolescents** or **adults**   experience more intense emotions.
4. The development of identity has been   **focused on** or **neglected** by researchers.
5. The "forgotten half" refers to youth who do not _____.
6. Research suggests that the most successful young adults have parents who strike a balance between continuing to provide support and _____ and allowing their children increasing _____.
7. For women in traditional roles, identity often develops out of _____.
8. Marital satisfaction   **increases** or **decreases**   following the birth of the first child.

9. Family members with happy relationships _____ negative comments and _____ positive ones.

10. Research shows that men but not women experience high emotional arousal as _____.

11. About _____ of all existing marriages will end in divorce.

12. **Whites** or **blacks** are more likely to remarry following divorce.

13. Androgynous couples had marriages that were **higher** or **lower** in satisfaction than nonandrogynous couples.

14. Research indicates that the Premarital Relationship Enhancement Program **is** or **is not** effective in increasing marital satisfaction over time.

15. Behavioral marital therapy has been shown to be more effective than other therapy approaches: **true** **false**

16. Couples therapy can be effective in alleviating a person's depression: **true** **false**

17. **Men** or **women** have a shorter life expectancy.

18. Older people are less satisfied with their lives: **true** **false**

19. Personality has been found to be consistent from middle age to old age: **true** **false**

20. Physical activity and physical health are some of the best predictors of psychological well-being among older adults: **true** **false**

21. Hormone replacement therapy increases the risk for cancer: **true** **false**

22. Visual acuity actually increases with age: **true** **false**

23. Older adults report fewer positive relationships and a declined sense of mastery over their environment than young and middle age adults: **true** **false**

24. Researchers have found support for the stages of bereavement proposed by Kubler-Ross: **true** **false**

25. Less intense bereavement predicts better long-term adjustment: **true** **false**

26. The prevalence of mental disorders increases with age: **true** **false**

27. The risk of completed suicide is higher among the elderly: **true** **false**

28. Men apparently benefit more from _____ while women benefit more from _____.

Multiple Choice Questions

The following multiple choice questions will test your comprehension of the material presented in the chapter. Answers are listed at the end of the chapter.

1) According to Lorna Benjamin, the foundation of this dimension of relationships is attack at one end and active love at the opposite extreme.

   a. interdependence
   b. enmeshed
   c. affiliation
   d. resolution

2) Which of the following groups has the highest suicide rate?

   a. teenagers
   b. young adults
   c. middle-aged adults
   d. adults over the age of 65

3) Which of the following includes various struggles in the process of moving from one social or psychological "stage" of adult development into a new stage?

   a. life cycle transitions
   b. transition to adult life
   c. developmental tasks of adult life
   d. family transitions

4) Approximately _____ of couples seen in behavioral marital therapy do not improve significantly.

   a. 30 percent
   b. 40 percent
   c. 50 percent
   d. 60 percent

5) According to Erikson, which of the following stages is the major challenge of adolescence and young adulthood?

   a. integrity versus despair
   b. generativity versus stagnation
   c. intimacy versus self-absorption
   d. identity versus role confusion

6) On the average, marital happiness declines following _____.

   a. the death of a family member
   b. the birth of the first child
   c. the emptying of the family nest
   d. the fifth year of marriage

7) Which of the following refers to youth who do not attend college and who often assume marginal roles in U.S. society?

   a. "Transient Youth"
   b. "Generation X"
   c. "Alienated Youth"
   d. "Forgotten Half"

8) When reviewing the various models of adult development, which of the following must be taken into consideration?

   a. that history, culture, and personal values influence views about which kinds of "tasks" are normal during adult development
   b. that transitions or "crises" may not be as predictable as the models imply
   c. some people may not pass through a particular stage of development
   d. all of the above

9) Research indicates that depression is more closely linked to _____ for women, while it is more closely liked to _____ for men.

    a. marital conflict; divorce
    b. divorce; marital conflict
    c. poor support system; financial difficulties
    d. financial difficulties; poor support system

10) The ratio of men to women _____ at older ages.

    a. increases
    b. decreases
    c. is approximately equal
    d. stays relatively the same across the age span

11) Erik Erikson highlighted _____ as a common theme that occurs throughout life cycle transitions.

    a. uncertainty   c. remorse
    b. conflict   d. acceptance

12) Estimates indicate that about _____ of all of today's marriages will end in divorce.

    a. 30 percent   c. 50 percent
    b. 40 percent   d. 60 percent

13) Epidemiological evidence indicates that the prevalence of mental disorders is _____ among adults 65 years of age and older as compared to younger adults.

    a. lower
    b. higher
    c. about the same
    d. it is unknown due to the difficulty in studying this population

14) Which of the following identifies people who are in the middle of an identity crisis and who are actively searching for adult roles?

    a. alienated identity achievement
    b. identity moratorium
    c. identify diffusion
    d. identity foreclosure

15) All of the following are emphasized by behavioral marital therapy EXCEPT:

    a. the couple's moment-to-moment interactions
    b. strategies for solving problems
    c. extensive clinical interview of relationship patterns in the couple's families
    d. the couple's style of communication

16) Family life cycle theorists classify adult development according to which of the following?

    a. the tasks and transitions of family life
    b. the adult's memories of their childhood and adolescence
    c. the tasks and transitions of psychological challenges of adulthood
    d. all of the above

17) Psychological research suggests that the most successful young adults have which kind of parents?

    a. parents who are strict and authoritarian
    b. parents who are supportive and could be characterized as their children's "best friend"
    c. parents who strongly encourage individuation and provide opportunities for their children to take on numerous responsibilities at an early age
    d. parents who strike a balance between continuing to provide support and supervision of their children while allowing them increasing independence

18) Which of the following individuals theorized that people have competing needs to move toward, to move away from, and to move against others?

    a. Erik Erikson   c. Karen Horney
    b. Daniel Levinson   d. Elisabeth Kubler-Ross

19) _____ struggles are attempts to change dominance relations, whereas _____ struggles are attempts to alter the degree of closeness in a relationship.

    a. Intimacy; power   c. Conflict; relational
    b. Power; intimacy   d. Relational; conflict

20) A study of adults over the age of 70 found that both men and women listed which of the following as the most common contribution to a negative quality of life in their later years?

    a. poor health   c. financial difficulties
    b. death of a spouse   d. interpersonal problems

21) All of the following are true of the "V codes" in the DSM-IV EXCEPT:

    a. they do not include an extensive summary of life difficulties
    b. they are similar to other diagnoses in the DSM in that they are diagnosed as mental disorders
    c. they include issues such as bereavement, identity problems, and phase of life problems.
    d. all of the above are true of "V codes"

22) Lisa and Mike have been married for four years. Recently, they have been arguing more than usual. Whenever they get into an argument, Lisa engages in a pattern of isolation and withdrawal, ignoring Mike's complaints and virtually ceasing all communication with him. According to the four basic communication problems identified by John Gottman, Lisa is engaged in which of the following?:

a. stonewalling
b. contempt
c. defensiveness
d. criticism

23) According to your text, all of the following are true of hormone replacement therapy EXCEPT:

a. it alleviates some of the psychological strains associated with adverse physical symptoms of menopause
b. reduces the subsequent risk for heart and bone disease
c. increases the risk for cancer
d. decreases symptoms of depression, which are often associated with menopause

24) Alternative lifestyles not withstanding, evidence indicates that _____ of the adults in the United States get married during their adult lives.

a. 40 percent
b. 60 percent
c. 75 percent
d. 90 percent

25) One criticism of Erikson's theories is:

a. the stages are inappropriate for certain developmental levels
b. the theories are too broad and general and are not applicable to a large proportion of the population
c. they are not very accurate in outlining developmental stages
d. the theories focus on men to the exclusion of women

26) According to Canadian psychologists Paul Wong and Lisa Watt, which of the following is associated with less successful adjustment in later life?

a. obsessive reminiscence
b. transitive reminiscence
c. instrumental reminiscence
d. integrative reminiscence

27) Family therapists and family researchers often blame difficulties in negotiating family transitions on which of the following?

a. low motivation
b. problems with communication
c. difficulty identifying problem areas
d. all of the above

28) Which of the following is NOT a stage of adult development in Erikson's model?

a. intimacy versus self-absorption
b. integrity versus despair
c. assurance versus apprehension
d. generativity versus stagnation

29) Research on identity achievement indicates that _____ may have rejecting and distant families, while _____ may have overprotective families.

   a. identity diffusers; identity foreclosers
   b. identity foreclosers; identity diffusers
   c. identity achievers; alienated identity achievers
   d. alienated identity achievers; identity achievers

30) All of the following are stages included in the Family Developmental Tasks through the Family Life Cycle EXCEPT:

   a. childbearing   c. aging family members
   b. launching center   d. death and dying

Understanding Research - Fill in the Blank

The Genetics of Divorce: The text presents a detailed description of a study by McGue and Lykken in the Research Close-Up on pp. 626-627. Finding the answers to these questions will help you get a good understanding of this study and why it is important. It is not necessary to memorize the answers; the process of finding them in the textbook will help you learn the material you need to know.

1. Behavior geneticists have increasingly emphasized that people make their own

_____. Some people are risk _____ who

constantly seek thrills, while others are risk-_____ who seek stable,

predictable environments. Family transitions may be partially determined by a

person's _____, which may be influenced by _____

factors. In this sense, _____ may be genetic. The sample in this

study included more than _____ MZ and DZ twin pairs. MZ twins with divorced

co-twins were more than _____ times as likely to be divorced as MZ twins with never-

divorced _____. For DZ twins, the risk was less than _____ times

higher if the co-twin was divorced than if the co-twin was never divorced. The

heritability of divorce was calculated at _____.

2. Clearly, there is no divorce _____. Since divorce does not occur at

random, children from divorced and married families differ in more ways than

_____. Over the past hundred years, divorce

rates have gone from _____ to _____. Environmental _____

can eliminate or increase divorce. Therefore, the issue is genes _____ environ-

ment. As well as personality traits, physical _____ or age

at _____ may be factors. People may find divorce more

_____ if their identical versus fraternal twin

has been divorced.

<u>The Concept of Heritability</u>: The text discusses this type of research in the Research Methods section on pp. 624-625. Finding the answers to these questions will help you get a good understanding of these issues.

3. The _____ is the most common method used in behavior genetics. Environmental factors are implicated in the etiology of a disorder when the concordance rate for MZ twins is _____. Why do some experts view the heritability ratio as representing a false dichotomy?_____

_____

4. Heritability estimates do not reflect the range of environments that are theoretically _____. If everyone had an identical environment, then all differences between people would be caused by _____. _____ may matter more than we are able to detect in contemporary research.

Brief Essay

As a final exercise, write out answers to the following brief essay questions. Then compare your answers with the material presented in the text.

After you have answered these questions, review the "critical thinking" questions that are presented at the end of the text chapter. Answering these questions will help you integrate important issues and themes that have been featured throughout the chapter.

1. Discuss the stages of Erik Erikson's model of adult development. What do you consider to be the strengths of this model? What are some of its weaknesses?

2. Outline the psychological, social, and biological factors that may contribute to difficulties in family transitions. Which factors do you think are most important when identifying the etiology of family transition difficulties?

3. Review the six categories of reminiscence identified by Paul Wong and Lisa Watt. Which categories appear to be related to successful aging? Which appear to be associated with less successful adjustment in later life? Which category do you think will best describe your reminiscence later in life? Why?

4. Discuss the various categories of identity conflicts as presented in your text. Presently, which category do you fit best in? Why?

ANSWER KEY

Answers to the exercises are listed below; page numbers where the information is referenced in the textbook are given in parentheses.

Key Terms - Matching #1

1. l (615)	11. b (610)
2. a (610)	12. n (615)
3. m (615)	13. i (613)
4. c (610)	14. r (616)
5. h (612)	15. o (615)
6. q (615)	16. e (611)
7. g (611)	17. d (611)
8. s (616)	18. p (615)
9. k (614)	19. f (611)
10. j (614)	

Names You Should Know

1. d (622)
2. b (615-6)
3. f (634)
4. a (612-5)
5. e (625)
6. c (617)

Key Terms - Matching #2

a. 14 (622)	m. 8 (621)
b. 22 (625)	n. 1 (616)
c. 7 (620)	o. 15 (623)
d. 6 (618)	p. 9 (621)
e. 18 (625)	q. 2 (618)
f. 23 (629)	r. 13 (622)
g. 12 (621)	s. 5 (618)
h. 17 (624)	t. 19 (625)
i. 4 (618)	u. 10 (621)
j. 20 (625)	v. 16 (624)
k. 11 (621)	w. 3 (618)
l. 21 (625)	

Key Terms - Matching #3

1. b (631)	10. j (633)
2. k (633)	11. o (635)
3. a (630)	12. r (637)
4. e (632)	13. m (634)
5. n (635)	14. d (631)
6. c (631)	15. i (633)
7. l (634)	16. h (633)
8. q (635)	17. p (635)
9. f (633)	18. g (633)

Multiple Choice

1. c	6. b	11. b	16. a	21. b	26. a
2. d	7. d	12. c	17. d	22. a	27. b
3. a	8. d	13. a	18. c	23. d	28. c
4. c	9. a	14. b	19. b	24. d	29. a
5. d	10. b	15. c	20. a	25. d	30. d

Review of Concepts

1. false (610)
2. psychological; social (615)
3. adolescents (617)
4. neglected (618)
5. attend college (618)
6. supervision; independence (619)
7. relationships (619)
8. decreases (621)
9. ignore; reciprocate (621)
10. negative (621)
11. half (623)
12. whites (623)
13. higher (625)
14. is (628)
15. false (629)
16. true (629)
17. men (630)
18. false (630)
19. true (631)
20. true (631)
21. true (631)
22. false (632)
23. false (632)
24. false (634)
25. true (634)
26. false (635)
27. true (635)
28. marriage; happy relationships (637)

Understanding Research

1. environments; takers; adverse; personality; genetic; divorce; 1,500; six; probands; two; .525

2. gene; their parents' marital status; zero; 50 percent; thresholds; and; attractiveness; marriage; socially acceptable

3. twin study; less than 100 percent; because all behavior is the product of genes and environment

4. possible; genetics; Environments

CHAPTER 18 - MENTAL HEALTH AND THE LAW

Chapter Outline

I. Overview
    A. Free Will versus Determinism
        1. Is Mental Illness a Myth?
        2. Rights and Responsibilities

II. Mental Health, Criminal Responsibility, and Procedural Rights
    A. The Insanity Defense
        1. M'Naghten Test
        2. Irresistible Impulse and the Product Test
        3. Legislative Actions
        4. Guilty But Mentally Ill
        5. Burden of Proof
        6. Defining "Mental Disease or Defect"
        7. Mental Health Professionals as Expert Witnesses
        8. Use and Consequences of the Insanity Defense
    B. Competence and Criminal Proceedings

III. Mental Hospitals and the Law
    A. Brief Historical Perspective: U.S. Mental Hospitals
    B. Libertarianism versus Paternalism in Treating Mental Patients
    C. Civil Commitment
        1. Grounds and Procedures
        2. Predicting Dangerousness and Suicidal Risk
            a. Clinical Assessment and the Prediction of Dangerousness
            b. Assessing Suicide Risk
        3. Commitment of Minors
    D. The Rights of Mental Patients
        1. The Right to Treatment
            a. *Wyatt v. Stickney*
            b. *O'Connor v. Donaldson*
        2. Treatment in the Least Restrictive Alternative Environment
        3. The Right to Refuse Treatment
            a. Almost a Revolution
    E. Deinstitutionalization
        1. Has the Pendulum Swung Too Far?

IV. Mental Health and Family Law
    A. Balancing the Interests of Children, Parents, and the State
    B. Child Custody Disputes Following Divorce
        1. Expert Witnesses in Custody Determinations
        2. Custody Mediation
    C. Child Abuse

V. Professional Responsibilities and the Law
    A. Professional Negligence and Malpractice

1. Informed Consent on the Efficacy of Alternative Treatments
   a. *Osheroff v. Chestnut Lodge*
2. Who is the Client?
B. Confidentiality
   1. Tarasoff and the Duty to Protect Potential Victims

Learning Objectives

After reviewing the material presented in this chapter, you should be able to:

1. Understand the "free will versus determinism" issue and its role in the insanity defense.

2. Distinguish the M'Naghten test, the irresistible impulse test, the product test, and the American Law Institute model legislation for determining insanity.

3. Describe the "guilty but mentally ill" verdict and explain the consequences of such a verdict.

4. Know the basic statistics surrounding the use of the NGRI plea and compare the consequences given the verdict of NGRI with that of a "guilty" verdict.

5. Understand the issue of "competence" and the role it plays in the legal system.

6. Contrast the libertarian position with that of the paternalist position regarding involuntary psychiatric commitment to an inpatient hospital.

7. Understand the reasons for the unreliability of dangerousness predictions and suicide risk predictions.

8. Describe the basic issues involved in the psychiatric patient's right to treatment, the right to the least restrictive alternative environment, and the right to refuse treatment.

9. Know some of the problems associated with the deinstitutionalization movement in psychiatry.

10. Describe the role of mental health practitioners in child custody disputes.

11. Delineate some of the most common types of malpractice cases that are filed against mental health practitioners.

12. List some situations in which psychologists are legally bound to break confidentiality.

Key Terms - Matching #1

The following terms related to mental health and the law are important to know. To test your knowledge, match the following terms with their definitions. Answers are listed at the end of the chapter.

a. Free will
b. Criminal responsibility
c. Determinism
d. Insanity
e. Insanity defense
f. M'Naghten test
g. Not guilty by reason of insanity
h. Irresistible impulse test
i. Deterrence
j. Product test
k. Guilty but mentally ill (GBMI)
l. Burden of proof
m. Standard of proof

n. Expert witnesses
o. Battered woman syndrome
p. Temporary insanity
q. Competence
r. Miranda warning
s. Moral treatment
t. Deinstitutionalization movement
u. Libertarian
v. Paternalist
w. Preventive detention
x. Civil commitment
y. Parens patriae
z. Police power

1. _____ a defendent's ability to understand the legal proceedings that are taking place against him or her and to participate in his or her own defense
2. _____ a legal term referring to a defendent's state of mind at the time of committing a crime
3. _____ the state as parent
4. _____ specialists who are allowed to testify about specific matters of opinion that lie within their area of expertise
5. _____ a person being held accountable when he or she breaks the law
6. _____ the attempt to care for the mentally ill in their communities
7. _____ the idea that people have the capacity to make choices and act freely on them
8. _____ the view that emphasizes the state's duty to protect its citizens
9. _____ confinement before a crime is committed
10. _____ the psychological effects of being chronically abused by a husband or lover
11. _____ the involuntary hospitalization of the mentally ill
12. _____ the principle for determining insanity of whether the person is prevented from knowing the wrongfulness of his or her actions by a mental disease or defect
13. _____ the stress of an event temporarily causes a person to be legally insane
14. _____ the idea that an accused person is not criminally responsible if his or her unlawful act was the product of a mental disease or defect
15. _____ a movement founded on a basic respect for human dignity and the belief that humanistic care would help to relieve mental illness
16. _____ the police must inform a suspect during arrest of his or her rights to remain silent and to have an attorney present during police questioning
17. _____ the idea that human behavior is determined by biological, psychological, and social forces

18. ____ the idea that people will avoid committing crimes because they fear being punished for them
19. ____ the degree of certainty required
20. ____ the principle that people could be found insane if they were unable to control their actions because of a mental disease
21. ____ the view that emphasizes protecting the rights of the individual
22. ____ whether the prosecution or the defense has the obligation to prove guilt
23. ____ an attempt to prove that a person with a mental illness did not meet the legal criteria for sanity at the time of committing a crime
24. ____ the finding by a court that a person is not criminally responsible for his or her actions because of a mental disease or defect
25. ____ the state's duty to protect the public safety, health, and welfare
26. ____ the finding by a court that a person committed a crime, was mentally ill at the time it was committed, but was not legally insane at that time

Key Terms - Matching #2

The following terms related to mental health and the law are important to know. To test your knowledge, match the following terms with their definitions. Answers are listed at the end of the chapter.

1. Emergency commitment procedures
2. Formal commitment procedures
3. Base rates
4. Sensitivity
5. Specificity
6. Informed consent
7. Substituted judgment
8. Revolving door phenomenon
9. Child custody
10. Physical custody
11. Legal custody
12. Sole custody
13. Joint custody
14. Mediator
15. Child's best interests standard
16. Divorce mediation
17. Child abuse
18. Physical child abuse
19. Child sexual abuse
20. Child neglect
21. Psychological abuse
22. Foster care
23. Professional responsibilities
24. Negligence
25. Malpractice
26. Confidentiality

a. ____ where the children will live at what times
b. ____ a court order that allows an individual to be involuntarily committed to a mental hospital for a long period of time, such as six months
c. ____ population frequencies
d. ____ repeated denigration in the absence of physical harm
e. ____ a legal decision that involves determining where children will reside and how parents will share legal rights and responsibilities for child rearing
f. ____ the ethical obligation not to reveal private communications
g. ____ a neutral third party who facilitates the parents' discussions
h. ____ more patients are admitted to psychiatric hospitals more frequently but for shorter periods of time
i. ____ parents meet with a neutral third party who helps them to identify, negotiate, and resolve their disputes during a divorce

j. _____ a temporary placement of the child outside of his or her home
k. _____ appointing an independent guardian to provide informed consent when a person is not competent to provide it for himself or herself
l. _____ when professional negligence results in harm to patients
m. _____ the standard that governs custody disputes
n. _____ allow an acutely disturbed individual to be temporarily confined in a mental hospital for a few days
o. _____ how the parents will make separate or joint decisions about their children's lives
p. _____ true positives over the sum of true positives and false negatives
q. _____ involves placing children at risk for serious physical or psychological harm by failing to provide basic and expected care
r. _____ a situation in which only one parent retains custody of the children
s. _____ involves sexual contact between an adult and child
t. _____ a situation in which both parents retain custody
u. _____ a legal decision that a parent or other responsible adult has inflicted damage or offered inadequate care to a child
v. _____ when a professional fails to perform in a manner that is consistent with the level of skill exercised by other professionals in the field
w. _____ true negatives divided by the sum of the true negatives and false positives
x. _____ involves the intentional use of physically painful and harmful actions
y. _____ a professional's obligations to meet the ethical standards of the profession and to uphold the laws of the states in which he or she practices
z. _____ the requirement that a clinician tell a patient about a procedure and its risks, the patient understands the information and freely consents to the treatment, and the patient is competent to give consent

Names You Should Know - Matching

The following people have played an important role in research and theory of mental health and the law. To test your knowledge, match the following names with the descriptions of their contributions to the study of abnormal psychology. Answers are listed at the end of the chapter.

a. Thomas Szasz   c. Lenore Walker
b. John Monahan   d. Henry Kempe

1. _____ researched the relation between violence and mental illness, and predicting dangerousness
2. _____ wrote about the "battered child syndrome"
3. _____ asserted that the concept of mental illness is a myth, and argued that abnormal behavior must be defined relative to some social or moral standard
4. _____ coined the term "the battered woman syndrome"

Review of Concepts - Fill in the Blank and True/False

This section will help focus your studying by testing whether you understand the concepts presented in the text. After you have read and reviewed the material, test your comprehension and memory by filling in the following blanks or circling the right answer. Answers are listed at the end of the chapter.

1. Mental health professionals typically assume which view:

    free will   **determinism**

2. Criminal law assumes which view:

    free will   **determinism**

3. The views of Thomas Szasz are widely accepted in the psychiatric community:

    true   **false**

4. The irresistible impulse test and the product test

    narrowed or **broadened**   the grounds for determining insanity.

5. The problem of circular reasoning was introduced when mental health professionals decided to include _____ disorder as one of the mental diseases that could be the basis of an insanity defense.

6. In federal courts today, the burden of proof of a defendent's insanity lies with the

    prosecution   **defense**

7. There remain some states in which a husband cannot be charged with raping his wife no matter what the circumstances: **true**   **false**

8. Approximately what proportion of female murder victims are killed by a husband or boyfriend?   **one-eighth**   **one-quarter**   **one-third**

9. About _____ percent of all criminal cases involve the insanity defense.

10. Most defendents who are found Not Guilty by Reason of Insanity spend substantially less time in a mental hospital than they would have spent in prison:

    true   **false**

11. The goal of commitment following an NGRI verdict is _____.

12. Competence refers to the defendant's _____ mental state and insantiy refers to the defendant's state of mind at the time of

    _____.

13. The poor conditions of mental institutions were brought to light shortly after World War II by _____.

14. American law provides for the confinement of someone who is about to commit a crime: **true**   **false**

15. What percent of the mentally disturbed have no history of violence? _____

16. Clinicians can usually predict violence quite accurately: **true**   **false**
17. Hospitals where minors are admitted constitute an independent fact finder, but they have a clear _____ interest in committing the minor.
18. Between 1980 and 1984 the number of juveniles admitted to private psychiatric hospitals increased by _____ percent.
19. Wyatt v. Stickney established that hospitalized mental patients have a right to

    _____.
20. Lake v. Cameron established the patient's right to be treated in the _____

    _____.
21. The development of resources to treat people in their communities grew rapidly with the deinstitutionalization movement: **true**   **false**
22. Many community mental health centers do not offer services to the seriously mentally ill: **true**   **false**
23. Many patients that would have been institutionalized before are now in jail or are homeless: **true**   **false**
24. Mental health law is mostly based on the state's _____ and family law is mostly based on the state's _____.
25. Several large-scale studies have shown that divorce itself has little negative effect on children's mental health: **true**   **false**
26. Research evidence suggest that conflict between parents is strongly related to maladjustment among children following divorce: **true**   **false**
27. Mental health professionals are not permitted to break confidentiality, even to report child abuse: **true**   **false**
28. One common ground for successful malpractice suits against mental health professionals is the existence of a _____ relationship.
29. The Tarasoff case established a mental health professional's duty to _____ a potential victim of their client.

Multiple Choice Questions

The following multiple choice questions will test your comprehension of the material presented in the chapter. Answers are listed at the end of the chapter.

1) Which of the following cases ruled that a state could not confine a non-dangerous individual who is capable of surviving safely on their own or with the help of willing and responsible family members or friends?

   a. Washington v. Harper
   b. Parham v. J.R.

   c. O'Connor v. Donaldson
   d. Lake v. Cameron

2) _____ commitment procedures allow an acutely disturbed individual to be temporarily confined in a mental hospital, typically for no more than a few days, while _____ commitment procedures can lead to involuntary hospitalization that is ordered by the court and typically lasts for much longer.

a. Formal; emergency
b. Emergency; formal

c. Medical; crisis
d. Crisis; medical

3) All of the following are true of the "guilty but mentally ill" (GBMI) verdict EXCEPT:

a. it holds defendants criminally responsible for their crimes
b. it helps ensure that the defendant receives treatment for the mental disorder
c. it was designed as a compromise to the "not guilty by reason of insanity" (NGRI) verdict
d. a defendant found to be GBMI cannot be sentenced in the same manner as any criminal

4) All of the following have been goals of deinstitutionalization EXCEPT:

a. to prevent inappropriate mental hospital admissions through arranging community alternatives to treatment
b. to release to the community all institutionalized patients who have been given adequate preparation for such a change
c. to decrease the influx of patients by not allowing them continued access to mental hospitals and thus encouraging independence
d. to establish and maintain community support systems for non-institutionalized people receiving mental health services in the community

5) Which of the following individuals argues that mental disorders are subjective "problems in living" rather than objective diseases, and thus believes that the concept of mental illness is a myth?

a. Thomas Szasz
b. E. Fuller Torrey

c. Bertram Brown
d. Henry Kempe

6) The majority of custody decisions are made by:

a. parents themselves
b. attorneys who negotiate for the parents outside of court
c. a judge and decided in court
d. mental health professionals who evaluate the case

7) All of the following are true of the parens patriae EXCEPT:

a. it is used to justify the state's supervision of minors and incapacitated adults
b. it is based on the state's duty to protect the public safety, health, and welfare
c. commitment under these rationales was virtually unknown to the United States until the early 1950s
d. it refers to the concept of the "state as parent"

8) Following a civil commitment to a mental hospital, mental patients' rights include all of the following EXCEPT:

a. right to treatment
b. right to design their own treatment plan
c. right to refuse treatment
d. right to treatment in the least restrictive alternative environment

9) Evidence suggests that the insanity defense is used in approximately _____ of all criminal cases in the United States.

a. 1 percent
b. 4 percent
c. 7 percent
d. 10 percent

10) All of the following stages are part of Lenore Walker's stages of the "cycle of violence" EXCEPT:

a. battering incident
b. tension-building phase
c. loving contrition
d. verbal reprimands

11) On the average, defendants who are found "not guilty by reason of insanity" (NGRI) spend _____ time confined in an institution as they would have if they had been given a prison sentence instead.

a. significantly less
b. twice as much
c. approximately the same
d. roughly three times as much

12) Which of the following terms is defined as the ethical obligation not to reveal private communication and is basic to psychotherapy?

a. confidentiality
b. private communications
c. classified information
d. privileged communications

13) Mental disorders and the actions that result from them are typically viewed as:

a. choices
b. conditions that are outside of voluntary control
c. responsibilities that the mentally disordered individual must assume
d. a and c

14) The acquittal of John Hinckley prompted all of the following EXCEPT:

a. the new verdict "guilty but mentally ill" (GBMI)
b. a revised definition of the insanity defense
c. shifting the burden of proof from the prosecution to the defense in federal courts
d. the creation of a much stricter standard of proof for the defense in the majority of states

15) All of the following are issues of special relevance regarding involuntary hospitalization of the severely mentally impaired EXCEPT:

a. criminal record
b. civil commitment
c. patients' rights
d. deinstitutionalization

16) Research indicates that approximately _____ of the mentally disturbed are not violent.

a. 30 percent
b. 50 percent
c. 70 percent
d. 90 percent

17) All of the following are grounds that tend to dominate commitment laws EXCEPT:

a. being dangerous to others
b. inability to care for self
c. being dangerous to self
d. inability to care for others

18) Over _____ of all reports of child abuse are found to be unsubstantiated after an investigation.

a. one-eighth
b. one-quarter
c. one-half
d. two-thirds

19) All of the following were key figures in instituting moral treatment reform efforts for the mentally ill EXCEPT:

a. Benjamin Rush
b. Lenore Walker
c. Phillipe Pinel
d. Dorothea Dix

20) Empirical research on children's adjustment after divorce indicates that:

a. a substantial portion of the difficulties found among children after divorce actually begins long before the marital separation occurs
b. the psychological functioning of children from divorced families does not differ from that of children from non-divorced families
c. the difficulties children experience are directly related to marital conflict and divorce
d. children from divorced families tend to have more internalizing problems than children from non-divorced families

21) Which of the following is known as the "product test" and indicated that "an accused is not criminally responsible if his unlawful act was the product of mental disease or defect"?

a. Parsons v. State
b. O'Connor v. Donaldson
c. Durham v. United States
d. Parham v. J.R.

22) One more common malpractice claim against mental health professionals is:

   a. the misuse of psychotherapeutic techniques
   b. the inappropriate use of electroconvulsive therapy (ECT)
   c. the failure to disclose therapeutic interpretations to clients
   d. inappropriate hospitalization

23) Confidentiality between a therapist and a client can be broken under which of the following circumstances?

   a. the client is threatening to harm another person
   b. the client has disclosed sexual or physical abuse of a child
   c. the client is threatening to harm himself or herself
   d. all of the above

24) Which of the following is NOT TRUE of the legal definition of "competence"?

   a. it refers to the defendant's ability to understand criminal proceedings
   b. it refers to the defendant's current mental status
   c. it refers to the defendants willingness to participate in criminal proceedings
   d. the "reasonable degree" of understanding needed to establish competence is generally acknowledged to be fairly low

25) In the case of Wyatt v. Stickney, the federal district court ruled that at a minimum, public mental institutions must provide all of the following EXCEPT:

   a. a humane psychological and physical environment
   b. a sufficient number of qualified staff to administer adequate treatment
   c. individualized treatment plans
   d. "reasonable" rates for inpatient services

26) Which of the following details a suspect's rights to remain silent and to have an attorney present during police questioning?

   a. Miranda warning   c. confidentiality
   b. informed consent   d. parens patriae

27) Evidence suggests that in child custody cases, mediation:

   a. does not necessarily reduce the number of custody hearings in court
   b. is more effective than the role that mental health professionals play in custody cases, and thus mental health professionals should limit their involvement in the legal system
   c. does not help parents reach decisions more quickly than if they were to go through custody hearings in court
   d. is viewed by parents as more favorable than litigation, especially fathers

28) Which of the following cases established the patient's right to be treated in the least restrictive alternative environment?

   a. Lake v. Cameron
   b. Osheroff v. Chestnut Lodge
   c. O'Connor v. Donaldson
   d. none of the above

29) Which of the following is TRUE regarding the idea that mental disability should limit criminal responsibility?

   a. it is a relatively new concept among mental health professionals
   b. it dates back to ancient Greek and Hebrew traditions and was evident in early English law
   c. it has emerged in our legal system within the past 50 years
   d. it surfaced following World War II when large numbers of veterans experienced post-traumatic stress symptoms and committed violent acts

30) In his research on the prediction of dangerousness, John Monahan has found which of the following to be several times higher among prison inmates as among the general population?

   a. major depression
   b. bipolar disorder
   c. schizophrenia
   d. all of the above

Understanding Research - Fill in the Blank

The Accuracy of Predictions of Violence: The text presents a detailed description of a study by Lidz, Mulvey, and Gardner in the Research Close-Up on pp. 657-658. Finding the answers to these questions will help you get a good understanding of this study and why it is important. It is not necessary to memorize the answers; the process of finding them in the textbook will help you learn the material you need to know.

1. Older studies on the prediction of violence were _____. This study examined _____ cases seen in a psychiatric _____ room in an urban area. Half the cases were predicted to have some _____ for violence by _____ clinicians who interviewed them; the other half were comparison cases who were not predicted to be violent. Patients were matched on age, sex, race, and hospital _____. The patient and someone that _____ them were later interviewed about subsequent _____ of violence. Interviews were conducted _____ times in the _____ months following their contact with the emergency room.

2. Investigators found that _____ percent of the predicted cases engaged in violence versus _____ percent of the comparison cases. Predictions of violence among _____ were less accurate, no better than chance, because of the clinician's

underestimation of the _____. The critical distinction was the decision of whether the potential for violence was _____ or _____.

<u>Base Rates and Predictions</u>: The text discusses this research issue in the Research Methods section on pp. 658-659. Finding the answers to these questions will help you get a good understanding of these issues.

3. The validity with which violence can be predicted depends on the _____ of the relation between the predictor and the outcome, and also by _____. Using a coin flip to predict violence results in a sensitivity of _____ percent and a specificity of _____ percent. With this method, the percentage of false positives is much _____. If the base rate is set at 50 percent, which would be better in the example given, the clinician's predictions or the coin flip? _____.

Brief Essay

As a final exercise, write out answers to the following brief essay questions. Then compare your answers with the material presented in the text.

After you have answered these questions, review the "critical thinking" questions that are presented at the end of the text chapter. Answering these questions will help you integrate important issues and themes that have been featured throughout the chapter.

1. Greg is a 35-year-old white male who was recently arrested for sexually abusing a seven-year-old girl. Although this is Greg's first offense, he has a history of "sexual addictions" that range from viewing pornography while masturbating to exhibitionism. Explain how you think criminal law would conceptualize Greg's behavior and how you think a mental health professional would conceptualize Greg's behavior. Discuss the similarities and differences of the two conceptualizations.

2. Briefly discuss Thomas Szasz's position on free will and determinism, mental illness, and the insanity defense. Do you agree or disagree with Szasz? Why?

3. What are the basic underlying principles of libertarianism and paternalism? Which view do you most agree with? Defend your position.

4. Discuss the implications of the Tarasoff v. Regents of the University of California case. If you would have been the therapist of Prosenjit Poddar, would you have handled the situation differently? Why or why not?

ANSWER KEY

Answers to the exercises are listed below; page numbers where the information is referenced in the textbook are given in parentheses.

Key Terms - Matching #1

1. q (651)	14. j (646)
2. d (644)	15. s (653)
3. y (654)	16. r (652)
4. n (648)	17. c (644)
5. b (644)	18. i (646)
6. t (653)	19. m (647)
7. a (644)	20. h (646)
8. v (654)	21. u (654)
9. w (654)	22. l (647)
10. o (649)	23. e (646)
11. x (654)	24. g (646)
12. f (646)	25. z (654)
13. p (650)	26. k (647)

Names You Should Know

1. b (656)
2. d (669)
3. a (645)
4. c (649)

Key Terms - Matching #2

a. 10 (667)	n. 1 (655)
b. 2 (655)	o. 11 (667)
c. 3 (658)	p. 4 (658)
d. 21 (670)	q. 20 (670)
e. 9 (667)	r. 12 (667)
f. 26 (673)	s. 19 (669)
g. 14 (667)	t. 13 (667)
h. 8 (664)	u. 17 (669)
i. 16 (668)	v. 24 (671)
j. 22 (670)	w. 5 (658)
k. 7 (663)	x. 18 (669)
l. 25 (671)	y. 23 (671)
m. 15 (668)	z. 6 (663)

Multiple Choice

1. c	6. b	11. c	16. d	21. c	26. a
2. b	7. c	12. a	17. d	22. b	27. d
3. d	8. b	13. b	18. c	23. d	28. a
4. c	9. a	14. d	19. b	24. c	29. b
5. a	10. d	15. a	20. a	25. d	30. d

Review of Concepts

1. determinism (644)
2. free will (644)
3. false (645)
4. broadened (646)
5. antisocial personality (646)
6. defense (647)
7. true (649)
8. one-third (649)
9. 1 percent (651)
10. false (651)
11. treatment (651)
12. current; the crime (651)
13. conscientious objectors (653)
14. false (654)
15. 90 percent (656)
16. false (657)
17. financial (660)
18. 450 (660)
19. treatment (661)
20. least restrictive environment (662)
21. false (663)
22. true (664)
23. true (664)
24. police power; parens patriae (666)
25. true (668)
26. true (668)
27. false (669)
28. sexual (671)
29. warn (673)

Understanding Research

1. flawed; 714; emergency; potential; two; admission; knew; episodes; three; six

2. 53 percent; 36 percent; women; base rate; present; absent

3. magnitude; base rates; 50 percent; 50 percent; higher; coin flip